CONTENTS

1 Gardens shaped with the earth's basic elements   7

2 A mountain view in your own garden   19
Picture essay: CREATING DRAMA WITH ROCKY DESIGNS   40

3 Water, the crowning touch   49
Picture essay: REFLECTIONS OF THE PAST IN CLASSIC POOLS   60

4 The bewitching beauty of water plants   71

5 An encyclopaedia of rock, water and bog plants   87

APPENDIX

Characteristics of 198 rock-garden plants   146
Characteristics of 56 bog and water plants   150
Acknowledgements   150
Picture credits   151
Bibliography   152
Index   153

Rock and Water Gardens

TIME
LIFE
BOOKS

THE SEAFARERS

WORLD WAR II

THE GOOD COOK

THE TIME-LIFE ENCYCLOPAEDIA
OF GARDENING

HUMAN BEHAVIOUR

THE GREAT CITIES

THE ART OF SEWING

THE OLD WEST

THE WORLD'S WILD PLACES

THE EMERGENCE OF MAN

LIFE LIBRARY OF PHOTOGRAPHY

THIS FABULOUS CENTURY

TIME-LIFE LIBRARY OF ART

FOODS OF THE WORLD

GREAT AGES OF MAN

LIFE SCIENCE LIBRARY

LIFE NATURE LIBRARY

YOUNG READERS LIBRARY

LIFE WORLD LIBRARY

THE TIME-LIFE BOOK OF BOATING

TECHNIQUES OF PHOTOGRAPHY

LIFE AT WAR

LIFE GOES TO THE MOVIES

BEST OF LIFE

Rock and Water Gardens

by

Ogden Tanner

and

the Editors of TIME-LIFE BOOKS

TIME-LIFE BOOKS (NEDERLAND) B.V.

THE TIME-LIFE ENCYCLOPAEDIA OF GARDENING

EDITORIAL STAFF FOR ROCK AND WATER GARDENS:
EDITOR: Robert M. Jones
Assistant Editor: Betsy Frankel
Picture Editor: Jane Jordan
Designer: Edward Frank
Assistant Designer: Edwina C. Smith
Staff Writers: Carol Dana, Bob Menaker,
Susan Perry
Researchers: Diane Bohrer, Margaret White
Dawson, Sheila M. Green, Lucinda Moore,
Marilyn Murphy, Susan F. Schneider
Editorial Assistants: Susan Larson, Maria
Zacharias

EUROPEAN EDITION

EUROPEAN EDITOR: Kit van Tulleken
Design Director: Louis Klein
Photography Director: Pamela Marke
Chief of Research: Vanessa Kramer
Special Projects Editor: Windsor Chorlton
Text Editor: Christopher Farman
Chief Sub-Editor: Ilse Gray
Researcher: Sheila Grant
Designer: Martin Gregory
Design Assistant: Adrian Saunders
Sub-Editor: Kathy Eason

Editorial Production
Chief: Ellen Brush
Quality Control: Douglas Whitworth
Traffic Co-ordinator: Helen Whitehorn
Art Department: Julia West
Editorial Department: Ajaib Singh Gill, Debra
Lelliott

ISBN 7054 0571 0

THE AUTHOR: **Ogden Tanner**, a former staff member of TIME-LIFE BOOKS, is
the author of *Garden Construction* and co-author of *Herbs* in THE TIME-LIFE
ENCYCLOPAEDIA OF GARDENING. An architectural graduate of Princeton
University, he has also written and edited books on natural history, science
and photography.

CONSULTANT, EUROPEAN EDITION: **Frances Perry** is a well-known gardening
authority whose books and broadcasts have gained her an international
reputation. She is a member of the Linnean Society, and was the first woman to
be elected to the Council of the Royal Horticultural Society; now a Vice-
President, she also holds the Society's coveted Victoria Medal of Honour. She
has lectured in Australia, New Zealand and America and has collected plants
in such diverse areas as Lapland, Africa and South America.

GENERAL EUROPEAN CONSULTANTS: **Roy Hay** is a horticulturist well known
for his articles in English publications, including *The Times* newspaper, and
for his monthly contribution to the French magazine *L'Ami des Jardins*. He
carries on a family gardening tradition—his father, Thomas Hay, was
Superintendent of the Central Royal Parks in London (1922-1940). Mr. Hay
is an Officer of L'Ordre du Merite Agricole of Belgium and France. **Pierre
Ebert** is chief gardener of the city of Paris. He is chief of the Fleuriste Municipal-
Auteuil and a member of the Association des Journalistes de l'Horticulture.
Since 1964 he has also been technical consultant for the magazine *Mon Jardin
et Ma Maison*. **Dieneke van Raalte** studied horticulture and landscape
gardening at the college of gardening in Fredriksoord in The Netherlands.
She is a regular contributor to European gardening magazines and is the
author of many Dutch gardening books. **Hans-Dieter Ihlenfeldt** is Professor
of Botany at the Institute of General Botany and Botanical Gardening in
Hamburg. He is co-editor of several botanical handbooks and has published in
scientific journals. **Hans-Helmut Poppendieck** is a custodian of the Botanic
Garden and lectures at the Institute of Botany in Hamburg. He has written
articles on plant taxonomy, tropical plants and South African succulents.

GENERAL CONSULTANTS: The late James Underwood Crockett, author of many
of the volumes in THE TIME-LIFE ENCYCLOPAEDIA OF GARDENING, was a graduate
of the Massachusetts' Stockbridge School of Agriculture. He lived in—and
cultivated a wide variety of plants in—California, New York, Texas and New
England and served as consultant to many nurseries and landscapers. Dr.
Robert L. Baker is Associate Professor of Horticulture at the University
of Maryland. H. Lincoln Foster, a past president of the American Rock Garden
Society, wrote the book *Rock Gardening*. Patrick Nutt is a specialist in aquatic
plants at Longwood Gardens, Philadelphia. Dr. William Louis Stern is Professor of Botany at the University of Maryland.

THE COVER: A rock and water garden, partially shaded by a Japanese black pine
(left), provides a soothing retreat from the midday sun. The pool, built on two
levels to create a series of small rippling waterfalls, is equipped with a pump to
recirculate the water. Primroses, grape hyacinths and daisies nestle among
the moss-covered rocks that line the pool's shore, while water lilies and a water
hawthorn float atop the pool itself.

CORRESPONDENTS: Elisabeth Kraemer (Bonn); Margot Hapgood, Dorothy
Bacon, Lesley Coleman (London); Susan Jonas, Lucy T. Voulgaris (New York);
Maria Vincenza Aloisi, Josephine du Brusle (Paris); Ann Natanson (Rome).
Valuable assistance was also provided by: Loral Dean (Atlanta); Tom and
Karen Horton (Honolulu); Enid Farmer (Lexington, Mass.); Diane Asselin
(Los Angeles); Carolyn T. Chubet, Miriam Hsia (New York); Janet Zich
(San Francisco); Carol Barnard (Seattle). The editors are indebted to Margaret
Carter, Jane Opper, Maggie Oster, Karen Solit, Lyn Stallworth and Sandra
Streepey, writers, for their help with this book.

Gardens shaped with the earth's basic elements

1

There is something about the idea of rocks and water in a garden that has an irresistible appeal. Partly it is the images they conjure up of mountain peaks and alpine meadows, of boulder-strewn streams and azure lakes. Rocks and water are the basic elements of nature's most stunning and memorable landscapes, and in a garden they supply, even in miniature form, a sense of nature's original plan. A well-placed rock or two can suggest the structural bones of the earth, solid, immutable, heaved and shaped by ancient geological forces. Water, their opposite, is quick, vital, changeable. In motion, it bemuses the eye and ear, blotting out other distractions. At rest, it brings the sky down to earth in its reflective surface and hints of dark mysteries concealed within its depths.

But the presence of rocks and water do more for the garden scene than enlarge its spiritual dimensions. Rocks and water also open up a whole new world of plants that are ideally suited to the limited scale of the average garden. An arrangement of rocks designed to simulate a mountain meadow gives the gardener a chance to experiment with alpine shrubs and wild flowers that normally grow above the tree line, where climatic conditions have kept the plants low and compact—without any sacrifice of the beauty of their flowers. In the same space that is customarily occupied by a dozen standard-sized garden specimens, one can grow as many as 40 or 50 alpine plants. And if the tiny alpine species are tucked into the crevices of a stone wall, the space they occupy in the garden is even smaller. Indeed, no other kind of garden offers the possibility of growing more plants of more different descriptions in so small an area.

If water is introduced into the picture, the range of plant materials broadens even further. Aquatic plants such as water lilies, sweet flag and water hawthorns, which grow in water and nowhere else, are available to the gardener, and so are water

Water lilies float on the glassy top of a man-made pool that is lined and edged with rocks collected from a nearby mountain. A wide variety of ferns and evergreens flourish on the pool's moist banks.

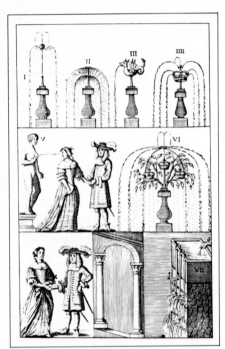

Garden-fountain designers of the 16th and 17th centuries were marvellously ingenious—though anything but subtle. Many elaborate water fountains were built, including an artificial tree with dripping leaves (centre, right) and a wall waterfall viewed through an arch (bottom). A favourite was the joke fountain (centre, left). Elizabeth I installed a joke fountain in her gardens at Hampton Court to "play upon the ladies and others standing by and give them a thorough wetting".

margin plants such as Japanese irises, arrowheads and reed-mace, which favour a wet, boggy soil. A beginner can start by growing miniature water lilies in a wooden tub and, as his skill and interest grow, may progress to more elaborate and permanent designs built into the framework of the garden itself.

An added attraction of rock and water gardens is that, with modern techniques and equipment, they generally require minimal upkeep. At the start, of course, there is a certain investment of time, labour and materials. But, once functioning, such a garden needs little pruning, fertilizing, watering or pest control. The major concerns are providing winter protection in cold climates, a good clean-up in spring and autumn and a certain amount of weeding to keep things neat.

Although rock and water gardens are now within the reach of everyone, they were almost exclusively the province of the rich when the design concepts used in creating such gardens were worked out hundreds and even thousands of years ago. In the ancient civilizations that sprang up along great rivers such as the Euphrates and the Nile, water was so central to existance itself, as irrigation for the fields, that it soon became a major motif in landscaping. Gardens from Egypt to India were graced with pools that were both reservoirs and decorative devices in which the sacred lotus often bloomed. Persian noblemen retreated from the desert heat into private walled gardens where flowers bloomed and fountains splashed. And in the earliest gardens of the Orient, cherished by emperors and poets, the natural landscape was evoked in stylized compositions that always included pools, as well as streams, rocks and mounds of earth surmounted by gnarled dwarf trees.

During the Middle Ages, Moorish Spain, drawing on Persian tradition, became famous for its courtyard gardens like those of the Alhambra and Generalife, where water from arching fountains spilled into catch basins and flowed through geometric channels symbolizing the rivers of life. During the Renaissance in Italy, the hillside villas of wealthy noblemen were adorned with grottoes and sculptured fountains; in one instance elaborate waterworks were kept constantly at play by diverting a river. This extravagance was soon imported into the rest of Europe and culminated in the gardens at Versailles, created in the 17th century for Louis XIV, where water mills and pumping machines tapped the Seine and drained the water table for miles around to feed the 1,400 fountain jets and fill the great axial canals on which the Sun King staged mock sea battles for his royal guests.

The introduction of water into European gardens naturally brought with it the cultivation of aquatic plants. A small white water lily native to Europe, *Nymphaea alba*, was grown in the pools of aristocrats. Late in the 18th century, a sweet-scented North American species, *Nymphaea odorata*, became popular among British gardeners. But it was not until the 19th century that water lilies became international favourites.

On New Year's Day, 1837, Robert Schomburgk, on expedition for the Royal Geographical Society, was travelling on the Berbice River in British Guiana. As his party reached a place where the river widened into a lake-like expanse of still water, it came upon an amazing sight: a flotilla of gargantuan plants with floating leaves, each 1.8 metres (6 ft) or more across with an upturned edge that made it resemble a gigantic platter. Enormous flowers, up to 38 centimetres (1¼ ft) in diameter, opened at dusk to release an intoxicating fragrance similar to that of crushed pineapple. The plants were unlike any Schomburgk had ever seen. The flowers, which first appeared creamy-white; changed colour almost as he watched. On successive evenings they passed from white to light pink to darker rose; before closing at sunrise on the third morning, they became a glowing purplish-red.

Schomburgk excitedly sent seeds of this vegetable wonder, as he termed it, back to England, where horticulturists tried to make them germinate. It was not until 1849, however, that Joseph Paxton, superintendent of the Duke of Devonshire's gardens at Chatsworth in Derbyshire, was able to bring a plant into flower in a specially created hot-house pool. This event created a sensation and was celebrated with an elaborate entertainment, during which Paxton's daughter, dressed as a fairy, was set afloat on one of the huge leaves.

The plant, named *Victoria regia* (now *Victoria amazonica*) in honour of the Queen, became so famous that portfolios of Victorian illustrations rarely failed to include a picture of a child in a sun bonnet, sitting demurely on a *Victoria* leaf. But exacting requirements limited the plant to the estates of the wealthy and the Royal Botanic Gardens at Kew. The giant needed a basin 9 metres (30 ft) across and 1.8 metres (6 ft) deep, generous amounts of fertilizer, plenty of sunlight and a water temperature of 27°C (80°F). Nevertheless, the Queen's lily stimulated European interest in water gardening, including the growing of smaller species imported from various parts of the world.

It remained for a Frenchman, Bory Latour-Marliac, to transform water-lily culture into a minor mania. Starting in the 1880s in southern France, Marliac amazed horticulturists by introducing one spectacular hybrid after another in a rainbow

Dressed in middy blouse and sailor's hat, a stalwart child pretends to go punting on the giant-sized pad of a Victoria *water lily in an illustration from a January 1885 issue of the* Gardeners' Chronicle. *Said to be strong enough to support a man, the* Victoria *lily pad gets its buoyancy from a network of radiating veins that project skeleton-fashion from its undersurface, trapping air in a honeycomb of interlocking pockets under the lily pad's skin.*

THE MARLIAC HYBRIDS

of hues. It is likely that he began hybridizing by crossing the white European water lily with a pink form found only in one Swedish lake; later he used *Nymphaea odorata* 'Rosea' from New England, as well as a yellow species called *Nymphaea mexicana*. No one can ever be sure, for he kept his records in his head and they died with him in 1911. The number of cultivars with Marliac in their names, however, testifies to his horticultural expertise.

His dedication was matched by that of another Frenchman, although the achievements of Claude Monet were of an altogether different type. In the early 1880s, the Impressionist painter moved to a country house, where he created a water garden. There he executed 236 paintings of his lily pond, probably the ultimate tribute of any one artist to a single flower.

AN ABUNDANCE OF OPTIONS

Thanks to the efforts of Marliac and later hybridizers, gardeners can choose from hundreds of cultivars of water lilies plus a number of other aquatic plants. The water-lily family includes all the true water lilies, members of the genus *Nymphaea*; the giant water lily *Victoria regia*, more correctly known as *Victoria amazonica*, and its cousin *Victoria cruciana*; the genus *Nelumbo*, which includes the lotus, the sacred flower of ancient India and China, a plant that holds its spectacular blooms and parasol-shaped leaves well above the water; and the genus *Nuphar*, called pond lily or spatterdock, with species that grow wild in ponds and streams of Europe and North America.

While interest in aquatic gardening was developing, another significant trend was under way. The grand formal gardens

(continued on page 14)

Pioneering with rocks and pools

In 1911, when the rage for alpine plants was at its height, the Royal Horticultural Society decided to construct a rock garden on a hilly site of approximately half a hectare (1¼ acres) that was part of its newly acquired property at Wisley, 32 kilometres (20 miles) south west of London. A novelty then—there had never before been a public garden devoted to these types of plants—Wisley was a challenge for its designer, J. L. Pulham. More than 500 tonnes of sandstone were carried to the site and 65,000 plants were gradually assembled.

Although several natural ponds already graced the property, Pulham added a series of concrete pools and waterfalls stepping down the hillside, and gave the lower pools shallow edges that overflowed from time to time to form small bogs because, he said, "a rock garden without damp and sedgy places . . . might as well be likened to Hamlet without the ghost." Wisley's plantings have changed and grown over the years, but it is still a classic example of what a rock garden should be.

A footbridge, its posts wrapped with wisteria, skims a lily pond at Wisley. Marsh marigolds brighten the boggy bank.

The grace that comes with age

White labels identify newly planted specimens in this 1914 Wisley photograph.

Though the rock garden at Wisley has acquired new paths and more plants, it still retains much of its original charm. Tall trees surround the garden, just as they did when it was new in 1911, and the contours of the rocky slopes are softened by the same kinds of small trees and shrubs.

On the cool and moist northern slope, ramondas are tucked into the rocky crevices, just as the garden's designer specified they should be. A weeping cherry that was a mere sapling in a 1914 photograph (*left*) has become a dense, cascading tree (*opposite*), and a Japanese larch—the oldest tree in the garden—is still standing at the edge of a pool, carefully pruned into cloud-like tufts.

At the height of its spring display, Wisley's terraced south-west slope is alive with the colour of plants tucked among its rocks. The large shrub on the left is a Lawson's cypress. Newer plantings include a rhododendron (lower, right), purple bugleweed, and pink and white spring heather.

Water pumped to the top of the rock garden and stored in an enormous tank camouflaged as a thatched cottage eventually works its way down to these natural lily ponds. A new flagstone path (left) winds round one of the ponds, past an evergreen berberis, spiny alyssum, St. John's wort and heather.

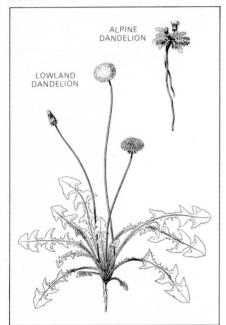

ALPINE
DANDELION

LOWLAND
DANDELION

Alpine plants, when compared with the same species growing in the lowlands, show extreme adaptations to the harsh climate of the heights. The alpine dandelion, grown as a rock-garden plant in Japan, has a more developed root system but smaller, more compact leaves than the lowland dandelion and is less than half its size. Long, thick roots enable the alpine dandelion to absorb moisture beneath rocks in arid surroundings; small, hairy leaves slow water loss from transpiration.

inspired by the Renaissance had reached their zenith, and a new cult of "naturalism" arose in reaction, chiefly in England. As early as 1711 the Earl of Shaftesbury predicted that the "mockery of princely gardens" would one day be supplanted by "rude rocks, mossy caverns, irregular unwrought grottoes, broken falls of water, and all the horrid grace of the wilderness itself". In 1772, a rockery was built at the Chelsea Physic Garden in London making use of some slabs of lava which had been brought home from Iceland by the British naturalist Sir Joseph Banks, together with an assortment of stones left over from a remodelling of the Tower of London.

It was not until the late 19th century, however, that gardening with rocks really became popular, and the impetus for it came from the thousands of British tourists, lured by cheap rail travel on the Continent, who went off to spend their holidays walking in the Alps. Marvelling at the daintiness and brilliant colours of the alpine flora, they took to popping specimens into empty biscuit tins and carrying them home to Kent and Sussex to plant in their gardens. The transfers did not always go smoothly, but in 1870 the would-be rock gardeners were helped by one of the great British gardening writers, William Robinson, who wrote a book on the subject, *Alpine Flowers for Gardens*. Perhaps slightly over-enthusiastically, Robinson stated that "there is no alpine flower that ever cheered the eye that cannot be grown in our island gardens."

By the turn of the century, rock gardening had become all the rage in the British Isles, so much so that it got rather out of hand. Some enthusiasts created whole mountain ranges in miniature by setting stones on edge, and one wealthy devotee at Henley-on-Thames constructed an exact scale model of the Matterhorn, complete with little goat-like chamois modelled in tin. In the hope of correcting some of these excesses, a 27-year-old rock gardener, Reginald Farrer, wrote a popular and influential book, *My Rock Garden*, in which he used humour and hyperbole to drive home his points.

"Now we have nothing but weak lines in our gardens," Farrer scolded, "vague, wibble-wobble curves that have no meaning nor explanation; our borders meander up and down and here and there, like sheep that have no shepherd, our silly lawns erupt into silly beds like pimples. All is uncertainty, formlessness—a vain, impotent striving after the so-called natural.

"The ideal rock-garden," he stated, "must have a plan. But there are three prevailing plans, none of which are good. The first is what I may call the Almond-Pudding scheme. You take a round bed; you pile it up with soil; you then choose out the spikiest pinnacles of limestone you can find, and you insert them thickly with their points in the air, until the general effect is that of a tipsy-cake stuck with almonds. In this vast petrified porcupine nothing will grow except Welsh Poppy, Ferns, and some of the uglier Sedums.

"The second style," Farrer's descriptions continued, "is that of the Dog's Grave. It marks a higher stage of horticulture, and is affected by many good growers of alpines. The pudding-shape is more or less the same in both, but the stones are laid flat. Plants will grow on this, but its scheme is so stodgy and so abhorrent to Nature that it should be discarded.

"The third style," he concluded, "is that of the Devil's Lapful. The plan is simplicity itself. You take a hundred or a thousand cartloads of bald square-faced boulders. You next drop them all about absolutely anyhow; and then you plant things among them. The chaotic hideousness of the result is something to be remembered with shudders ever after."

Farrer then described the proper way to build and plant rock gardens, guidelines that still hold good (*Chapter 2*). In *My Rock Garden* and subsequent volumes, he led his followers up one alp after another in pursuit of new botanical treasures. ("I regard the British craze for exercise as a superstition," confided the short, portly Farrer, "but walk I must, and walk I do.") His quest for the elusive, dwarf, blue-flowered cushion plant (*Eritrichum nanum*) was recounted with all the melodrama of a Victorian romantic epic: "Ah, *Eritrichum* is near! Down, beating heart! In another moment I am on my knees before the nearest tuft of blue, babbling inanities into its innumerable lovely faces. There is no colour that I know exactly like that of *Eritrichum*. It is blue—the absolute blue!"

In 1914 Farrer set out with a professional plant hunter, William Purdom, to seek new species in the forbidding mountains of China's Kansu province. On the first of two expeditions they made some notable finds, including *Rosa farreri* and *Geranium farreri*. Mounted on an evil-tempered pony named Spotted Fat and equipped with a complete set of Jane Austen's books, Farrer aroused the suspicions of Tibetan monks who jealously guarded their hills against gold hunters. After delicate negotiations with the chief lama, Farrer congratulated himself on his success, unaware that at that very moment the lama "was busily issuing a proclamation that we were all to be murdered in the night with as little fuss and unpleasantness as might reasonably be". The party escaped the murderous monks, then nearly collided with a mad Chinese rebel general named White

PLANT-HUNTING HAZARDS

Wolf, who was destroying every village in his path. Their second collecting season was relatively uneventful with one exception: the discovery of *Gentiana farreri*, a pale blue flower that Farrer considered worth the cost of the entire expedition.

Back in England during World War I, Farrer worked at the Ministry of Information by day and at night completed a two-volume work, *The English Rock Garden*, which catalogued all his knowledge of alpine plants and was the first definitive work on the subject. With the end of the war he began collecting again, this time in upper Burma. Farrer plunged through rain-shrouded passes where no plant collector had ventured before, accompanied by a servant he called The Dragon. There he fell victim to a fever that sapped his strength and reduced him to a diet of whisky and soda. In October 1920, the man known as "the prince of alpine gardeners" died aged 40 in the mountains he had made his life.

All through the 1920s rock gardening was something of a mania in both Britain and the United States, producing—despite Farrer's strictures—a certain number of Almond Puddings, Devil's Lapfuls and Dog's Graves. The movement languished during the 1930s and World War II, but then it re-emerged in the post-war years, newly infused with landscaping ideas from the Orient. These were chiefly based on the highly developed art of rock and water gardening practised by the Japanese. In America, the cool coastal shelf of the north west, from northern California through Oregon, Washington and British Columbia, proved especially well suited to this new kind of gardening. Indeed, so many alpine species flourished there that Seattle and Vancouver were soon vying for the title of "rock garden capital of North America".

In Europe, the same feverish activity prevailed. Scotland proved an ideal place for rock gardens, as did Switzerland and parts of Germany and France.

CONSTRUCTION AIDS

An important factor behind this revived interest in rock and water gardening was undoubtedly the ease with which water, at least, could be introduced into the garden. The availability of such materials as plastic and concrete, and the development of submersible pumps and pool liners made it possible for gardeners to build their own streams, ponds and waterfalls. But in the course of discovering the delights of alpine and aquatic plants, many amateurs have learned—sometimes the hard way—that creating a setting with rocks and water is not the same as digging and planting an ordinary flower bed. A great deal more planning and judgement are required if the result is not to look

ROCK GARDENS IN THE RUBBLE
Thousands of plants sprang out of the London ruins of World War II, creating natural rock gardens that both surprised and heartened the city's war-weary inhabitants. "Cellars and courts shattered into rubble by the German raids of 1940-41 have been taken over by an army of weeds which have turned them into wild gardens, sometimes as gay as any tilled by human hands," reported Lewis Gannett, a London correspondent for the New York Herald Tribune. *Musk mallow, larkspur, candytuft, groundsel, evening primrose, poppies, fleabane, ferns, purple-flowering nightshade—all thrived among the rocky debris.*

awkward, artificial or just plain silly. Nothing betrays lack of forethought more surely than the rock garden that simply resembles a rock pile, or the "natural" pool with a trite kidney shape surrounded by a regular row of small, uniform stones, or the stage-set mountain cave, complete with spouting waterfall, rising abruptly from the flat expanse of a suburban lawn.

To avoid such mistakes, you should first take stock of the natural attributes of your property—slopes, outcrops or depressions—that lend themselves to the introduction of rocks and water. It is not a bad idea, either, to devote some time to examining how nature itself arranges things in the area where you live. Take along a camera and make photographic notes on how rock strata lie in the land and align themselves in ledges, how real streams flow through the landscape, how water spills and collects in pools.

As your ideas for the garden begin to crystallize, seek out nurseries and suppliers who specialize in rock and water plants and the materials needed to grow them. Local garden centres may stock a handful of the more popular rock and bog-garden species, but for any choice you will have to go to nurseries that specialize in alpine plants and dwarf shrubs and to growers of water lilies and other aquatic plants. The latter will usually stock, as well, the pool liners, pumps, pipes, heaters, lights and chemicals needed for water gardens—and even decorative fish.

Would-be rock gardeners might benefit from joining the Alpine Garden Society. In addition to a quarterly bulletin of articles and news on rock plants, membership enables them to obtain seeds of uncommon plants, to take part in study groups and field trips abroad and to consult the Society's library. In Scotland, enthusiastic rock gardeners may be interested in joining the Scottish Rock Garden Club.

STARTING A ROCK GARDEN

Like most amateurs who have come to specialize in one aspect of horticulture, rock gardeners are a dedicated, even passionate breed, sharing an abiding fascination for what Reginald Farrer fondly referred to as "the little people of the mountains". The smaller and rarer the specimen, the keener the glint in the eye. Consequently, as members congregate round the show benches at the Royal Horticultural Society halls and at other exhibitions, they chat like old and best friends. Not without reason, rock gardening has been called all-consuming. "It never ceases to amaze me," says one rock gardener, "that in my own small garden I can grow botanical treasures of every description from almost every mountain range on earth."

THE THRILL OF THE CHASE

A mountain view in your own garden

A rock garden may take many forms. It may spread over several hectares, encompassing an alpine meadow, a massive ledge and a tumbling stream, or it may occupy a single hollowed-out rock or an old stone sink large enough to hold only a few tiny plants. A drystone wall, made without mortar, can be a rock garden, and so can a paved terrace with soil-filled crevices between the stones. Some rock gardens are islands or raised beds in conventional gardens; some are miniature landscapes in trough-like containers; and some are built round nothing more than a few exceptionally sculptured stones. Theoretically there could even be rock gardens without rocks—since what basically defines a rock garden is less the presence of rocks than the nature of the soil and the plants.

To purists, those plants are alpine materials, native to cold, high altitudes above the tree line. The ultimate reward for alpine plant enthusiasts is finding a rare and beautiful specimen from the roof of the world, and coaxing it to grow—even for just a year or two—in a sea-level garden. The greater the risk, the greater the pleasure, for the likelihood of defeat makes success all the sweeter. And some of the wild fledglings have never survived captivity. Not even the skilled rock gardener Reginald Farrer could persuade the blue-eyed *Eritrichum nanum* to become domesticated. "There rises before me, like King Richard's ghosts on the eve of Bosworth," he wrote, "a long and expensive train of phantoms—all the *Eritrichums* I have loved and lost, despite care and pains unutterable."

Happily, most of the difficult alpine plants have less demanding close relatives, which makes life for the new rock gardener much easier. Also, there are a number of familiar lowland plants that seem to fit naturally into rock gardens—dwarf shrubs, small flowering bulbs, herbs, ferns, succulents. What constitutes a proper rock-garden plant is in fact mainly a matter

Dwarf conifers—no more than 1.5 metres (5 ft) tall—provide a backdrop for a colourful alpine garden. Large boulders are encrusted with yellow cotyledons, purple aubrieta and pink phlox.

of common sense. Experts seem to agree that it is any plant that does not look out of place in a natural rocky setting. This generally rules out the large showy hybrids which, in any case, do not take kindly to the shallow soil—though certain smaller azalea and rhododendron cultivars fit into the larger rock gardens as naturally as if they had been there all along.

THE ESSENTIAL ALPINES

Alpine wild flowers, however, are the backbone of a rock garden, so it is well to know something about their nature and how they behave. Anyone who treks in spring in the Alps or Appennines, or even on Snowdon, will be amazed by the fact that any plant, let alone plants so seemingly delicate, can survive among barren rocks in a situation exposed for much of the year to intense cold and gale-force winds. Yet there they are, springing from crevices and spreading intricate tapestries of colour over the stony ground, colour that seems all the more spectacular because the flowers are often disproportionately large in comparison to the size of the plant.

Actually, these appealing characteristics are simply adaptations for survival. By growing close to the ground, often in the lee of rocks, alpine plants avoid the full brunt of the wind and make maximum use of the sun's heat, which warms the rocks and in turn the plants near them. In winter, these plants have the added protection of a thick, constant blanket of snow to insulate them from the cold. Together, these conditions compress the plants into typically tight cushions, or "buns", with streamlined shapes that deflect the wind and keep temperatures within the plants somewhat higher. The leaves themselves are often small, and rounded or needle-thin, exposing the least possible surface to the elements. On many plants the leaves have a thick, waxy surface and an inner structure of water-storing cells, like those of desert plants, or are covered with soft woolly hairs that shield the leaf pores from the drying effects of wind and sun.

BEAUTY FOR SURVIVAL

Just as extremes of climate stunt mountain trees into gnarled shrubs and mountain shrubs into low-growing ground covers, so these mountain flowers are dwarfed. But the dwarfing effect involves primarily their vegetative growth. The flowers, which appear in the spring when the weather is most benign, are close to full size but seem even larger because the plants themselves are so small. Large flowers too have survival value. In the high mountains' short growing season, which rarely lasts for more than four months, and frequently only for two or three, reproduction must happen in a hurry. In order to survive, a plant must burst into bloom almost the moment it pushes through the snow, and put on a floral display bright enough to lure insects to do their work of pollination quickly.

Another equally interesting adaptation of alpine wild flowers to their harsh environment is one walkers never see. Plants that are found in close association with rocks—called saxicoline or saxatile, from the Latin word *saxum*, for rock— typically send down deep roots to anchor themselves in the gravelly, fast-draining soil, and to get at the moisture and nourishment they need. A plant only 5 to 7.5 centimetres (2 to 3 in.) high may have roots 60 to 90 centimetres (2 to 3 ft) long, and may even force tiny hair-like feeder roots into rock fissures.

DANGERS IN MUGGY CLIMATES

Transplanted into the garden, these tough little wild flowers demand the same kind of quick drainage and cool root runs they are accustomed to in the mountains; they cannot tolerate excessive heat or excessive moisture round their stems. Nor can they adjust, after so many years of adversity, to very rich soils. Though a few may accept the soft life for a while, the great majority will turn into lustreless, over-fed weaklings and quickly expire. The same is true of their reaction to tropical humidity. For alpine plants, the arch-enemy is muggy weather— long spells of sultry summer heat punctuated by thunderstorms. Unless plants have perfect drainage and access to some shade and moving air, this relentless combination of humidity and heat will quickly reduce them to a mildewed mess. Indeed, in some parts of Europe, alpine plants can be grown successfully only in cool or "alpine" greenhouses.

Bearing in mind these natural proclivities of alpine plants, you can begin to plan the siting of your rock garden. If your property is punctuated by a jutting rocky ledge, by all means exploit it—lawn grass will not thrive on it in any case. Do a little exploratory digging round the ledge to see how far it extends in case you want to expose more of it to view. Scrape out the tangle of old turf and weeds from between the crevices, and clean the rock further with a forceful spray from the high-pressure jet of a water hose. You may be able to create planting pockets right in the face of the stone. But, if you plan to do this, be sure to get rid of all the roots of existing plants—which otherwise could return to plague you. It is also a good idea to replace the existing soil in these pockets with the ideal mixture for rock plants described on page 34.

BRINGING THE ROCKS IN

If your property does not have a ready-made stone outcrop— and few gardens do—you will have to import stones. But that gives you the option of siting your rock garden exactly where you want it. At the turn of the century, when rock gardening was young, the idea was to place these gardens where they would be encountered unexpectedly as one strolled over the grounds of a large estate; they were supposed to be "surprises of nature". It is a little difficult to create surprises of this kind in a small suburban garden, and anyway the concept of rock gardens has changed. Once they were conceived as naturalized gardens; now they are often openly man-made affairs, incorporating such rectilinear architectural elements as stone walls, raised beds and paved paths and steps.

Where you site a rock garden depends partly on your personal preference: you will naturally want to place it where you will most enjoy looking at it. But you will save yourself a great deal of trouble later if you also consider the needs of the plants. With a few exceptions, rock plants need plenty of sun. They should be exposed to it for at least half the day. This rules out the proximity of trees, which are also apt to invade rock gardens with their roots, robbing the plants of vital nutrients.

LIGHT WITHOUT HEAT Although they require sun, most alpine plants need to be protected from baking heat. In places where summers are truly cool, such as the far north of Europe, a rock garden can face in almost any direction. But elsewhere, an eastern or northern exposure is advisable. If a southern or western exposure is unavoidable, the hot sun of midday and late afternoon should be filtered through the foliage of trees—but trees distant enough to avoid the problems of root invasion. And particularly sensitive plants, such as saxifrages and androsaces are best grown in the shade of rocks or low shrubs that are part of the garden.

Because good drainage is probably the single most important growing condition for alpine plants, a rock garden should take advantage of the land's natural contours. A slope, even a slight one, will help to move rainwater downhill after it has percolated into the ground. But if the site is nearly level or the soil is heavy clay, some additional measures may be needed. One way to improve drainage is to excavate the garden to a depth of 45 to 60 centimetres ($1\frac{1}{2}$ to 2 ft), and put in a layer of assorted stones, broken rocks and coarse gravel, 15 to 30 centimetres (6 to 12 in.) deep. Top this with 5 centimetres (2 in.) of stone chips or coarse sand to prevent soil from washing down and clogging the drainage bed. Then lay down the rocks and soil that will form the garden's surface.

THE NATURAL LOOK These surface rocks are of course the garden's very foundation, the elements that establish its essential character, and their selection and grouping are critical. Today, as in Reginald Farrer's day, the most common mistake in working with them is creating a "dog's grave"—using too many rocks too small in size, and of too many different kinds. The result is a garden that looks more like a geological display than a natural feature of the landscape. But this can be avoided with a few simple guidelines. First, limit the choice of rock to a single kind, and choose a kind that is relatively neutral in colouring. Also, avoid rocks that have been too obviously finished by human hands—a rock garden is not a showcase for the quarryman's craft. And finally, if possible, choose a rock that is indigenous to your area. Not only will it look more at home in your garden, but it will also save you transportation costs.

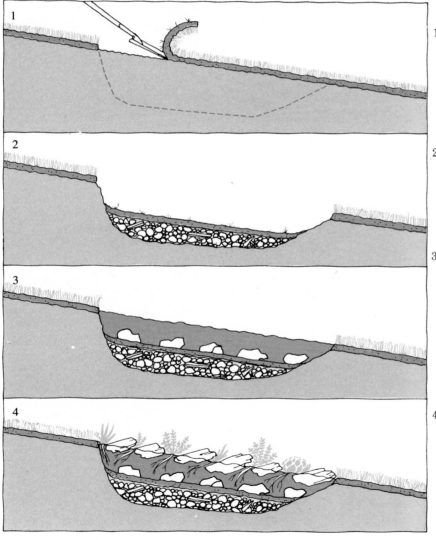

STARTING ON A SMALL SCALE

1. *To build a small, easy-to-care-for rock garden on a gentle slope, strip turf and topsoil from an area no larger than 1.8 by 1.8 metres (6 by 6 ft). Then dig a hole with sloping sides that is about 45 cm (1½ ft) deep at the centre. Reserve debris for later use.*

2. *Line the hole with a 15 cm (6 in.) layer of coarse drainage material such as broken bricks or stones. Top with the turf, upside down, to keep soil from sifting into the drainage bed. Stone chips or coarse sand can be substituted for turf.*

3. *Top the drainage layer with good-sized rocks to support other rocks that will be exposed to view in the finished garden. Mix the excavated soil with equal parts of leaf-mould and gravel, fill the hole with this mixture and rake smooth. Moisten and let it settle for a few days, filling any low spots that develop with additional soil mixture.*

4. *Embed several large rocks in the soil with their broadest sides down and angled so that water will drain back into the soil. Cover the rocks to at least one third their depth with the soil. Set plants between the rocks.*

Mountain gems

The exquisite colour and delicacy of alpine plants belie their ability to exist in the sparsest of surroundings. In fact, the brilliance of their hues is an insurance against destruction in the dry winds and hot sun of a mountain-top environment. Flying insects, attracted by the bright colours, pollinate the flowers which produce thousands of seeds, at least some of which will survive the winter to germinate the following year.

CANDYTUFT
Iberis sempervirens

DRUMSTICK PRIMROSE
Primula denticulata

MOSSY SAXIFRAGE
Saxifraga hypnoides

GOLD DUST
Alyssum saxatile

AUBRIETA
Aubrieta deltoides

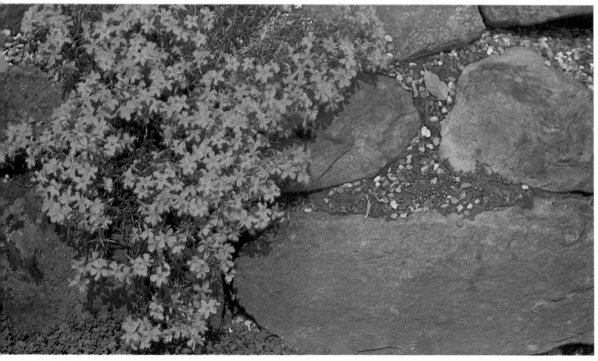

MOSS PHLOX
Phlox subulata 'Scarlet Flame'

25

VIRTUES OF SANDSTONE

One of the best and most widely distributed rocks for rock gardens is sandstone. It is a pleasing yet unobtrusive colour, ranging from a light yellowish-grey to a dark reddish-brown, depending on where it is found. Sandstone is a strong rock but it is soft enough to weather into interesting stratified patterns, and porous enough to retain moisture—a benefit during hot, dry weather to plants growing round it. And because its chemical composition is relatively neutral, it will accommodate plants with a wide spectrum of soil preferences.

Another good choice is limestone, which is usually grey in colour. It, too, weathers into interesting patterns of cracks and crevices, and is porous and water-retentive. True, a small amount of lime will leach out of it, which could be a problem for plants that need acid soils, such as heathers and azaleas. But many choice alpine plants are native to limestone mountains. If you want to make sure that acid-loving plants are not harmed by the lime, they should be placed at the top of the rock garden, above the level of the lime run-off.

FROM GNEISS TO TUFA

Other rocks, found in some parts of Europe, that are suitable for gardens are gneiss, a layered rock that usually comes in a handsome, dark grey colour with wavy lighter bands running through it, and both shale and schist, though certain kinds of these rocks are soft and brittle, and tend to crumble around the edges. Two porous rocks that are occasionally available are lava, a volcanic rock, and tufa, formed of limestone sediment in springs and streams. Granite, exceptionally hard and fine grained, weathers very slowly and, being non-porous, is less hospitable to plants. However, many gardens have been built of granite when it is the only rock available. Glacial boulders, commonly of granite, are not only hard but also rounded and smooth. They are ideal for simulating a boulder-strewn alpine meadow, but are less easy to work with than craggy rocks with flat tops and many crevices.

Rock gardens look best when the rocks are few and relatively large, and are buried deep in the ground. But handling large rocks calls for some special precautions. Wear heavy gloves with leather palms and strong shoes with reinforced steel toes. When lifting any rock, squat in front of it, grasp it firmly and then stand up, keeping your back straight; this will force your leg muscles rather than your back to take the brunt of the load. Unmanageable rocks can be slid along the ground with the help of a crowbar and rollers, or a piece of plywood (*page 28*). By such means you can probably manoeuvre rocks weighing 50 kilograms (100 lb) or more into place by yourself.

The key rocks in a fair-sized ledge garden, however, may weigh as much as half a tonne; for these you will clearly need the help of a contractor with mechanized equipment.

STARTING AT THE BOTTOM

To avoid unnecessary work it is a good idea to sketch out various arrangements of rocks on paper, and then plot them on the ground, using newspaper, stakes and string. When the plan seems right, begin to set the rocks in place, starting at the bottom of the slope and working upwards—much as you would construct a wall. Not only is this a more natural way to work but it makes the job simpler. To place a rock, cut a step into the slope so that the rock, when resting on its broadest face, tilts slightly backwards; rainwater will then run into the soil. Then pack soil round the narrow rear end of the rock so that not more than two-thirds of it is exposed. Besides giving rocks stability, this is the way they are most often found in nature.

Many rocks used for rock gardens have, in fact, a natural structure, which should be taken into account in their siting; as a group they are known as sedimentary rocks, built up in layers called strata, aeons ago. When exposed by the movement of the earth's crust or by erosion, these layers are visible as horizontal lines running through the face of the rock. Furthermore, wherever vertical cracks occur, they too follow a distinctive pattern, running through the layers in continuous lines, from top to bottom. Seen in cross-section, the rock face appears to have been composed of building blocks. This composition suggests how they should be placed in a rock garden—with all their strata lines lying in one direction, and with their vertical cracks lined up, from stone to stone.

RAINWATER TO THE ROOTS

As you place the rocks, tilt them slightly into the slope, so that their outer edges will catch the rain and carry it back into the soil to water the roots of plants. Also, it is a good idea to vary the spaces between the rocks, leaving narrow crevices for smaller plants and wider spaces for shrubs and plants with spreading roots. Remove enough soil for each rock so that at least a third of its bulk will be buried; even two-thirds is not too much. As you replace the soil, pack it firmly round the rock; and to make sure the rock is well bedded, stand on it and shift your weight.

If your rock garden is small, you can probably tend it simply by stepping from stone to stone, but for larger gardens you may want to put winding paths and even steps among the rocks. These should be unobtrusive; paths can be as narrow as 45 centimetres ($1\frac{1}{2}$ ft). As surfacing, some gardeners use organic materials such as shredded bark—but these can offer a haven for slugs, one of the main enemies of alpine plants. Far safer, and more natural looking too, are stone chips, gravel or crushed stone. In fact, these can often be extended into the garden proper, as a mulch for the plants. Whether as paths or as mulch, these materials should be about 7.5 centimetres (3 in.) deep. If you incorporate steps into the steeper parts of the path, keep them wide and shallow, ensuring that the width of the treads measures much more than the height of the risers. Old railway sleepers and sections of timber are good for making steps, but even more appropriate are flat pieces of the same kind of rock used in constructing the garden.

In such a setting, designed to resemble a rocky mountain meadow, alpine flowers are immediately at home. But a natural

MOVING ROCKS SINGLE-HANDED

1. *One man can move a rock weighing 50 kg (100 lb) or more by using a dolly made from a 90 by 120 cm (3 by 4 ft) piece of 18 mm (¾ in.) plywood laid over lengths of 10 cm (4 in.) plastic drainpipe. To start, tilt the plywood towards the rock by placing a single length of pipe at the far end. Roll the rock on to the middle of the board. For safety, wear gloves with leather palms and shoes with steel-capped toes. Bend your knees as you push so that the leg muscles do the work rather than the weaker back ones.*

2. *Roll the plywood and the rock forward on to additional lengths of pipe. Then using the pipes as rollers, push the rock along the ground until the rear pipe is free of the plywood. Move that pipe in front of the dolly and push the rock again, manoeuvring the pipes until the rock is just short of its prepared destination. Tilt the plywood as you roll the rock off and into place.*

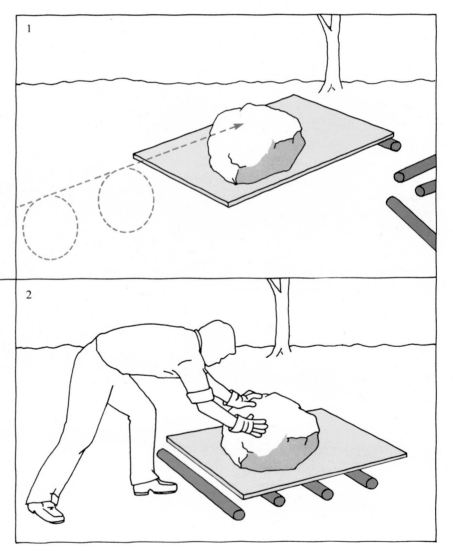

rock garden is not the only environment for these plants. Faced with such insuperable problems as a flat site, a soil that drains poorly, or too little space, gardeners have created ingenious substitutes. One of the most popular is the dry-wall garden and its close relative, the raised bed. Both literally rise above the problem of an excessively moist soil by getting the plants off the ground, into the air, and providing a maximum floral display near eye level in a minimum of space. "If I could have only one small rock garden," says one expert, "it would be of the wall or raised-bed type."

A wall garden fits advantageously into any situation where there is a change in ground level—at the point where the sloping ground round a house foundation joins the lawn, for instance, or along a bank viewed from a road. It is essentially the same as a stone wall, with narrow spaces between the rocks, except that those spaces are filled with soil rather than mortar. This means, of course, that the wall is less stable, which dictates precautionary measures in its construction. For safety, it should be not more than 60 to 90 centimetres (2 to 3 ft) high, and the stones used to build it should be relatively flat. Use stones as large as you can comfortably handle, since a section of wall composed of a few large stones tends to be sturdier than one made of many small stones. As you proceed from course to course, set the stones back slightly, so that the finished wall will have a backward pitch of at least 2.5 centimetres (1 in.) for every 25 centimetres (10 in.) of height; for walls at the base of a steep slope, this pitch can be as much as 5 centimetres (2 in.). Occasionally a stone can be inserted lengthways—like a stretcher—to make for greater stability.

To build the wall, first establish the position of its face by stretching a piece of string between stakes. Excavate the slope behind this line to a depth of 15 to 30 centimetres (6 to 12 in.) below ground level, and extend the excavation into the slope at least 30 centimetres (1 ft) beyond where the back of the wall will be. Fill this trench to within 5 centimetres (2 in.) of the top with coarse gravel or broken rubble, for drainage, and slant the top of this filling material slightly into the slope; this will tip the subsequent rocks slightly into the slope too— for greater stability and to channel rainwater to plant roots.

As with conventional rock gardens, the best rocks for a wall garden are sandstone and limestone. Because rocks, like bricks, can vary in colour from quarry to quarry—a variation that might be disconcertingly apparent in the finished wall—you should have enough on hand to complete the job. For every 3 square

A CLEVERLY WEDGED LEDGE

By artfully arranging rocks that have clearly defined strata and fracture lines, such as limestone or sandstone, you can create the illusion of having a rock outcrop in your garden. Using flat pieces small enough to lift easily, pile the rocks on top of one another against a slope, lining up both the horizontal (strata) and the vertical (fracture) lines as evenly as possible. Scoop soil round the stack and set plants in the crevices. Only a close inspection will reveal that the work is yours and not that of nature.

BUILDING A WALL GARDEN

metres (approx. 33 sq. ft.) of wall surface, you will need roughly a tonne of stone. Set the largest, flattest rocks in a line, to form the bottom course of the wall, and fill in the spaces between them with the standard soil mixture described on page 34. Add a few odd stones or rubble here and there to improve drainage, and be sure to tamp in the soil firmly round the back of the wall, filling in the excavation as you go.

PLANTING AS YOU BUILD

A dry-wall garden, unlike a conventional rock garden, is best planted in the course of construction because planting is much more difficult after the wall is completed. Therefore, as you complete each course, leave gaps here and there, and fill these with small plants, knocked out of their pots and inserted sideways; then cover the roots with 1 centimetre ($\frac{1}{2}$ in.) of soil, and lay another course of rocks on top. Stagger the rocks so that their joints do not line up with those of the course below, and fill in uneven spaces with soil or small slivers of rock.

As you complete every few courses, wet the entire wall with a fine spray of water, to settle the soil between the rocks and moisten the plant roots. When the entire wall is complete, spread a layer of crushed stone or gravel on the surface of the soil behind it, strategically position a stone or two, and set more plants along the top, extending your alpine garden back from the face of the wall to whatever depth you desire.

A raised garden can be built against an existing house wall or be entirely free-standing, and can be square or rectangular and of any size, though a bed no more than 90 centimetres (3 ft) high and 120 centimetres (4 ft) wide is easier to reach across for tending than a larger one. The construction is identical to that of a wall garden, except that the wall is built round a raised bed (*drawings, right*). The plants in the top of the bed are, of course, at the garden's centre stage, with those on the sides of the wall serving as supporting players.

ALTERNATIVES FOR ROCK

In some regions where natural rocks are scarce, gardeners have carried the concept of man-made wall gardens one step further and have created walls and raised beds without rocks. Sometimes the structural members are heavy, rot-resistant timbers, such as railway sleepers. On a gentle slope, these wooden members can be set wide apart, to create shallow terraces; on a steeper gradient, they can be placed close together, forming narrow planting pockets. And, on level ground, they can be staggered or stacked log-cabin style to create a raised bed.

Another substitute for natural stone, concrete block, comes in muted colours with textured surfaces, but these always look artificial. In Scotland, particularly, peat blocks are often used in place of stone and are ideal for acid-loving plants.

For some alpine plant enthusiasts, the man-made rock garden takes the form of a miniature landscape, planted in a suitably rustic container. The idea originated in Britain, and the favourite containers were old stone sinks or water troughs. As these antique items became increasingly difficult to find, gardeners made artificial ones out of concrete, substituting moss peat for the gravel, and vermiculite or perlite for the sand usually used in making concrete. This mixture, together with cement and water, gives the trough a stone-like appearance; it also helps to make the container more porous and lighter in weight than it would otherwise be.

Using the same formula, a few gardeners varied the theme and made artificial rocks ranging in size from stepping-stones to billiard-table-sized boulders with built-in planting pockets. The latter are hardly a do-it-yourself project, but smaller rocks are easy to cast and use. First, make a form by digging a hole in the ground, leaving the bottom somewhat irregular. Press small pieces of oiled stone into the soil here and there, to create planting pockets. Then mix the concrete, using 1 part portland cement to $1\frac{1}{2}$ parts fine moss peat and $1\frac{1}{2}$ parts perlite or vermiculite; you can tint this mixture to dark earth tones by adding one of the cement colouring powders available at hardware shops or builders' merchants. Add water little by little, stirring the mixture well, until it has the consistency of cottage cheese.

CAST OF CONCRETE

WALLING A RAISED BED

On level ground, a raised bed 60 to 90 cm (2 to 3 ft) high will ensure the quick drainage needed by most rock plants. Start with a trench 15 to 30 cm (6 to 12 in.) deep in the desired shape (insets). Place the largest stones in the trench, tilted slightly towards the centre of the bed. As each row of the drystone wall is built, use soil like cement, packing it into crevices. Fill the bottom of the bed with ordinary garden soil. Fill the top of the bed with a 25 cm (10 in.) layer of equal parts garden loam, leaf-mould and gravel. As you build, put plants in some of the crevices. Plant the bed and mulch with 5 cm (2 in.) of crushed stone.

Rock gardens in miniature

In the 1930s, British rock gardeners discovered that old stone watering troughs made good and appropriately rough-hewn containers for finicky alpine plants that did not adapt readily to life in a conventional rock garden. When the supply of these period pieces was exhausted, inventive gardeners began to fashion their own from lightweight concrete. Today, rock gardeners still make similar troughs—but sometimes for a different reason: they want to introduce a note of rugged beauty into a man-made setting.

Foreshadowing a rocky slope across the lawn, a trough garden mulched with pebbles displays an assortment of succulents.

Trailing plants cascading over the rim of a concrete trough blend a miniature garden into its rocky surroundings.

Sedums, sempervivums and golden erigeron surround a collection of rocks and driftwood in a rough raised trough.

33

Pour the mixture gradually into the prepared hole until the hole is filled, stirring it gently with a spade from time to time to remove air pockets. Leave the mixture to harden for several days, then pry up the concrete lump and loosen the stones embedded in it to create planting pockets; if they do not slip out easily, tap them with a hammer. Set the lump aside to cure further for another four or five days, covering it with a piece of damp hessian or canvas; keep the covering damp, since concrete requires moisture to cure properly. Finally, soak your artificial rock in a tub of water for several days to leach out the lime in the concrete, or let it stand out of doors through several heavy showers. At the end of this treatment, clean off any remaining bits of soil and loose concrete with a stiff wire brush—and your imitation rock is ready for planting.

A BASIC SOIL MIXTURE

Once the basic structure of the rock garden is established, you are ready to deal with the final components—soil and plants. While alpine flowers grow in a variety of soils, almost all are found in soil that is relatively porous, fast-draining and not over-fertile. Soils are usually a mixture, in varying proportions, of clay or loam, humus from rotting leaves or other vegetation, and particles of mineral matter in the form of broken rock, gravel or sand. Following nature's general pattern, a standard mixture for rock gardens consists of 1 part garden loam, 1 part well-rotted leaf-mould and 1 part stone chips, broken crocks, crushed stone or gravel.

Coarse sand can be substituted for the stone or gravel, although drainage will not be quite as good, and garden compost can be substituted for leaf-mould, although it tends to be somewhat rich for alpine plants and may in addition contain weed seeds. You can also use moss peat instead of leaf-mould, but since moss peat has almost no nutritive value, it is a good idea to enrich every 36 litres (8 gal.) of soil with two handfuls of dried manure, two handfuls of bone-meal or a cup of fertilizer high in phosphorus. Moss peat also makes the soil more acid, which suits only some plants. To make the soil less acid, add two handfuls of ground limestone to the same quantity of soil as above.

TAILORED PLANTING MIXTURES

In a number of cases you may want to alter this basic soil mixture to suit areas of the garden given over to certain kinds of plants. For gentians, heaths and heathers, for instance, which grow best in acid soils, the proportions should be changed to 2 parts of loam, 5 parts of leaf-mould (preferably from the leaves of oak or beech trees, which are very acid), and 1 part of coarse sand. Moss peat can be substituted for all or part of the leaf-mould, but if a great deal of moss peat is used, the mixture should be enriched with fertilizer, as previously described.

Other plants with special soil needs are the pinks and saxifrages, which are usually found on limestone ledges and consequently do better in an alkaline soil. For such plants the proportions can vary to 1 part loam, 1 part non-acid leaf-mould, 1 part gravel or sand, and 1 part limestone chippings or crushed sea shells. And there are, in addition, alpine plants with very special drainage needs. One group, which includes the drabas, androsaces and edraianthus, is often found in what geologists call scree, or talus, the rocky debris that accumulates at the base of ledges and cliffs. Another group, which includes some edraianthus and alpine poppies, favours a moraine, the mixture of rock and earth scraped up by glaciers and left behind as the ice melts and recedes.

SCREES AND MORAINES

Both scree and moraine conditions can be simulated in a rock garden, preferably as they are found in nature—fanning out at the base of a slope. And both require, above all, first-class drainage. Excavate the area to a depth of at least 60 centimetres (2 ft) below the eventual soil level, and line the excavation with a 20 centimetre (8 in.) layer of coarse stones, broken bricks or building

POCKETED PLANTS IN A TOWER OF TUFA

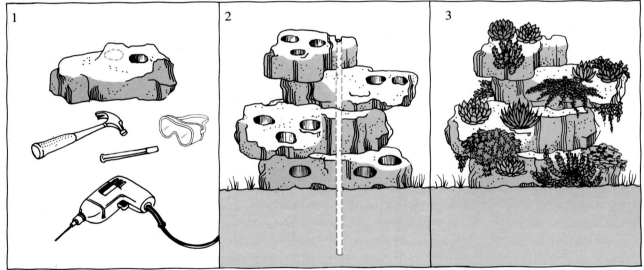

To plant in lava rock or tufa, wet the rock and make pockets 7.5 to 15 cm (3 to 6 in.) deep with an electric drill and masonry bit or with a hammer and cold chisel. Wear gloves and goggles. Remove dust from holes.

To assemble several rocks to look like a natural formation, drill a hole through each and thread them on an aluminium rod long enough to drive into the ground; or use a reinforcing rod as used in masonry work.

With rocks arranged, line each plant pocket with moss to prevent the porous rock from drying the pockets. Fill the pockets with plants in a mixture of 1 part soil, 1 part gravel and 1 part leaf-mould. Water often.

rubble, such as bits of concrete. Over this drainage bed place a layer of unrotted leaves or gravel, to prevent the soil from sifting down into it. Then prepare the soil. First, blend together 1 part garden loam with 2 parts leaf-mould or moss peat, adding a handful or two of dried manure or bone-meal for enrichment. Then combine this soil mixture with gravel or stone chips, using 4 parts of gravel or chips to 1 part of soil.

For a scree garden, this mixture is simply placed on top of the drainage bed, but for a moraine garden some sort of constantly moving underground water must be provided. In dry periods, it must come from your own plumbing system. In one arrangement it flows in a steady trickle during the growing season from perforated pipes which have been buried in the drainage bed (*drawing, right*).

POSITIONING PLANTS   By dividing a rock garden on paper into a number of such planting areas, each with slightly different growing conditions, you can combine plant materials with as much freedom and imagination as a painter manipulating pigments. You can play colours, textures and forms against one another to create close harmonies and unexpected contrasts and, since the garden is a living painting, you can also vary its visual effects from week to week by taking into account the plants' periods of bloom. Nevertheless there are certain design guidelines that experienced rock gardeners follow. Purists among them insist that tall plants should be placed at the bottom of the slope, as they are found in nature, and that plant material should diminish in size as it moves up the slope, ending with the tiny tufts found on the mountain top, above the timber line. This is fine when the garden is large, but on slopes of more modest size it can easily result in taller plants blocking out the view of the smaller ones. Consequently the reverse order may be better.

In a natural rock garden it is also advisable to avoid setting plants in too regular or geometric a pattern, which quickly destroys the desired natural effect. So too will the intermixing of too many species with different foliage and flower colours in too small a space. Instead, group together plants of a single kind, but leave enough room between groups so that the plants will spread into irregular drifts of foliage—and then of massed colour—when they are in bloom.

OFF-SEASON COLOUR   Because most alpine plants bloom in spring and are relatively drab for the rest of the year, the garden design should include some plants that vary from the norm. Look for species that bloom earlier than usual, such as the Kabschia saxifrages, or that have brilliant autumn foliage, most alpine geraniums, for example. Also, look for alpines whose leaves are as interesting as their flowers—either in texture or colour; the sempervivums and ajugas are typical examples. To extend the garden's period of bloom, add some non-alpine plants to its composition. Small bulbous plants such as snowdrops, cyclamen, winter aconite, dwarf iris and crocus—all of which bloom very early in spring— blend naturally into an alpine garden. So do such summer-flowering perennials as the campanulas; and for autumn and winter colour, there are ceratostigmas and heathers.

When the garden has been created on paper, it is time to create it outdoors. This can be done at any time during the growing season, though it is best to avoid the hot and humid weather of summer, which is equally hard on you and the alpine plants. Some rock gardeners like to start their gardens in spring, when plants are most readily available. But this means condensing a great deal of work into a relatively short span of time, since the preliminaries to planting—the actual creation of the rocky setting—can take several weeks. Also these preliminaries should include a thorough soaking and a resting period of a week or more, to allow the soil to settle into place.

A garden started in autumn has the advantage of encouraging the development of strong roots, since the plants at that stage have completed their top growth and are preparing themselves for the winter. If you decide to plant in autumn, plan to do so at least a month before the first heavy frost is expected, so that the tender new roots will not be torn by heaving ground.

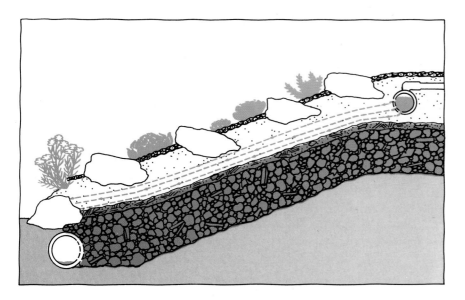

MAKING A GLACIAL MORAINE

Alpine plants native to a moraine— rocks and soil deposited by a melting glacier—need quick drainage and a constant flow of water round their roots during the growing season. To simulate such an environment on a slope, dig a bed 45 to 60 cm (1½ to 2 ft) deep and lay 1.8 to 2.4 metres (6 to 8 ft) of perforated plastic drainpipe. Cover pipe and bed with a 20 cm (8 in.) layer of stones and a layer of gravel. At the top, lay a second length of pipe, capped at one end and connected at the other to a water supply. Cover pipe and bed with a mixture of 1 part soil and leaf-mould to 4 parts gravel. Add plants and rocks and let water trickle constantly through.

THE PLANTING TECHNIQUE

The actual planting should proceed from large plants to small; plant dwarf trees and shrubs first, then work down the scale to the smallest specimens. Be sure to make the holes large enough to accommodate the deep roots of most alpine plants. Loosen the roots of pot-grown plants and set them in the soil at the same depth they occupied in the pot. Fill in round the roots with the planting mixture, packing it down to eliminate air pockets. When the hole is about two-thirds full, fill the remaining third with water; then, when this has trickled through, add soil to the surface level. Dress the top of the soil with 4 centimetres (1½ in.) of gravel or crushed stone, surrounding the plant like a collar.

In the moderately cool weather and normal rainfall of spring and autumn, most rock-garden plants adjust to their surroundings with no special care. However, if the weather is unusually hot or dry, young plants may need regular watering. Make a thorough job of this, so that the water reaches down to the feeding roots and, for best results, water in the morning so that the leaves and stems can dry off before nightfall. In excessively bright sun, young plants may also benefit from some temporary shade at midday. You can erect a screen between the plant and the sun, using stakes and cardboard.

WATER IF LEAVES WILT

Once established, rock-garden plants have few problems. In periods of drought, they may need watering—a good rule of thumb is to water only when the leaves appear wilted. In periods of high humidity, they may develop mildew, which can generally be controlled with a dusting of sulphur or of a chemical fungicide. Few pests attack them, but you should keep a sharp look-out for slugs. They come out of hiding at night to chew tender stems and are especially troublesome in humid weather.

You can somewhat discourage slugs by keeping the garden mulched with gravel and free of dead leaves and debris, their favourite hiding places. You can also control them with baits and pesticides made specifically for this purpose, or with home-made remedies. Some gardeners trap slugs by leaving lettuce leaves or raw potato slices as bait, then collecting and dropping them into a can of water topped with paraffin oil, where they drown. Others set out saucers of beer or grape juice as lures—and the slugs drown themselves.

ROOTING OUT THE WEEDS

One chore that should never be postponed in the rock garden is weeding. When weeds gain a foothold among rocks or in cushion-like plants, they are very difficult to eradicate. In a newly planted garden, the surest way to deal with them is simply to pull out any seedlings that appear among the plants. Later, the distinctions are not so easy. Many rock-garden plants seed themselves, and this self-seeding should generally be encouraged, especially if the plants are short lived, like the alpine poppy. If you have trouble spotting the difference between a weed and a cultivated plant, allow the mystery plant to flower; if it is a weed, pull it up before it has a chance to go to seed.

Finally, like all perennials, those that grow in rock gardens benefit from extra attention in spring and autumn, as they begin and end the growing season. In late autumn, after the last blooms have faded and the leaves have dropped from the trees, give the garden a thorough clean-up.

A SPRING BOOSTER

Also, in spring, another clean-up may be in order, to remove the debris of winter storms and to repair patches of soil eroded by heavy rain or melting snow. Most rock gardens are improved by fertilizing annually in spring. An excellent mixture for this purpose is equal parts of leaf-mould and gravel or coarse sand, plus a handful or two of dried manure or bone-meal; spent mushroom compost is an excellent alternative. Spread a 1 centimetre ($\frac{1}{2}$ in.) layer of this mixture over the surface of the soil. Your rock garden is now ready to reward you through another season with its constantly changing display of colour.

POSITIONING PLANTS TO THEIR BEST ADVANTAGE

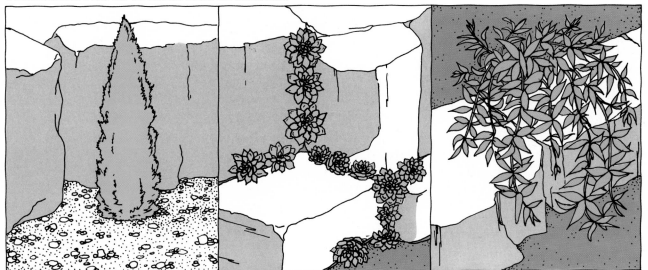

A slender dwarf conifer must be sensitively positioned in order to best display its delicate beauty in a rugged rock garden. Plant it where it will be entirely silhouetted against a large, dark rock or rock outcrop.

Succulents that grow in rosettes and spread by runners, like sempervivums, thrive in rock crevices. Here the drainage of rainwater is swift and the rocks hold the rot-prone plant crowns safely above the damp soil.

Rock plants that have trailing stems, such as prostrate campanulas and aubrietas, should be planted at the top of a rocky ledge or retaining wall. They will cascade down and produce a lavish display of flowers.

Creating drama with rocky designs

For centuries, rocks and the plants that thrive among them have fascinated gardeners. The Chinese designed rock gardens over 2,000 years ago. When discovered by Europeans in the 17th and 18th centuries, these gardens had a great influence on the "naturalism" garden movement then sweeping Europe.

"The sides of the canals, or lesser streams, are not faced (as they are with us) with smooth stone and in a straight line," wrote Father Attiret, a French missionary, in 1743, "but look rude and rustic, with different pieces of rock, some of which jut out, and others recede inwards; and are placed with so much art, that you would take it to be the work of nature. The banks are sprinkled with flowers, which rise up even through the hollows in the rock work, as if they had been produced there naturally. They have a great variety of them, for every season of the year."

More than two centuries later, most rock gardens are still designed to imitate nature's informality. Plants appear singly or in groups—not in formal rows. Paths are laid out to wander casually through the garden and are covered with such natural materials as pine needles, shredded bark or stone chips. Stepping-stones are blended into the garden with creeping thyme or other ground-hugging plants. Even more formal wall gardens (*pages 42-43*) are draped with trailing plants to soften their man-made appearance.

With proper planning, a rock garden can be built almost anywhere—squeezed, for instance, into a narrow, restricted area between a path and a fence or a wall, or spread over a rambling woodland outcrop (*page 46*). Such gardens can be practical as well as beautiful. The addition of rocks and rock plants to a steep bank can help stop erosion. A barren field of boulders can become a colourful alpine meadow. A ledge garden, consisting of a few flat rocks and low-growing plants, can add interest and colour to a large, sweeping lawn. And a raised rocky bed can make an excellent foundation planting round a house, for rock plants are generally small and unlikely to outgrow their allotted space.

Candytuft, aubrieta, ferns, saxifrage, alyssum and blue gentian, planted among jagged outcrops of closely-packed schist, create a rock garden of subtle contrasts.

**When gardeners
set the scene**

A rock garden totally man-made—whether a wall garden or a simulated stone outcrop—should draw its inspiration from nature. For an outcrop, irregularly shaped rocks are preferable to small, spherical ones, which often do not look natural. Quarried rocks, with raw, unweathered surfaces, should be confined to wall gardens, bridges, steps, paths or similar structures. A rock garden should exhibit all the elements of good garden design: unity, balance, accents, a variety of colour and texture. Avoid using too much stone—a rock garden is not a collection of rocks but a collection of the plants that will grow among them.

Lined at top and bottom with retaining walls built of quarried stone, a steep gravelly slope is transformed into a colourful rock garden. Phlox subulata carpets the lower edge of the garden with vivid spring flowers.

Most of the plants in this terraced rock garden were chosen for their ability to withstand drought as well as for their beauty. The lower wall displays succulents while the upper wall hides behind blue-grey rosemary.

*Dwarf conifers give a vertical note
to a rock garden that is dominated by
low-growing alpines and succulents. The
combination of alpine and lowland plants
extends the garden's period of bloom.*

*Conifers, including a weeping hemlock
(right), blend with craggy rocks of
granite. To produce the best effect, rocks
should be few and relatively large,
and buried deep in the ground.*

When nature takes the lead

A natural outcrop or rocky slope can be transformed from an eyesore into an eye-catching display of dazzling rock plants—often with only minor modifications. A few rocks may have to be removed or added to provide better planting pockets, or native soil may have to be replaced with more suitable prepared soil (*page 34*); but, in general, gardeners with rocky sites need only start stocking them with their favourite plants. Aggressive plants, such as aubrieta and ajuga, can be kept in check set between large rocks. Trailing plants, *Phlox subulata*, for example, can cascade over elevated surfaces. Small alpines grow best when planted alone in small crevices.

A variety of predominantly evergreen plants, including a dwarf weeping hemlock, are planted among moss-covered granite boulders to create a year-round rock garden that is rich in contrasting textures.

A breathtaking array of spring-blooming rock plants, including forget-me-nots, primroses, candytufts and columbines, rise from a natural granite outcrop. In summer, ferns and heathers prevail.

Water, the crowning touch 3

There is no rock garden—or any other kind of garden, for that matter—that cannot be made more delightful by the introduction of water. This addition can be as simple as a wall tap or wall fountain dripping musically into a trough banked with pots of bright geraniums, as scenic as a series of waterfalls cascading into a woodland pond, or as exotic as a display of water lilies blooming on the glassy surface of a formal pool. Add water, by almost any means, and the garden suddenly becomes more alive.

The key word, however, is "almost". Some enthusiasts become so preoccupied with concrete, pumps and other mechanical aspects that they fail to capitalize on the qualities that give water its appeal. The most obvious—yet often overlooked—is the way water can act as a mirror, reflecting not only sky and clouds but also upside-down images of nearer objects such as flowers and tree branches. A garden pool will be largely wasted if it is tucked away where its reflections cannot be enjoyed—or if those reflections emphasize an unsightly clothes line instead of a lovely yellow waterside iris.

Elements in the background of a garden pool or pond—rocks, flowers, shrubs, trees, perhaps even a piece of sculpture—are as important as the pool itself and should be considered carefully before a spit of earth is turned. Moreover, the site of the pool should be close enough to a major viewing point such as a terrace for the angle of view to permit the water surface and its reflections to provide a constant source of pleasure.

If you plan to have water lilies or other aquatic and bog plants in or around the water, make sure the site gets ample light. Hardy water lilies (*Chapter 4*) require at least six hours of direct sunlight a day and tropical varieties in indoor or warm Mediterranean pools need even more. So avoid placing a lily pool close to trees or buildings that will block the sun for much

A tranquil pool 60 cm (2 ft) deep and bordered with stone slabs offers a reflective surface for fragrant 'Rose Arey' water lilies. Spikes of red cardinal flowers rise from the pool's boggy edge.

of the day. If you want to have fish in your pool, check the position of nearby deciduous trees. They drop leaves and other debris; when enough of such refuse reaches the bottom of a pool and rots, it releases gases that can harm fish, especially in winter when the pool is iced over. Trees and other plantings will not be a problem if they are sited north of the water and far enough away not to create a litter problem. Indeed, an evergreen hedge or a garden wall will shelter a pool against early north winds, allowing the water to warm up sooner in spring.

POSITIONING THE POOL

When you plan a garden pool, try out its site, size and shape by outlining the space with a length of rope or garden hose laid out on the ground. In the case of a more formal rectangular pool, use stakes and string. Leave the outline in place long enough to determine how many hours of sunlight will fall on the pool, how well the size and shape work with the rest of the garden and its traffic patterns, and whether the pool and its background will present a pleasing picture from a main viewing point. With a little experimenting you may find an ideal solution by slight alterations or by pruning back a few tree branches.

For maximum enjoyment, consider the depth and bottom treatment of your pool as carefully as its top. A miniature pool

REFLECTIONS ON A REFLECTING POOL

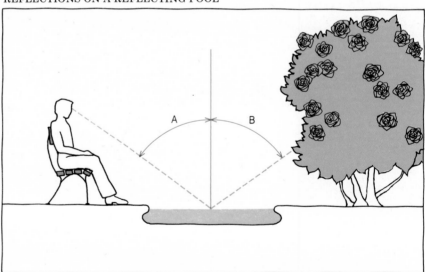

Just where you should position an object that you want to see reflected in a garden pool can be estimated with reasonable accuracy. Exactly equal angles are formed with an imaginary perpendicular line by a reflection coming from a point on a mirroring surface ("A" above) and any image-bearing light rays that strike that point ("B"). Therefore, a bush planted as shown above would be reflected to the man's eyes.

designed primarily to capture reflections or to serve as a catch basin for a fountain need be only a few centimetres deep. For garden pools up to about 10 square metres (approx. 100 sq. ft) in surface area, a depth of 40 to 45 centimetres (16 to 18 in.) looks better and will accommodate water lilies and fish. A larger pool or pond can be 60 to 90 centimetres (2 to 3 ft) deep, but any pool is likely to create a hazard for small children. While the children are still toddlers, it may be advisable to delay making a pool for a year or two, or else to fill it with sand and let them use it as a temporary sand-pit.

Since garden pools are generally shallow, the treatment of the bottom is important if the water is to yield a mirror effect. A white or sky-blue finish causes the water to sparkle in the sun, but reflects so much light that it all but eliminates surface reflections. It also looks unnatural and turns dark through fallen debris. Therefore, make the bottom neutral or dark by using natural stones, a dark plastic liner or concrete that is coloured grey or black. Then images of clouds and flowers will be sharper and the shallow water will give the impression of being mysteriously deep. As a practical matter, the inevitable stains, algae and accumulations of silt on the bottom will be less visible against the dark background, and the water will tend to warm up faster in spring and hold its warmth well into autumn.

    Another basic quality of water is its ability, when in motion, to produce a range of dramatic effects. There are few sights more beautiful than the sun striking a mountain lake just as a morning breeze ruffles the surface and turns its reflection into pinpoints of sparkling light. Even a modest garden pool, positioned with an eye to sun angles, can capture some of the same fleeting beauty on a miniature scale. Running water—a waterfall, stream or fountain—also refracts sunlight in endless patterns and adds a bonus of sound to absorb attention and conceal less pleasant background noises. On a hot day, waterfalls and fountains have another soothing effect: evaporation may actually lower nearby air temperature a few degrees—and the psychological cooling may seem even greater.

Finally, water in the garden can create an environment that will provide further dividends in the form of water-loving plants and animal life. Even a shallow water dish on a garden wall will attract birds to drink, splash and preen. A larger pool will soon attract its own colony of residents as frogs move in and dragonflies dart above the surface. With encouragement, an impressive array of water-loving plants from Japanese iris to

TO SIMULATE MORE DEPTH

NEW FLORA AND FAUNA

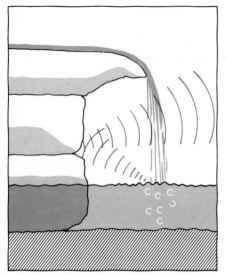

Although you can never turn a waterfall into a cello or guitar, you can borrow the sound-chamber concept of these instruments to enhance a waterfall's musical murmurs and babbles. Experiment with the amount of rock overhang that lets the water fall free at the top, the height of the fall, and the slant of the rocks behind the fall. The best combination will create reverberations and send out a pleasant musical echo.

SMALL SUNKEN POOLS

pickerel weed will flourish in the pool, in the shallows, or in moist pockets of soil round the edge of the pool.

How you use water in your garden will, of course, depend not only on the effects you want but also on budget and terrain. If you are fortunate enough to have a small stream crossing your property, all you may need to do is to prune away scruffy undergrowth, rearrange a few boulders to create a sparkling riffle and plant some bog plants and ferns. You may also want to build a small dam to form a reflecting pool and waterfall, but first check the local bye-laws applying to stream-bed alterations and flood control. And if the stream is bordered by a low, marshy spot, you may have the makings of an attractive bog garden in what was previously an eyesore.

Lacking a natural water course, you have an even wider choice of possibilities for incorporating water into the landscape. Water gardens, like rock gardens, offer an almost unlimited range of sizes, shapes and treatments, but they generally fit one of two broad categories: they are either informal and naturalistic or formal and obviously man-made. In the naturalistic type, the gardener attempts, with a little sleight of hand and artful concealment of mechanics, to create an illusion that nature has done the job. This is not as easy as it might seem, particularly if the garden is small and the gardener has limited landscaping experience. Many "natural" pools do not look natural at all. It may be simpler to stylize nature rather than simulate it, with no pretences at all.

To have water in your garden, you need only two things: water and a container to hold it. Surprisingly attractive small gardens can be made with a modest volume of water held in some inexpensive object salvaged from the attic or basement: an old stone sink, bath or laundry boiler, a metal bowl from an old outdoor grill or the cut-off end of a discarded boiler tank. Among the more widely available containers, stocked by many garden centres, is a wooden-staved tub made by sawing an old wine or beer barrel in half. If the fumes of the barrel's former contents have not dissipated, let the barrel weather in the sun and rain for a few months. Then scrape the inside clean and fill it with an initial tubful of water to swell the wood and tighten the seams. On a corner of a terrace, a half-barrel can become a bubbling fountain with the addition of a miniature submersible pump, or a pocket-sized water garden with the addition of a miniature water lily or some water fringes.

Such a tub pool—or one made from an old galvanized washing tub, cast-iron sink, even a bathtub—can also be set in the ground and made an integral part of the garden design. Unattractive edges and bottoms can be camouflaged with plants and rocks. If you plan to put fish in the pool, do not paint the inside—as lead-based paints will poison them. Also, for the same reason, do not use a copper container or copper plumbing.

For a larger sunken pool, there are several kinds of containers, including prefabricated shells, pool liners of flexible plastic and the traditional poured concrete. Prefabricated shells are made of durable plastic reinforced with fibreglass mesh. They come in circular, kidney, rectangular and free-form shapes, in sizes from 60 centimetres (2 ft) in diameter up to 3.6 metres (12 ft) or more in length. Those that are dark grey or black give the best surface reflection and a greater illusion of depth, as well as fitting less obtrusively into the garden scene. Such pools are easy to install in a matter of hours; moreover, they are virtually indestructible, even in regions of severe frost.

To assure good results, excavate a hole 15 centimetres (6 in.) or so wider and deeper than the pool all around. Remove any projecting stones and tamp the earth smooth, then line the

Water dripping into a hand-hewn oak trough captures rippled reflections, then spills over the edges to moisten the soil for bog primroses that are growing in the crevices of a limestone ledge below.

bottom of the excavation with a 5 centimetre (2 in.) layer of sand. This will make it easier to level the pool and will help to drain ground water away in winter. Place the shell in the hole and pour a bucket of water into it; using the water as a level, adjust the shell evenly on the sand base. Then fill the pool with water from a garden hose, at the same time filling the gap around the sides with well-packed soil to equalize the weight and pressure of the water building up inside. Prefabricated pools are generally sold without drains or overflow pipes. Use a hose to replenish water lost by evaporation. When the pool needs cleaning, you can syphon or pump the water out.

Less expensive than a prefabricated pool, and almost as easy to install, is one made with a flexible pool liner, plastic sheeting that you can buy in almost any size and then trim with scissors to create a pool in the shape you want. The first pool liners on the market were made from sheets of polythene plastic, which tended to become brittle, tear and spring pinhole leaks. Today, polythene has been largely supplanted for pool use by tougher compounds such as butyl rubber or polyvinyl chloride, called PVC. A PVC liner, woven with nylon for strength, is elastic enough to conform to uneven pool bottoms and to stretch rather than split under the pressure of ice or frost. If accidentally punctured, it can be mended with a repair kit. PVC comes in various colours, and with a smooth or pebble-like finish.

FITTING A PLASTIC LINER

To make a pool with a PVC liner, buy one large enough to fit the pool's surface dimensions plus at least twice its maximum depth. A pool 2 by 5 metres, $\frac{1}{2}$ metre deep, for example, requires a liner 2 plus $\frac{1}{2}$ plus $\frac{1}{2}$ metre on one side, and 5 plus $\frac{1}{2}$ plus $\frac{1}{2}$ metre on the other, or a total of 3 by 6 metres (or a 7 by 16 foot pool, $1\frac{1}{2}$ feet deep, requires a liner 7 plus $1\frac{1}{2}$ plus $1\frac{1}{2}$ feet on one side, and 16 plus $1\frac{1}{2}$ plus $1\frac{1}{2}$ feet on the other, or a total of 10 by 19 feet). Firms will make such liners to the required size, using heat-sealing to join the lengths. Mark the pool's outline and excavate to a uniform depth or series of depths if marginal aquatics are envisaged. Some water plants need 75 centimetres ($2\frac{1}{2}$ ft) of water, others only 7.5 to 15 centimetres (3 to 6 in.). Small pools of simple geometric shapes such as rectangles or circles generally look best in a formal setting if the sides are vertical. For large pools and those of irregular form, a bowl-shaped depression with sloping sides suggests the look of a natural pond. Make sure the rim of the pool is at the same level all the way round so that when it is filled, high parts of the liner will not show. Remove any stones, sticks or roots that could pierce the plastic, then line the bottom with a 2.5 centimetre (1 in.) layer of sand. Spread the liner smooth and taut across the top of the hole—the plastic becomes more flexible as it is warmed by the sun and filled with water—and use large, smooth stones, bricks or other small weights to hold the edges in place.

THE FINISHING TOUCHES

Start filling the liner at its centre with water from a garden hose; the weight of the water will slowly stretch the plastic down, moulding it to the contours of the excavation. You may have to fold and smooth the liner into any sharp corners as the filling proceeds. When the pool is filled, trim off the excess liner, leaving a flap 15 to 20 centimetres (6 to 8 in.) wide round the edge. To finish the pool, dig a sloping slit trench and tuck the flap into it, covering the trench with plants or turf to give the appearance of a natural pond. In a rock-garden setting, trim the edge with small boulders and plant marginal aquatics about 23 centimetres (9 in.) beneath the surface. For more formal designs, edge the pool with a coping of flagstones, concrete paving stones, bricks, tiles or even wooden planks, all of which should extend up to 5 centimetres (2 in.) over the pool edge.

LINING A RAISED POOL

PVC liners can also be used to hold water in above-ground pools. For a small, raised pool, build a rectangular enclosure

SPEEDING A STREAM ON ITS WAY

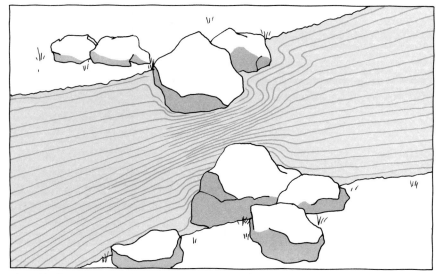

A swift-flowing stream enhances any garden. If you have a stream that is sluggish, you can speed it up with a partial dam. When the water is at its lowest level, usually in summer, place several large rocks along each side of the stream, leaving the centre of the channel open. Use smaller stones to chink crevices on the upstream side. This will concentrate the flow in the same way that partially blocking a hose creates a jet of water.

about 45 centimetres (1½ ft) high, using concrete blocks, bricks, timber or railway sleepers. In cold regions, provide masonry enclosures with a footing that goes down to the frost line or below, but elsewhere the construction materials can be set directly on the ground. Make sure the top of the enclosure is level. Line the bottom with sand and fit the liner inside, folding it into corners and draping the excess over the top. Then fill the pool, let it settle, trim off liner edges and conceal them under a coping of brick, flagstones, tiles or wood. Such pools are naturally more vulnerable to frost and heat than sunken pools.

One or more such plastic liners can also be used to water-proof the bottom of a small man-made stream bed or a series of cascade pools; just smooth the material into place, cut it to fit and conceal the edges. You can also use a plastic liner to create a bog garden for plants such as Japanese kaempferi irises, arums, calthas and water forget-me-nots that grow where soil is constantly wet. Dig out a low area to a depth of about 30 centimetres (12 in.), lay down the liner and cover it with about 15 centimetres (6 in.) of a mixture of equal parts of moss peat, soil and sand. To ensure a constant water supply when it is most needed, snake out a canvas hose or perforated plastic drainpipe over this layer of soil. Then cover with additional soil mixture. The plastic membrane of the liner will normally retain rainwater round the roots of the plants, but during dry periods the buried watering system can be connected to an outside tap to keep the bog garden soggy.

MASONRY MADE TO LAST   Despite the relative ease and low cost of using prefabricated shells or pool liners, some gardeners prefer the solidity and permanence of a masonry construction, which permits building a pool of any size and shape, in or out of the ground. A simple rectangular pool can be built of brick or concrete blocks, but mortar joints may leak unless a plastic liner is used. A more satisfactory choice for a masonry garden pool is poured concrete, the conventional material used for building swimming pools. Properly mixed and placed, concrete provides a durable, seamless container that will last for years. If the rim of a submerged concrete pool is exposed, it can be concealed with rocks or plantings or a coping of brick or stone. (Keep any juncture between concrete and rock above the water line; their different rates of expansion can cause leaks even in well-mortared joints.) Similarly, concrete can be used with other kinds of masonry to create a formal, raised pool—a handsome feature that lessens the risk of toddlers falling into the water and allows you to sit comfortably on the edge to tend water lilies or feed fish. If the raw concrete of the outside walls of the pool seems unattractive, you can incorporate a cement colouring into the mixture or coat the finished pool with a cement paint; or the concrete exterior can be covered with brick or stone.

The easiest kind of concrete pool to build is a simple bowl that does not require a wooden form and can be poured and trowelled in place right on the ground. A circle 90 to 120 centimetres (3 to 4 ft) across and 30 centimetres (1 ft) deep at the centre is adequate for a small reflecting pool; a larger size, 1.8 to 2.4 metres (6 to 8 ft) across and 45 centimetres (1½ ft) deep, will accommodate a collection of plants and fish. Small pools and those built in generally frost-free areas can be made of a layer of wire-reinforced concrete 10 centimetres (4 in.) thick laid directly on well compacted soil. For larger pools and those in colder areas, the excavation should be lined with a 10 centimetre (4 in.) layer of well tamped cinders, gravel or crushed stone; the shell should be 15 centimetres (6 in.) of reinforced concrete.

    Outline the pool on the ground with rope or hose, allowing an extra 10 to 15 centimetres (4 to 6 in.) for the thickness of the concrete rim and another 10 centimetres (4 in.) for the gravel bed if one is needed. Mark the outline with a spade and start digging from the edge, slanting the sides of the pool at an angle no steeper than 45° from the vertical (an even shallower 60° is safer) so that the wet concrete will hold without slipping when it is put in place. Firm the base, then cut and bend a piece of 15 by 15 centimetre (6 by 6 in.) wire reinforcing mesh to fit the

THE SIMPLE CONCRETE BOWL

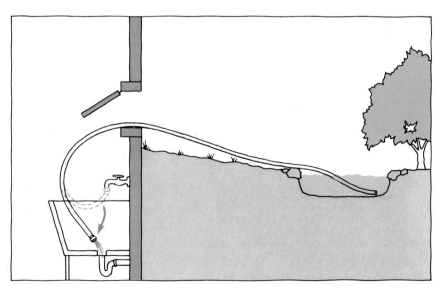

HOW TO DRAIN A POOL
A garden pool without a drain can easily be emptied for cleaning or repair by syphoning the water to any place lower than the bottom of the pool—for example, into a basement sink. Place one end of a hose in the pool at its deepest point and attach the other end to the basement tap. Run water from the tap until it begins to flow into the pool, indicating that the hose is full. Then, with the tap off, unscrew the connector from the tap and insert it into the sink drain. With the hose in this position, the water from the garden pool will be syphoned off into the drain.

excavation and prop it 5 to 7.5 centimetres (2 to 3 in.) off the bottom with small stones or pieces of brick. To control the thickness of the concrete shell as you pour it, drive temporary stakes at intervals round the bottom and sides, marking each at a point 10 to 15 centimetres (4 to 6 in.) from the ground, depending on the thickness desired for the concrete shell. Set a plank across the hole as a platform and you are ready to start pouring.

POURING AND SHAPING   A good concrete formula for a pool is 1 part portland cement, 2 parts sharp builders' sand and 3 parts gravel of various sizes from 6 to 18 millimetres ($\frac{1}{4}$ to $\frac{3}{4}$ in.), with just enough water to make the mixture evenly moist but stiff enough not to slump and run down the sides. Small batches can be mixed by hand, using a wheelbarrow and shovel, but for a pool of any size hire a portable power mixer or use ready-mixed concrete. Pour the concrete into the hole, then use the back of a flat shovel to work it around and up so that it covers the reinforcing mesh. When you reach the marks on the stakes, remove the stakes and fill in the holes they leave. Form the top rim into a rounded edge extending up to 5 centimetres (2 in.) above ground level to keep surface water and silt from washing into the pool during heavy rains. You can leave the surface of the concrete as it is or, for a smoother finish, go over it lightly with a wooden mason's float. At the same time, before the concrete hardens, you can, if you wish, add colouring powder to darken the bottom of the pool. To keep the concrete moist while it cures and hardens, spread sacking or canvas over the surface and sprinkle this covering occasionally with water from the garden hose for at least a week.

Even after it has cured, fresh concrete covered with water will release lime in quantities toxic to fish and plants, so do not introduce them immediately. There are various sealing agents on the market, which give a waterproof finish as well as seal off the lime. These should be painted over the whole of the pool's interior. Many professional pool-builders, however, rely on an older, but slower method: they fill the pool with water and let it stand for a week to leach out the lime, then drain and repeat the process twice more. Finally, they empty the pool and scrub it with a wire brush and an acid solution. You can do the same with chemicals sold for this purpose, or scrub with 1 part malt vinegar to 10 parts water. Then rinse the pool clean.

BUILT-IN DRAINAGE   To simplify cleaning out pools, many gardeners build in a drainage system. To do so, before pouring the concrete, set a brass coupling at an inconspicuous place near one side of the pool so that its top is slightly below the deepest point. Into this coupling screw a 5 centimetre (2 in.) galvanized pipe long enough to reach the surface at the water level you want to maintain, and cap the pipe with a screen. Using an elbow-shaped pipe fitting, attach the bottom of the coupling to a sloping run-off pipe leading to a drain or to a soak-away filled with coarse gravel. The standing pipe in the pool will take care of overflow; when it is unscrewed from the coupling, the water from the pool can be drained off completely.

To replenish the water in your pool, you can also equip it with an inlet pipe attached to the house water supply. The tap can be strictly utilitarian, concealed behind a rock or shrub, or it can take the more decorative form of a playing fountain or small waterfall that you can turn on and off as you like.

Pumps are available in many different sizes and include some that can be mounted outside the pool and others that are set in the water. A submersible pump with a capacity above 700 litres (150 gal.) an hour is large enough to power a small waterfall or a fountain jet up to 1 metre (3 ft) high. All you need to do is to set the pump in the bottom of the pool (propping it up on bricks if necessary to get a fountain jet at water level), lead the waterproof cable over the side to a buried and insulated electric outlet and plug it in.

THE SUBMERSIBLE PUMP

You may also want outdoor lighting to dramatize fountains, waterfalls and pools at night. The easiest and safest to install are low-voltage sealed fixtures that can be placed on the bottom of the pool or hidden behind a shrub or under a lily pad. An illuminated waterfall or fountain makes a handsome display. If waterproof lighting fixtures are placed behind the water sprays, the droplets will sparkle with refracted light to create even more entrancing results.

Landscape architects often advise their clients that the simplest schemes usually turn out to be the best: a small pool of uncomplicated shape, modestly planted, may bring more pleasure over the years than a large one with complex angles and a jungle of landscaping. Determine whether your design is to be primarily naturalistic or formal, then stick to your choice.

Finally, if you light your garden, do it with restraint. Modern equipment makes it possible to rival the fountains of Versailles. But unless you want your garden to resemble Disneyland, leave such projects to the designers of showpieces in public amusement parks and limit your installation to one or two well-concealed bulbs, shaded white. The water in your garden will take on quite enough magic by the light of the moon.

MODESTY IN LIGHTING

Reflections of the past in classic pools

For almost 3,500 years, ever since gardeners along the River Nile discovered that irrigation ditches could be beautiful as well as practical, decorative pools and fountains have played a role in garden design. Ancient Egyptian pools were rectangular or T-shaped and were stocked with fish and aquatic plants, especially water lilies, which the Egyptians harvested for medicinal uses. Most of the pools were small, for water was scarce, although Pharaoh Amenhotep III built one 1.6 kilometres (1 mile) long and almost half a kilometre ($\frac{1}{4}$ mile) wide that he used for boating and water festivals.

Centuries later, across the Arabian peninsula, the Persians carved decorative pools out of their sun-scorched soil. After Muslims conquered Persia in the 7th century, these pools took on a distinctly Islamic character with a particular emphasis on geometric designs. Water was drawn down to the desert from the mountains through an ingenious system of underground channels. The channels, some of them several kilometres long, emptied into narrow canals, which often sliced each garden into four areas of equal size. These canals usually crossed at a central pool. As the water descended from a higher level, gravity-fed jets often sent it arching into the air.

When the Muslims invaded Spain in the 8th century, they took their designs for water structures with them. Palatial gardens were divided into small walled patios—each bisected by a canal or with a fountain at the centre.

In contrast to the ancient Egyptians and Muslims, who built pools with geometric shapes, the Japanese re-created in their gardens the asymmetric ponds and lakes of nature. Each pond, lined with pressed clay and banked with stones and small evergreens, often had an island connected to the shore by an arched bridge. Soon, streams and waterfalls were added.

Modern pools are more often lined with cement or plastic than with clay or marble, but they frequently borrow from these designs of the past—designs that still soothe and refresh, whether rigidly formal or as asymmetric as nature herself.

A rectangular pool filled with water lilies and aquatic birds was an essential element of ancient Egyptian gardens, as shown in this detail of a garden about 1400 B.C.

Islam's rules for Persian pools

Persian gardens were greatly influenced by the Islamic religion. In the Koran, the Islamic holy book, Muhammad commanded that water be kept in motion. As a result, the Muslims devised ingenious schemes for moving water from one part of the garden to another, including sloping stone chutes cloaked with shallow running water. Fountains were simple, unadorned jets of water, for religious beliefs forbade making likenesses of living things.

A chute, rippling with clear water, connects a Persian pavilion with a tranquil garden pool in this 1847 drawing. Water was circulated under the stone floors of many pavilions in order to cool them.

A wall fountain, a modern version of the ancient Persian water chute, offers a steady cascade of rippling water. A pump recirculates the water through copper pipes that are concealed within the brickwork.

Spain's geometric gardens

Of the 50,000 villa gardens built in Spain during the reign of the Muslims only a handful have survived. One of the most beautiful is the Generalife, a 13th-century summer palace for Granada's Moorish kings (*below, left*). Perched on a mountainside, the Generalife has seven terraced gardens with inter-connecting canals. Moorish designs influenced many modern water gardens, including one that graces a New Orleans estate (*opposite*).

A small fountain at Longue Vue in the USA draws upon Moorish heritage for its geometric design. Pebbles for the pool and surrounding courtyard were imported from Spain and set in a foundation of concrete.

Arching jets of water mimic the stone arches of a neighbouring arcade in the Generalife's Court of the Canal. Beds of cypress, myrtle, oleander and roses border the canal in a pattern developed more than 600 years ago.

Inspired by a Generalife garden, the Canal Garden at New Orleans' Longue Vue estate features a narrow canal and simple jet fountains. Potted plants, including tulips and liriopes, add colour to the clay-tiled banks.

Arching jets of water, identical to those used for centuries by the Moors, frame columns of a loggia, or outdoor sitting room, at Longue Vue.

Japan's homage to nature

By the 9th century, a lake was considered an essential element of a Japanese garden. Some lakes were large enough for boating. Most, however, were small and featured one or two islands and a path that wound around the lake to offer different viewpoints of the water. One of the most famous of these stroll gardens is the Ginkakuji garden in Kyoto (*right*), designed by Sho-ami, a 15th-century Japanese tea expert, painter and landscape architect.

A multi-level waterfall sends sheets of water cascading into a small pool in this modern Japanese garden. A simple rustic bridge—for centuries an important element of Japanese water gardens—spans the pond.

Coniferous shrubs and trees, clipped into fanciful shapes, surround the rocky shores of a Japanese-style pond in Southern California. Such clipping was introduced by Sho-ami, the creator of the Ginkakuji garden.

Designed for a Japanese shogun (or general) in 1480, the garden of the Ginkakuji, or Silver Pavilion (shown here in an 1893 etching), features a stream, lake and waterfall. Two islands adorn the centre of the lake.

The bewitching beauty of water plants

Of the many plants that can be grown in a water garden, water lilies are the most enchanting. They all belong to a single generic grouping, the *Nymphaea*, but the diversity among them is startling. There are the so-called hardies, those that will survive winter at the bottom of a frozen pond, some as far north as Alaska and Sweden. And there are the tropicals, so tender that they must be lifted and replanted or replaced each year. Among these tropicals, some bloom by day and others by night. There are miniatures, with flowers only 2.5 centimetres (1 in.) or so in diameter, and there are giants, with spectacular blooms as large as a dinner plate.

Among the most fascinating are the hardy water lilies listed in catalogues as "changeables", "autumn shades" or "sunset shades". These are one colour when they open, but by the end of the first day have already begun to change to a darker hue, which continues to deepen on successive days. A large-flowered Marliac cultivar called 'Comanche', considered by some water gardeners to be the finest of the changeables, starts out a rich rose-apricot colour and becomes darker and more vivid until it finally turns a glowing coppery bronze, with what one admirer has called "a heart of fire".

The hardy lilies are the lilies native to temperate zones in Europe, Asia and North America—and their hybrids and cultivars. They have smooth, round leaves of moderate size—5 to 20 centimetres (2 to 8 in.) in diameter. Their flowers, which come in every colour except blue, green and purple, open during the day, close at night, then re-open on a second and third day and sometimes on a fourth. The flowers generally float at water level, although when growing under crowded conditions, they may rise above the water on their stems.

Hardy lilies have large rhizomes, which are tuber-like underground stems, and will survive under a 30 centimetre (1 ft)

The lotus, much prized for its serene beauty and rich scent, flourishes in shallow ponds and bogs. Buddhists view the flower's rise from the mud as a symbol of spiritual ascent and purity.

layer of ice as long as the rhizomes themselves do not freeze. All hardy lilies are perennials, and because of this they are popular with gardeners who favour plants that come up year after year with a minimum of care.

The other broad category of true water lilies includes species that come from warmer regions. Although they will not survive winters north of such places as North Africa, they are just as popular as the hardy lilies—sometimes more so—for they can be grown in many northern gardens as annuals or in indoor pools under glass. The tropical lilies do just about everything that hardy lilies do—but even more flamboyantly. Their leaves are larger, and are often beautifully coloured and veined, with crimped, fluted or frilled edges. Their flowers come in a spectrum of colours that includes blue and purple; some tropical species produce four or five times more flowers per season than hardy types. The flowers of most of them are held above the water on tall, strong stems.

BLOOMS BY DAY OR NIGHT

Most of the tropical water lilies that flower in the daytime open before noon and close around dusk, and almost all of them are fragrant. The night-blooming varieties open at about the time that day-blooming lilies close, and stay open until midday. When illuminated by the moon—or by spotlights hidden in plantings around the pool—night-blooming lilies put on a magical display for summer garden parties.

The two kinds of water lilies, tropical and hardy, have different growing requirements. In Britain and over much of northern Europe, hardy lilies can be planted as early as mid-April without fear of damage from frost, and can tolerate cool, deep water. Tropical lilies, on the other hand, must be planted in late spring, and need warm, shallow water to get started. Also, many of them require twice as much pool space as hardy lilies. Once started, the tropical lilies come into bloom quickly, soon catching up with their hardier cousins. And they continue to bloom late into the season, to the end of autumn if the pool is indoors or is in a warm climate and sheltered from the wind.

FLOWERS IN SUCCESSION

Despite these differences, gardeners with pools of sufficient size grow lilies of both kinds. According to climate and to accommodate the tropical varieties, they prepare raised platforms and plant the tender lilies only when the water warms up. By so doing, they have a continuous floral display. In early summer outdoors, the earliest hardy lilies appear—*N. odorata* 'Gigantea', a large fragrant white, for example—followed by later blooming hardy cultivars in red, yellow and changeable shades, such as the garnet-red 'Attraction'. However, in indoor pools or in very favoured situations outdoors, the first of the day-blooming tropical lilies make their debut by early summer, to be joined in midsummer by the night-blooming types.

All water lilies, including those that flower at night, need a measure of full sun in order to produce the largest, most abundant bloom, but in warm places, such as the Mediterranean, some will perform reasonably well in partial shade. 'Comanche' and 'Chromatella' are good examples of shade-tolerant hardy lilies, and the cultivars named 'Director George T. Moore' and 'Isabelle Pring' are examples of shade-tolerant tropicals. Several lilies are smaller than normal, making them good choices for tub gardens and pools of limited size. Among the most popular hardy lilies for this purpose are the Laydekeri section, with small leaves and flowers of purplish-red, pink or rose, about 10 to 15 centimetres (4 to 6 in.) in diameter. Other small-scale hardy kinds include the pygmy lilies, whose white, pink and yellow flowers are only 2.5 to 5 centimetres (1 to 2 in.) across.

Among the tropical lilies adapted to small pools and tub gardening is *Nymphaea* x *daubenyana*, a fragrant, light-blue hybrid from whose leaves spring tiny miniature plants, complete with miniature blooms. These piggy-back or viviparous plants bear young that can be removed and repotted (*below*). Another small tropical with this attribute is *N. micrantha*.

In many small pools and tub gardens, these diminutive lilies are combined with other aquatic plants that are similar in

MINIATURE TROPICALS

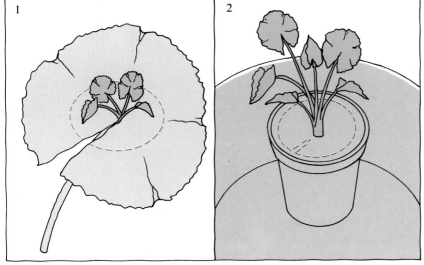

PLANTLET INTO WATER LILY

1. *A miniature offspring produced on the leaf of a tropical viviparous water lily is ready to be transplanted when a plantlet sends out roots. To remove the plantlet, snip a circle of leaf around its base 2.5 cm (1 in.) in diameter.*

2. *Place the plantlet and leaf fragment on moist soil in a 10 cm (4 in.) pot, pinning the leaf down with toothpicks or hairpins. Submerge the pot in a shallow bowl until 2.5 to 5 cm (1 to 2 in.) of water covers the soil. When the young water lily is well rooted, transplant it in a full-sized container and set it in a warm-water pool.*

scale. Among the tropicals, one of the most decorative is the tropical water poppy, *Hydrocleys nymphoides*, which produces a profusion of small yellow flowers all summer long and has a similar appearance to the soil-growing California poppy. The water poppy is also useful as a foil for larger lilies in larger pools. In fact, although water lilies will undoubtedly be the mainstay of your water garden, you should not restrict yourself to them. There are many other useful and beautiful aquatic plants. In addition to the floating poppy, the surface of the pool could be decorated with water lettuce, *Pistia stratiotes*, which has rosettes of pale blue-green leaves and dangling, free-floating roots that permit the plant to skim around the pool's surface at the whim of the breeze. There is also the hardier *Nymphoides peltata*, the water fringe, with lily-pad leaves and yellow flowers. The water hyacinth, *Eichhornia crassipes*, is another lovely floating plant, which has lavender-blue flowers that are shaped like those of its soil-dwelling namesake, but it has gained such a bad reputation for clogging waterways that it cannot be grown with impunity in frost-free climates.

OXYGEN FOR THE FISH A number of plants should be considered if you plan to put fish in your water garden. The most important of these are the submerged oxygenating plants such as the *Elodea* and *Myriophyllum* species, which are suitable for cold-water pools, and the *Sagittaria* and *Vallisneria* species for warm-water pools. These underwater plants help to keep the pool water in proper chemical balance by absorbing carbon dioxide produced by the fish and converting it into oxygen, which the fish need. Occasionally you can see the oxygen form tiny silver bubbles on the surface of the foliage. Besides providing oxygen, these underwater plants compete with algae for the pool's nutrients and sunlight and thus help to keep the water clear. And their attractive foliage supplies fish with food, a bed for their spawn and a hiding place for their young.

For shallow water near the edges of pools and the moist adjoining land, there is another group of plants that lends colour to a water-garden scene. But only in warm areas can gardeners grow the most dramatic of them—the lotus, whose richly perfumed flowers are often 25 to 30 centimetres (10 to 12 in.) across and held on sturdy, elegant 0.9 to 1.5 metre (3 to 5 ft) stems. The lotus flowers come in shades of pink, red, yellow and white, and, like those of the water lilies, open over a period of about three days, becoming wider each day. The plant dies down in winter in temperate areas, but will come up the following spring provided that the water has not frozen round its roots.

Other favourites for the edges of a pool are the many varieties of water iris, whose red, white, blue, purple or yellow flowers open in late spring and early summer; the handsome arrowhead, with arrow-shaped leaves and white flower spikes; and the pickerel rush, with blue-violet blossoms and spear-shaped leaves. For early and late colour, there are the yellow marsh marigolds, the first of the bog plants to come into bloom, and the fiery red cardinal flower, *Lobelia cardinalis*, which blooms from July until September. For striking foliage, there are various typhas and reeds, some of them variegated, and the sweet flag, *Acorus calamus*, with iris-like leaves and brown, arum-type flowers. Other choices include such familiar water plants as bogbean, bog arum and flowering rush.

Whatever your choice of aquatic plants, it is imperative to plant them as soon as possible after they arrive. This means that their arrival should coincide with the air and water conditions that are best for their growth, and in fact most suppliers of aquatic plants do not deliver stock until it is safe to plant outdoors. In Britain, for example, you will generally receive hardy water lilies in late April or May. But, if the winter has been unusually long or severe, the supplier may not send out plants until later. Tropical lilies, on the other hand, will normally not reach you until mid-June, when the water in the pool will have warmed up enough to plant them.

Most water lilies need a very rich soil; this is especially true of the tropicals. Soggy debris and river mud may seem ideal,

COLOUR AT THE WATER'S EDGE

DELIVERY TIMED TO CLIMATE

LILY IN A BASKET
To plant a water lily in a plastic aquatic basket, line the container with sacking or nylon sheeting and fill with moistened heavy loam mixed with bone-meal or cow manure. Place the rootstock of a hardy lily horizontally or upright (according to type), the rootstock of a tropical lily (inset) vertically. Press the soil down firmly, with the growing tip or crown exposed. Add 2.5 cm (1 in.) of coarse sand and submerge the basket so the sand is just below the water surface, supporting it on bricks if necessary. Gradually remove the bricks until 25 cm (10 in.) of water covers the sand.

but they are not necessarily good choices. They generally lack sufficient nutrients and may also produce harmful gases that turn the water sour and are toxic to fish. The same is true of soils containing leaf-mould, garden compost, moss peat or fresh manure. The best growing medium for water lilies is a good heavy topsoil containing some clay to act as a binding agent. To every 5 parts of this topsoil, add 1 part of decayed cow manure or $\frac{1}{8}$ part of coarse bone-meal.

If your water garden is a small pool or a tub, you can spread a 15 to 20 centimetre (6 to 8 in.) layer of soil on the bottom of the container. Cover it with a piece of sacking anchored with stones while you fill the container with water. Then remove the sacking and set the plants so that only their growing tips are exposed. Finally, cover the soil, except for a small area around each growing tip, with 1 centimetre ($\frac{1}{2}$ in.) of clean, pea-sized shingle to prevent the water from becoming muddied.

A PLANT IN A ROLL In larger natural ponds, professional growers sometimes use the "hot dog" technique to plant aquatics. They wrap the root in a thick piece of turf, grass side out, add some fertilizer, and bind it with cloth tape—something like a hot dog in a roll. Then they toss the plant into the pond, relying on the weight of the turf to carry it to the bottom, where it will take root and grow. For amateurs, a more dependable technique is to plant the roots in baskets, then put them in the water (*page 75*).

Setting plants in special aquatic baskets rather than in a soil-lined pool has many advantages. In the first place, it is

(continued on page 81)

The rewards of good breeding

In the 1800s, when the first tropical water lilies opened their flowers in botanical gardens in Europe and America, people travelled for miles to see them. Special illumination was installed and newspapers reported the flowering as a major event. Yet, despite the enormous interest in the plants, few people put them in their own pools. "A gardener practically needed a small lake to grow them," one expert explains, "and besides, their colours were not all that exciting."

Both objections were laid to rest early in the 20th century by a number of dedicated hybridizers—chief among them George Pring of the Missouri Botanical Garden. Over the years, he and other hybridizers introduced tropical water lilies in an incredible array of hues, sizes and shapes. Pring used pygmy water lilies from Africa to attain lilies of a size appropriate to the average garden pool. Still, the search for the perfect lily continues unabated. No one has yet bred a hardy lily that blooms for 24 hours a day, nor a blue one.

Four types of day-blooming tropical water lilies live side by side with five hardy water lilies in this natural-looking rock and reed-edged tropical pool.

76

A medley of tropical bloom

The conditions required for growing tropical water lilies in Europe are best met in a heated greenhouse. You may have an amazing variety of plants to choose from, ranging in size from 'Missouri' (*below*), which may cover almost a square metre (10 sq. ft), to the pygmy (*opposite, below right*), small enough for a fish bowl. Equally varied is the range of colours—from white to pink through deepest red to palest lavender. Foliage may vie with flowers for attention, and many types are scented.

The magnificent 'Missouri', a Pring cultivar, opens at dusk to display gleaming white blooms up to 35 cm (14 in.) across.

The day-blooming 'Blue Beauty' unfurls petals stroked with lilac; individual pads measure 30 cm (1 ft) across.

The scented flowers of the day-blooming 'Panama Pacific' change colour daily over their lifespan.

Renowned for its purple and chestnut flecked foliage, night-blooming 'Evelyn Randig' has magenta flowers.

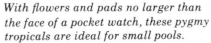

With flowers and pads no larger than the face of a pocket watch, these pygmy tropicals are ideal for small pools.

much easier to work at a potting bench than to wade around in cold murky water, burying roots by touch. The use of baskets also permits you to prepare the pool in early spring, long in advance of the plants' arrival—to clean it, refill it and allow the water to warm up to the desired temperature. Containers, in addition, allow you to adjust the depth of each plant individually, by propping them up on bricks or flat stones, and to change the position of plants at will. And they make it simple to fertilize plants, to lift them for propagation, to clean the pool, and to remove the less hardy ones for winter storage. Finally, baskets confine more vigorous species, preventing them from taking over the pool at the expense of less robust plants.

Almost any kind of basket, tub, bucket or crate makes a good container, provided it is sturdy. There are also plastic water-lily baskets on the market, which have holes punched out round the sides. Avoid copper containers, however, and any wooden ones contaminated with oily substances that could be toxic to plants or fish. If you are building your own containers, use well-seasoned or weathered wood.

The size of the container depends on the size of the mature plant. For most lilies, containers 45 to 60 centimetres ($1\frac{1}{2}$ to 2 ft) across and 23 to 25 centimetres (9 to 10 in.) deep are ideal, although many hardy lilies will live in smaller containers, 23 centimetres (9 in.) deep and 28 centimetres (11 in.) in diameter. Miniature lilies can be planted in orchid flower pots which have holes in the sides and are only 15 centimetres (6 in.) across.

SIZING LILY CONTAINERS

With the pool filled and warming in the sun, and with containers and soil ready and waiting, you will be able to start planting as soon as the plants arrive. If that is not possible, open the packages immediately, wet down their contents and cover them with a piece of wet sacking, placing them temporarily in a shady spot. They must be kept wet at all times. For planting, fill each container with soil to within 2.5 to 5 centimetres (1 to 2 in.) from the top, and use fairly moist soil so that it will be easier to press round the rhizomes or roots. Make a depression in the surface of the soil. If you are planting hardy water lilies, study their roots first. Some grow upright and should be planted that way, others have fleshy, iris-like rhizomes, each of which should be positioned so that its base is near the edge of the container and the growing tip is just above soil level. The roots of tropical water lilies should be planted virtually in the centre of the tub, with the crown just above soil level. Place a flat stone on top, to hold it in place after the container is submerged. Then cover the soil with gravel to prevent muddying the water.

A night-blooming tropical lily unfurls its pink petals beside day-blooming white lilies that have stayed open longer than usual.

SUBMERGING THE PLANTS

As each container is planted, lower it gently into the pool. If growth has barely started, prop up the container so that the water just covers the growing tips; otherwise, set it so that at least three leaves are floating on the surface. The other leaves, beneath the surface, will adjust to the water level as they grow. When the plant has become established, and new stems and leaves begin to appear, gradually lower it to its optimum depth.

In the case of bog plants, planting depth is generally no more than 2.5 to 5 centimetres (1 to 2 in.) below the surface of the water. But lotus and tropical lilies can be covered by as much as 15 to 30 centimetres (6 to 12 in.) of water, and hardy lilies by as much as 45 centimetres ($1\frac{1}{2}$ ft); some kinds are robust enough to take water depths of 60 to 90 centimetres (2 to 3 ft). No plant, however, should be more than 15 centimetres (6 in.) below water level if it is growing in partial shade; otherwise its growing tips will not get enough light.

A NEED FOR OPEN SPACES

The number of plants you put in a pool is also critical. One of the most common mistakes in water gardening is overplanting —covering the surface of the pool with so much foliage that there are no clear spaces. No more than half the surface of a pool should be covered by the leaves and flowers of plants; with a few preliminary calculations you can arrive at this ideal open area in advance.

First, estimate the size of the water surface; a 3 by 4 metre (10 by 13 ft) pool, for example, will have 12 square metres (130 sq. ft), giving you 6 square metres (65 sq. ft) to work with. Most hardy lilies spread over an area of 1 square metre (10 to 12 sq. ft), while medium-sized lilies will cover 0.8 to 1 square metre (8 to 10 sq. ft), and the smaller lilies will occupy 0.4 square metre (4 sq. ft) or less. So your pool will accommodate three or four wide-spreading plants, five or six medium ones, or as many as 10 miniature plants.

Having filled and planted the pool, new water gardeners are often dismayed by a natural occurrence: almost immediately the clear water turns an unattractive green and scum forms on the surface. Millions of algae spores and other tiny organisms, thriving on sunlight, and the nutrients leaching out of the planting soil, are multiplying at an incredible rate. Do not be tempted to empty the pool and change the water. The pool is simply in the first stages of achieving an ecological balance that the addition of new water would only delay. As the water lilies and other cultivated plants begin to spread, they will gradually shade the algae from the sun and compete with them for nutrients. The tadpoles, frogs and toads that take up residence in and around the pool will consume large quantities of these tiny organisms—as will any fish that you may introduce.

But do not expect the pool ever to be crystal clear. Although it will become less murky, it will always be slightly cloudy and green—even when it has achieved a healthy ecological balance. When that balance is about right, you will barely be able to see your hand about 30 centimetres (1 ft) beneath the surface.

A NATURAL CLOUDINESS

If the algae offend you, you can scoop out much of the scum with a folded newspaper or a broom. Or you can prevent the build-up by installing a recirculating pump and filter. You can also use the pump to power a gentle bubbling jet that will aerate the water for fish, placing it far enough from water lilies not to disturb them. There are also several algicides on the market that are harmless to fish and plants if they are used as directed.

Fish are likely to be the finishing touch for your pool. They keep the balance of life in the pool under better control. Fish eat algae but they also consume great quantities of other small organisms, as well as insects and their larvae. They are especially effective in keeping the pool from becoming a mosquito breeding ground.

FISH FOR ORNAMENTS

Some owners of large ponds stock them with tench and carp; both these tend to live at the bottom of the pool, where they stir up the mud and are rarely seen. Most water gardeners prefer more visible and decorative species, such as golden orfe, goldfish and koi carp, which have been specifically bred for ornamental use. The hardier varieties of goldfish and golden orfes will live and breed for many years in an outdoor pool 60 centimetres (2 ft) or more deep, provided the water does not freeze all the way to the bottom in winter, and provided the fish are not over-crowded or overfed and have plenty of submerged oxygenators.

Once fish are in the pool, they practically take care of themselves. The water contains so many edibles that they need only light feeding. Some water gardeners feed their fish only once every two or three days, and claim that their fish are livelier and live longer than those fed more often. But others feed their fish once a day with a high-protein fish food, giving them only what they can consume in five minutes. After this time, remove the surplus to keep it from decomposing and fouling the water.

AN EASY-CARE GARDEN

One advantage of a water garden is the simplicity of its care. The fish are not demanding; and the plants do not require any of the weeding and watering associated with conventional gardening—neither are they particularly afflicted by the pests and diseases that attack other sorts of plants. You will occasionally need to top up the pool from the garden hose to replace water lost through evaporation. And you will need to trim dead leaves and flowers and prune back foliage that appears to be getting too crowded. Do this close to the roots, to prevent dead stems from rotting in the water. Spray with the hose to wash off any aphids; once they hit the water, the fish will do the rest.

Two kinds of care you will have to provide without fail are plant fertilizing and winter protection. Water plants, especially fast-growing tropical water lilies, use up nutrients in their planting soil very rapidly. Fertilize these once a month during the growing season, and give them a booster feed even more frequently if flower production seems to slow down, or if leaves are smaller than usual and have a yellow cast.

WHEN WINTER COMES

In all but temperate climates, water plants also need protection from winter cold. Plants such as the hardy water lilies can be left in the pool if the water is deep enough for ice not to form round the bases of the plants, but many gardeners take the added precaution of removing any brick and stone props under the plants and lowering them to the bottom of the pool.

In very cold areas, it is preferable to move the less hardy plants indoors for the winter. One way to do this is by moving containers into a cool place, such as the garage or an unheated cellar, where they should be covered with plastic sheeting, wet sacking or damp moss peat to preserve the moisture. Or they can be immersed in a tub of water with the plants about 5 centi-

CHOOSING THE YOUNGEST

1. *A water lily's stamens change position as the flower ages. On the day the flower opens—the best day for cutting for a flower arrangement—stamens stand erect and the central disc is visible.*

2. *Over the flower's three to five-day lifespan, stamens gradually bend inwards over the disc until—on the last day of the flower's life— the centre is completely covered by the innermost rows of stamens.*

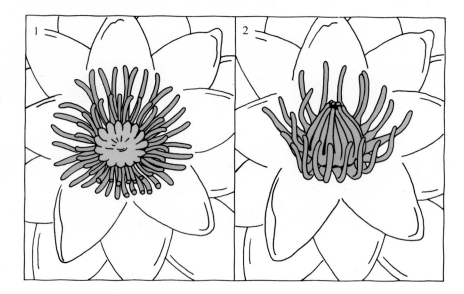

metres (2 in.) below the surface. Another way of overwintering them indoors is to lift the roots or rhizomes from the containers and bury them in clean, damp sand. Before burying, wash them thoroughly and remove any old stems and dead roots. The roots of tropical lilies can be overwintered, but most gardeners throw them away and start with new stock the following season.

TO DRAIN OR NOT TO DRAIN

If the pool is small, you may prefer to drain it in winter, netting the fish as the water level sinks and transferring them to an indoor aquarium that contains water from the pool. But simply leaving everything in place has its advantages. The weight of the water in the pool is a deterrent to frost-heaving and may spare you cracks in pool walls.

If you are going to let the water remain in the pool all winter, take certain precautions. When the water freezes, the pressure of ice within the pool can crack the walls, especially if they are vertical (in pools with sloping sides, the expanding ice simply moves up the incline). One way to absorb the pressure is to put a few logs or other compressible material into the pool. Another precautionary technique is to keep a small area of the pool open. This, in fact, is necessary if you intend to leave fish in the pool all winter; otherwise they will be deprived of oxygen. Do not attempt to provide this area of open water by breaking a hole through the ice every few days; the fish can be injured by the pounding. Instead, install a small electric pool heater made for this purpose. Float it on the surface of the water, and set the thermostat to turn the heater on at a temperature just above freezing. The heater will not raise the water temperature enough to disturb the dormant fish, but it will keep ice from forming in a circle round the heater itself.

STARTING A NEW SEASON

When winter is over and spring comes again, you will need to do some clearing up to give your pool a fresh start. As the weather warms, drain the pool, clean out accumulated debris and inspect the walls for leaks and cracks. If these are small, fill them with sealing paint; larger breaks will need to be plugged with concrete. While such work goes on, transfer the fish to a temporary container filled with water from the pool.

This is the time, too, to divide and replant hardy lilies in fresh soil, a procedure that should take place every two or three years. Wash off the rhizomes or roots and cut them into 15 to 20 centimetre (6 to 8 in.) sections with a sharp knife, making sure that each section has at least one "eye" or growing point. Then plant the sections in separate containers and lower them into the pool for another season of bloom.

An encyclopaedia of rock, water and bog plants

Anyone planning a rock and water garden has a world's worth of plants to choose from. A blue gentian from the Swiss Alps, an Atlas daisy from the mountains of Morocco, a Himalayan primrose will all thrive in the man-made mountain meadow of a suburban rock garden. Tropical water lilies from African and South American lagoons will bloom throughout the summer in warmed greenhouse pools of northern climates, and the ancient Egyptian papyrus that sheltered the baby Moses will root with ease at a pool's edge.

To help you narrow your choices, the encyclopaedia that follows lists 254 outstanding rock, water and bog plants, selected for their availability from local nurseries and specialist suppliers. The entries, which are divided into rock-garden plants, starting on the next page, and aquatic plants, beginning on page 131, are arranged in alphabetical order by the plants' botanical names; the common names are cross-referenced to the Latin equivalents in the index. Each entry contains information on the physical characteristics, the uses in the garden and the growing requirements of the plant.

For rock-garden plants the entries generally include specific preferences for soil acidity or alkalinity, since many alpine plants grow in dry soils with a high limestone content, while rock-garden plants native to moist woodlands tend to need soils rich in leaf-mould and moss peat. Similarly, the entries for aquatic plants include optimum water depths and temperatures. Some water lilies thrive in 45 centimetres (1½ ft) of water, for instance, but others, such as the pickerel weed, need shallower water. The latter, however, survives in pools that freeze in the winter, while the tropical water lilies may be damaged if the water temperature falls below 21°C (70°F).

On pages 146-151, characteristics charts summarize the information in the encyclopaedia for quick reference.

A sampler of rock and water plants swings in an arc around a water lily. At the top, among bog plants, are arrowhead and umbrella grass, while rock plants below include a mountain avens and a blue gentian.

WOOLLY YARROW
Achillea tomentosa

BUGLE
Ajuga reptans

Rock-garden plants
A

ACHILLEA

A. chrysocoma, also called *A. aurea*; *A. tomentosa* (woolly yarrow)

Achilleas thrive in a sunny rock garden and will flower even in poor, gritty soil as long as there is good drainage. *A. chrysocoma* has downy, grey-green, fern-like leaves which form a dense mat at ground level, spreading to 25 cm (10 in.), and are aromatic if crushed. In summer, tiny deep yellow flowers appear in dense, flat-topped clusters, 5 to 7.5 cm (2 to 3 in.) wide, on top of 10 cm (4 in.) flower stalks. *A. tomentosa* has similar foliage and lighter yellow flowers in heads up to 7.5 cm (3 in.) wide and is 15 to 30 cm (6 to 12 in.) tall. If the stems are cut down to the ground after the plants have flowered, the foliage of this sturdy perennial remains evergreen.

HOW TO GROW. Achilleas are fully hardy. They need full sun and a well-drained, rather poor, slightly acid to neutral soil with a pH of 6.0 to 7.0. Set plants out in spring, spacing them 30 to 60 cm (1 to 2 ft) apart. Plants require little attention, even during hot, dry summers and do not need to be fertilized. However, some types spread so rapidly that clumps may need to be divided every year or two to prevent overcrowding. Division is also the preferred method for propagating new plants; this should be done in spring or autumn, after flowering.

AJUGA

A. pyramidalis; *A. reptans* (bugle)

These two ajugas form thick mats of shiny oval leaves, 5 to 10 cm (2 to 4 in.) long, in either dry or moist soil and are useful perennials for planting in the crevices of rocks as well as for growing as ground covers. Both these species bear small flowers on 12.5 to 15 cm (5 to 6 in.) spikes in late spring and early summer, and their leaves turn bronze in the autumn. In Britain, this bronze colour remains throughout the winter, but in colder climates the leaves drop off.

A. pyramidalis spreads freely from underground stolons. It usually grows 5 to 15 cm (2 to 6 in.) tall but may reach a height of up to 23 cm (9 in.); its flowers are generally blue, although rare pink and white cultivars are also available. One particularly decorative cultivar, *A. pyramidalis* 'Metallica Crispa', has rich blue flowers and metallic-looking, purple-brown, puckered leaves.

Bugle grows 10 to 15 cm (4 to 6 in.) tall and spreads rapidly; thus it is advisable not to plant this and the previous species where they will intrude on other plants. The original species has dark green foliage and bright blue flowers, but there are several named cultivars. Some have red or white flowers; others come with reddish-purple leaves or with leaves of variegated colours—green splashed with white, or green splashed with pink and purple. These are available under such names as 'Rainbow', 'Burgundy Glow' and 'Multicolour'.

HOW TO GROW. Ajugas grow in almost any soil, rich or poor, and in full sun or shade. Those with metallic-coloured foliage, however, do best when they are planted in full sun in a damp situation. They are relatively indifferent to soil chemistry but grow well in a slightly acid to neutral soil with a pH of 6.0 to 7.0. Set plants out in spring or autumn, spacing them 15 to 30 cm (6 to 12 in.) apart. Ajugas do not require special care but 'Metallica Crispa' needs to be lifted, divided and replanted about every two years.

Propagate by dividing plants in spring or autumn; cut off sections of runners and replant them at once.

ALLIUM

A. beesianum, also called *A. sikkimense*; *A. moly*; *A. tuberosum*, also called *A. senescens*

These three ornamental members of the onion family are relatively small and thrive in a sunny rock garden. Their grass-like foliage grows from clumps of underground bulbs; their flowers form tight, fluffy clusters of tiny blooms at the tops of tubular stalks, with the exception of *A. moly*. All species bloom from late spring throughout summer.

A. beesianum produces two to four flat, purple-tinged leaves, up to 15 cm (6 in.) tall, and its 5 cm (2 in.) clusters of bright blue or purplish-blue flowers appear on stalks 23 to 30 cm (9 to 12 in.) tall.

A. moly has only two strap-like, blue-green leaves, 30 cm (12 in.) tall and up to 5 cm (2 in.) wide. Its loose umbels of bright yellow flowers, 5 to 7.5 cm (2 to 3 in.) wide, cap stalks 23 to 30 cm (9 to 12 in.) tall.

A dwarf species well suited to a rock garden, *A. tuberosum* grows 15 to 20 cm (6 to 8 in.) tall. It has narrow leaves in dense tufts and bears pink, violet or near purple flower umbels 5 to 7.5 cm (2 to 3 in.) wide. All three species are perennials and spread moderately slowly.

HOW TO GROW. Alliums as a group are hardy in Britain and grow best in full sun, although *A. moly* and *A. tuberosum* will also tolerate partial shade. They need a rich, well-drained soil with a pH between 5.5 and 7.0. Plant bulbs in autumn, setting them about 7.5 cm (3 in.) deep and 10 cm (4 in.) apart. Keep the soil moist during the growing season. Propagate by dividing clumps of bulbs in the spring, replanting them immediately, or by lifting and replanting small bulbs that develop round the larger ones. Additional plants may also be started from seeds collected and sown as soon as they are ripe, but it will take them two or three years to flower.

ALYSSUM

A. montanum; *A. saxatile* (gold dust); *A. spinosum*, also called *Ptilotrichum spinosum*

Alyssums grow naturally on limestone cliffs and are among the most popular rock-garden plants, fitting easily into a moraine as well as between the stones of a wall. As a group, these three perennial species usually form mounds less than 25 cm (10 in.) tall, spreading wider than their height. They have small grey-green leaves and bear masses of tiny flowers in late spring or early summer.

A. montanum is a compact plant, seldom growing more than 7.5 to 15 cm (3 to 6 in.) tall, although it can reach 25 cm (10 in.). It spreads up to 30 cm (1 ft) wide and is especially attractive on a drystone wall. Its rambling stems bear fragrant, 5 cm (2 in.) clusters of yellow flowers.

A. saxatile is a shrubbier plant with woody stems 15 to 30 cm (6 to 12 in.) tall and a spread of 30 to 45 cm (1 to 1½ ft). Its deep yellow flowers are packed densely in 10 to 15 cm (4 to 6 in.) flower spikes. Cultivars, in addition to the species, include 'Citrinum', with pale yellow flowers; 'Compactum', of close habit; 'Plenum', with double flowers; 'Tom Thumb', which grows only 7.5 to 10 cm (3 to 4 in.) tall; and a variegated kind with yellow-marbled foliage.

A. spinosum is actually a dwarf shrub. It grows 15 to 30 cm (6 to 12 in.) tall and equally wide or wider. Its flowers are white or pale pink, and one cultivar, 'Roseum', has dark pink flowers. When the flowers drop off, the remaining part of the flower head hardens into tiny white spines that decorate the plant throughout winter. Alyssums seed themselves if faded flower heads are not removed and can also be propagated from cuttings; the latter is the better method for named cultivars.

Allium moly

GOLD DUST
Alyssum saxatile

ATLAS DAISY
Anacyclus depressus

ROCK JASMINE
Androsace sarmentosa

HOW TO GROW. Most alyssums are hardy. All grow best in full sun, in well-drained, gritty soil with a pH of 6.0 to 7.5. In very cold areas, plant them out in spring; elsewhere, in autumn or spring. Space plants about 20 to 30 cm (8 to 12 in.) apart. For bushier growth, pinch back stems after flowering. Alyssums do not need to be fertilized. Propagate from stem cuttings of new growth, taken in summer, or by sowing seeds in spring.

ANACYCLUS
A. depressus (Atlas daisy)

Ideally suited to scree or moraine conditions, the Atlas daisy is native to the Atlas Mountains of Morocco. From a carrot-like root, it forms low clumps only 5 to 7.5 cm (2 to 3 in.) high, but its fern-like, grey-green leaves, up to 4 cm (1½ in.) long, grow on branching prostrate stems that fan out like the spokes of a wheel to cover an area 30 cm (1 ft) across. Its daisy-like flowers, 2.5 cm (1 in.) wide, bloom profusely in summer; the petals are dark red on the undersides and white on top, so that in bud the daisy is one colour and in bloom another.

HOW TO GROW. Atlas daisies are hardy in Britain, but dislike wet soil conditions. They grow best in full sun and in a well-drained, dry and gritty soil with a pH of 6.0 to 7.5. Set plants in the ground in spring, spacing them 30 cm (1 ft) apart. Keep roots barely moist during the growing season. Do not overwater; if plants have too much water, they may die. To prolong flowering, snip off faded blooms. Propagate from seeds sown in the autumn as soon as they are ripe. It is best to start them in a seed bed, later transferring them as seedlings to pots, and then to the open garden. Additional Atlas daisies can also be propagated from stem cuttings taken during the growing season and rooted in a mixture of moss peat and sand. Mature plants cannot easily be moved.

ANDROSACE
A. carnea; *A. sarmentosa*. (Both called rock jasmine)

These delicate alpine perennials, which seldom exceed 10 cm (4 in.) in height, flourish in a moraine or on a rocky ledge or bank. They bear clusters of tiny circular flowers, less than 6 mm (¼ in.) wide, from late spring to summer. *A. carnea*, the smaller of the two, grows only 7.5 cm (3 in.) tall and spreads 15 to 23 cm (6 to 9 in.) wide. Its shiny green leaves, 18 mm (¾ in.) long, grow in a rosette from a plump underground rhizome; its flowers are pink or white with yellow centres and grow on stems 2.5 to 7.5 cm (1 to 3 in.) tall. There are several good named forms, such as *A.c.* ssp. *brigantiaca*, which has soft pink flowers, and *A.c.* ssp. *laggeri*, which bears pink flowers with yellow eyes and freely seeds itself.

A. sarmentosa becomes 10 cm (4 in.) tall and up to 30 cm (1 ft) wide. Its leaves, up to 4 cm (1½ in.) long, are covered with silvery down when young, turning brighter green in summer, and its flower clusters are pink, capping 10 cm (4 in.) stems. It spreads rapidly by means of runners to form dense mats.

HOW TO GROW. Rock jasmines are hardy in Britain. All grow best in full sun but *A. sarmentosa* can also tolerate partial shade. They need a gritty, well-drained, slightly acid soil with a pH of 5.5 to 7.0. Do not put them near more aggressive creeping plants such as alyssums, which will crowd them out. Set out plants in spring or autumn, spacing them 15 to 30 cm (6 to 12 in.) apart. Keep their roots moist during the growing season, but do not allow the leaves to remain wet or they will rot. It is a good idea to pile granite chippings round the crowns to keep these dry in winter. Propagate by dividing large clumps in autumn or spring. *A. sarmentosa* can also be increased by cutting off and transplanting the small plants that develop at the end of runners. It may also be grown from seed, but germination is slow.

ANEMONE
A. apennina; *A. blanda*; *A. nemorosa* (wood anemone)

Among the earliest spring flowers, anemones are used in woodland gardens tucked between stones or massed at the top or bottom of a rocky slope. Their delicate bowl-shaped flowers are actually petal-like sepals that surround the colourful seed heads; there are no true petals. Anemones have either deeply lobed or fern-like leaves. All the species are hardy perennials.

A. apennina comes from southern Europe and has ferny foliage and clear blue, many-rayed flowers on 10 cm (4 in.) stems in early spring. There are also white and double-flowered cultivars.

A. blanda is the earliest to bloom, producing its rich blue flowers, often 2.5 to 4 cm (1 to 1½ in.) wide, from December onwards. It is deeper in colour than *A. apennina*. Forms that have pale blue, mauve, white and pink flowers are common; 'Radar' is red with white centres; and 'Atro-caerulea' is deep blue. All these plants grow up to about 10 cm (4 in.) tall.

Wood anemone becomes 15 to 25 cm (6 to 10 in.) tall and normally bears single white, 2.5 cm (1 in.) flowers. However, there are variants: 'Alba Plena' has double, white flowers; 'Allenii' has lavender-blue flowers; 'Rosea' has red-purple blooms; and 'Robinsoniana' has two-toned flowers, pale blue inside, yellow outside. The compound leaves die soon after the flowers fade.

HOW TO GROW. All these anemones are hardy even in cool climates. They do best when grown in a partially shaded position and appreciate soils that are slightly acid to neutral with a pH of 6.0 to 7.0.

Plant anemones in autumn, setting them 15 to 30 cm (6 to 12 in.) apart. Keep the soil moist while plants are in flower. Scatter a mixture of leaf-mould and bone-meal occasionally on the ground after they have flowered.

The easiest way to propagate anemones is from seed, freshly gathered after flowering and sown immediately. Sow in trays of seed compost, scattering the seeds thinly to prevent overcrowding. The following spring, transplant the pricked out seedlings to their permanent positions in the rock garden. Plants that are started from seed will not flower until the third year.

ANEMONE PULSATILLA See *Pulsatilla*
ANEMONE THALICTROIDES See *Anemonella*

ANEMONELLA
A. thalictroides, also called *Anemone thalictroides* and *Thalictrum anemonoides* (rue anemone)

An American woodland flower often found growing among rocks, the rue anemone flourishes on a rocky embankment, between paving stones or in a rock garden in the shade. This rather delicate beauty grows only 10 to 15 cm (4 to 6 in.) tall and has round-lobed leaves like those of the herb after which it is named. Its small white or pink flowers, 1 cm (½ in.) wide, appear in spring in loose clusters on branching stems. These delicate-looking flowers usually last about two weeks. Like those of its relative, the anemone, the flowers of this plant consist of bright sepals, not petals. Rue anemones grow from finger-like tubers that

WOOD ANEMONE
Anemone nemorosa

RUE ANEMONE
Anemonella thalictroides

COLUMBINE
Aquilegia flabellata

WALL ROCK CRESS
Arabis caucasica

become dormant when the leaves die down to the ground in midsummer.

HOW TO GROW. Rue anemones are hardy in southern Britain and similar regions, but need partial shade and a position sheltered from the wind. They do best in a rich, well-drained, peaty soil with an acid pH of 5.0 to 6.0, but can tolerate more neutral soils. Plant tubers in autumn, setting them 2.5 cm (1 in.) deep and 10 cm (4 in.) apart. Cover them with a light winter mulch of leaves. During the flowering season, keep the soil moist. To propagate, divide tuber clusters when plants are dormant, or sow seeds as soon as they are ripe. Rue anemones will seed themselves if faded flowers are not cut off, but plants grown from seed take three years to flower.

AQUILEGIA
A. bertolonii; *A. canadensis*; *A. flabellata*; *A. scopulorum*. (All called columbine)

Columbines have a special affinity for rocky settings. Depending on their size, they are suitable for scree gardens, rock ledges or drystone walls. Their finely cut, grey-green or blue-green leaves make lacy mounds 10 to 24 cm (4 to 10 in.) tall from which, in late spring or early summer, rise flower stems of various heights—as low as 15 cm (6 in.) and as tall as 1 metre (3 ft). Funnel-shaped flowers with long spurs dangle gracefully from these stems high above the foliage; they are followed by seed-filled capsules.

A. bertolonii forms a mound up to 10 cm (4 in.) high and equally wide. It produces blue-violet flowers, 5 cm (2 in.) wide, one to a stem.

A. canadensis, an American species, has a foliage mound 15 to 20 cm (6 to 8 in.) tall. Its flower stems are 30 to 90 cm (1 to 3 ft) tall and bear red-and-yellow flowers about 6 cm (2½ in.) long.

The basal leaf mound of *A. flabellata* ranges from 15 to 25 cm (6 to 10 in.) tall and spreads 15 to 20 cm (6 to 8 in.) wide. It bears 4 to 5 cm (1½ to 2 in.) violet-and-white flowers on stems up to 45 cm (1½ ft) tall. One small cultivar of this species, 'Nana Alba', has thick-petalled, white flowers on 15 to 20 cm (6 to 8 in.) stems.

A. scopulorum, a tiny alpine columbine native to western America, grows only 10 to 15 cm (4 to 6 in.) tall and wide, with 2.5 to 4 cm (1 to 1½ in.) blue-purple flowers capping 15 to 25 cm (6 to 10 in.) flower stems.

HOW TO GROW. Columbines grow in Britain and the milder parts of northern Europe. They do best in partial shade but can tolerate some sun in cooler, drought-free areas. They thrive in moist, well-drained gritty soil with a pH of 5.0 to 7.0.

Plant columbines in early spring as soon as the soil can be worked, or in autumn when plants are dormant. Space smaller alpine species 15 cm (6 in.) apart, larger kinds 20 to 30 cm (8 to 12 in.) apart. Water thoroughly in summer, but allow the soil to become almost completely dry to the touch between thorough waterings.

In very cold spells in winter, protect plants with a light mulch of leaves or straw. Columbines seed themselves readily and should be allowed to do so, for plants have a short life. If started from seed in spring or summer, the plants will produce flowers the following spring.

ARABIS
A. alpina; *A. caucasica*, also called *A. albida* (wall rock cress); *A. ferdinandi-coburgii*

Useful little plants for drystone walls, plantings between paving stones or for alpine conditions, arabis form compact mounds of jagged-edged leaves, covered in early spring with airy clusters of tiny flowers on 15 to 25 cm (6 to 10 in.) stems. In mild climates, the foliage remains green throughout the winter.

A. alpina is a compact plant with rosettes of hairy leaves; it spreads 30 cm (1 ft) wide and grows 15 cm (6 in.) high. Flowers of the species are white, but this plant also comes with pink blooms or white-splashed leaves.

A. caucasica also grows to 15 cm (6 in.) high and spreads to cover an area as much as 45 cm (1½ ft) wide. Its leaves are grey-green and downy, and its flowers are white and very fragrant. There are cultivars with larger flowers or flowers of different colours, including pink and lavender, such as 'Coccinea', crimson, and a fine double, 'Flore Pleno', whose clear white flower spikes resemble miniature stock; some types also have woollier leaves.

A. ferdinandi-coburgii, a mat-forming species, has grey-green leaves and white flowers on 15 cm (6 in.) stems; the finest kind, however, is 'Variegata', an outstanding cultivar with green and white variegated leaves.

HOW TO GROW. Arabis are hardy in northern Europe. They grow best in a well-drained sandy or gritty soil with a pH of 6.0 to 7.5 and normally need full sun, although in hot, dry areas they do better in partial shade. Set plants out in early spring or autumn spacing them 25 to 30 cm (10 to 12 in.) apart. After flowers fade, cut back stems by half to encourage new leaves.

Propagate from stem cuttings taken immediately after flowering or by dividing plants in autumn. Arabis can also be started from seed.

ARCTOSTAPHYLOS
A. uva-ursi (bearberry)

A low evergreen shrub with trailing branches, bearberry is ideally suited for planting round rocks, on walled terraces or as ground cover over stony banks. It grows 15 cm (6 in.) tall, and spreads by taking root where branches touch the soil, forming new shoots that may eventually blanket an area up to 4.5 metres (15 ft) wide. The shiny dark green leaves are 2.5 cm (1 in.) long and in autumn turn bronze-red. Clusters of tiny bell-shaped, white or pink flowers, 6 mm (¼ in.) long, tip the branches in spring; they are followed by long-lasting red berries that remain well into winter. This hardy plant can withstand wind, severe drought, cold and polluted air.

HOW TO GROW. Bearberry is native to Britain and northern Europe and grows in full sun or partial shade. It does best in a well-drained sandy or gritty soil with an acid pH of 4.5 to 5.5; however, it can also tolerate near neutral soils. Set out plants in spring or autumn, spacing them 30 to 60 cm (1 to 2 ft) apart. Provide young plants with a permanent mulch of chunky moss peat or pine needles to conserve moisture and keep weeds down; older plants need no special attention.

Bearberry is very difficult to transplant, and, if additional plants are wanted, it is best to buy new ones that have been container-grown. Cuttings of new growth may be rooted in a mixture of equal parts of sand and moss peat.

ARENARIA
A. grandiflora; *A. montana*. (Both called sandwort)

The sandworts are mountain plants, forming low mounds or tufted mats of foliage that is often evergreen except in extremely cold winters. They are well suited to scree conditions or rocky ledges, or may be tucked between the paving stones of a terrace or path. The plants themselves are seldom more than 5 to 10 cm (2 to 4 in.)

BEARBERRY
Arctostaphylos uva-ursi

SANDWORT
Arenaria montana

high, although their flower stems may be up to 25 cm (10 in.) tall. In late spring and summer, they bear great numbers of small, five-petalled, white flowers, which bloom singly or in loose clusters on slender stems. The foliage varies from species to species: in some it resembles grass, in others needles or moss.

A. grandiflora forms tufts 5 to 7.5 cm (2 to 3 in.) tall and spreads on creeping stems to cover an area up to 30 cm (1 ft) wide. Its bright green, needle-like foliage is thick and leathery, and its 2.5 cm (1 in.) flowers top stems 15 cm (6 in.) tall. The species takes root wherever the creeping stems touch the ground.

A. montana has narrow, glossy, grey-green leaves, up to 2.5 cm (1 in.) long and forms thick mats 5 to 10 cm (2 to 4 in.) tall and 45 cm (1½ ft) wide. Its plentiful flowers, 1 to 2.5 cm (½ to 1 in.) wide, appear on branching stems 15 to 20 cm (6 to 8 in.) tall. Unlike other creeping sandworts, its cascading stems do not root and are most effective when they are allowed to tumble over stony walls or large rocks.

HOW TO GROW. Both species are hardy in Britain and northern Europe and grow best in full sun except in very hot areas, where they need light shade. They need a moist, well-drained, sandy or gritty soil. *A. grandiflora* thrives in soils with a pH of 6.0 to 7.5, while *A. montana* benefits from acid soils with a pH of 5.5 to 6.5. Plant sandworts in spring, spacing them about 15 cm (6 in.) apart. They seed themselves readily and may be propagated from seed. Sandworts with creeping stems may also be propagated from stem cuttings taken in early summer, or by dividing established plants in spring.

ARISAEMA
A. candidissimum; *A. dracontium* (green dragon); *A. sikokianum*; *A. triphyllum*, also called *A. atrorubens* (Jack-in-the-pulpit)

These handsome arum-style flowers make unusual additions to a moist, shady garden on a woodland site. The spring flowers consist of a finger-like spadix that is protected by a hood called a spathe. In late summer or autumn, the hood usually withers and dies, revealing a club-like spike of tightly packed orange or red berries. The plants grow from tuberous roots.

A. candidissimum is a Chinese species, whose pure white spathes are striped inside with pink, but are green on the outside. Unlike the other species, this plant blooms in midsummer and has broad three-lobed leaves. There is also a white cultivar.

Green dragon grows up to 90 cm (3 ft) tall, and has a tail-like spadix that extends well beyond the unarched, 5 to 10 cm (2 to 4 in.) green spathe. Its curious leaves are actually a single leaf that divides into three leaflets and then sub-divides into five or more smaller leaflets.

A. sikokianum is 20 to 30 cm (8 to 12 in.) tall and has mottled leaves, 15 cm (6 in.) long, which are divided into two to five sections. Its 5 cm (2 in.) long, ivory-white spadix is backed by a white-lined, dark purple hood, 12.5 to 25 cm (5 to 10 in.) long, that is flecked and streaked with green and white.

Jack-in-the-pulpit, from eastern North America, grows 30 cm (1 ft) tall and produces two leaves, 10 to 23 cm (4 to 9 in.) long, that divide into three parts. Its 7.5 cm (3 in.) long spadix, the Jack, stands under a 10 to 17.5 cm (4 to 7 in.) green or purple arched hood with purple, green or white stripes. All these plants are perennials, dying down to the ground in winter and reappearing in early spring.

HOW TO GROW. All the species mentioned are hardy in sheltered parts of Britain and temperate northern Europe.

JACK-IN-THE-PULPIT
Arisaema triphyllum

They do best in partial shade in moist, rich, well-drained soil with an acid pH of 5.0 to 6.5. Plant in spring or autumn, setting them at least 15 cm (6 in.) deep and 15 to 20 cm (6 to 8 in.) apart. Or start plants from seeds sown in autumn after the fleshy covering is removed, covering them with 6 to 12 mm ($\frac{1}{4}$ to $\frac{1}{2}$ in.) of seed compost; plants that have been started from seed will bloom in the third year. If desired, transplant seedlings in the late summer or autumn of the first year.

ARMERIA
A. juniperifolia, also called *A. caespitosa* (juniper thrift); *A. maritima* (thrift, sea pink)

Thrifts are plants accustomed to dry, sandy soils; they take naturally to rocky ledges and stone walls. Each plant forms a dense mound of stiff evergreen leaves, which rise in multiple tufts like small pincushions from a single taproot. In late spring and summer, tiny pink, white or lilac flowers bloom in globe-like clusters, 1 cm ($\frac{1}{2}$ in.) across, above the foliage.

A. juniperifolia has clumps that are only 5 cm (2 in.) tall, and its leaves are short and needle-like, only 1 cm ($\frac{1}{2}$ in.) long. The flower stalks are sturdy and very short— 5 to 15 cm (2 to 6 in.) high.

A. maritima, which grows wild on rocky seashores, is a somewhat larger plant; its foliage clumps are 10 cm (4 in.) high and its leaves are grass-like, growing up to 15 cm (6 in.) long. The wiry flower stalks are 15 to 30 cm (6 to 12 in.) in height. Several cultivars are available: 'Alba', with white flowers; 'Merlin', soft pink; 'Perfection', large, bright pink flower heads; and 'Vindictive', with deep pinkish-red flowers.

HOW TO GROW. Thrifts are hardy plants which grow best in full sun and a deep, dry, gritty soil with a pH of 6.0 to 7.5. Good drainage is essential; they cannot tolerate excessive moisture. Set plants out in spring, spacing them 23 to 30 cm (9 to 12 in.) apart. As plants age, the centres of the clumps may rot and die out. Sometimes this can be prevented by sprinkling a gritty mixture of stone chips over the plants to keep the crowns dry. Older plants may be regenerated every three years, in spring or autumn, by cutting off tufted sections and rooting them in sand. Propagate in the same way. *A. maritima* may also be started from seeds, sown as soon as they ripen in summer. The seeds of named cultivars, however, rarely breed true to the parent plants.

ARTEMISIA
A. schmidtiana 'Nana'

A. schmidtiana 'Nana' is a dwarf version of a garden perennial that is noted for its finely cut, silvery-grey leaves. It grows 7.5 cm (3 in.) tall, with glistening silver, filigree foliage, and is an excellent plant for alpine rock gardens and scree conditions. The branching stems form mounds 23 to 30 cm (9 to 12 in.) wide that can be left undisturbed indefinitely. Late summer is the period of bloom, but the sprays of tiny, ball-like, yellowish-green flowers of this plant are inconspicuous and far less decorative than the foliage.

HOW TO GROW. This artemisia is hardy only in warm sheltered parts of Britain and does well in the south. It thrives in a well-drained sandy or gritty soil with a pH of 6.0 to 7.5 and prefers full sun but will tolerate partial shade. Set plants out in spring, spacing them 30 to 45 cm (1 to 1$\frac{1}{2}$ ft) apart. They may need light watering during the growing season, but the soil round the roots should never be wet; in winter, wet soil will kill the plants. To encourage

THRIFT
Armeria maritima

Artemisia schmidtiana 'Nana'

WILD GINGER
Asarum europaeum

SWEET WOODRUFF
Asperula odorata

thicker foliage, cut off the flower stems before the flowers open. Propagate in spring or summer from stem cuttings rooted in damp sand.

ASARUM

A. canadense; *A. caudatum*; *A. europaeum*. (All called wild ginger)

The heart-shaped leaves of the wild gingers are useful for carpeting a woodland rock garden or a shaded area under shrubs or trees on a slope. These hardy perennials usually grow 15 cm (6 in.) tall from fleshy underground stems or rhizomes, which have a ginger-like scent and flavour. They spread rapidly, and in mild climates the foliage of all but *A. canadense* is evergreen. In spring, small, cup-shaped, brown or red flowers, about 2.5 cm (1 in.) long, bloom on short stems under the foliage; sometimes they appear even before the leaves unfold completely. The flowers remain in bloom for as long as four weeks.

A. canadense has soft, hairy leaves, 5 to 17.5 cm (2 to 7 in.) wide, and 2.5 cm (1 in.) brownish-purple flowers whose cup-shaped bases open into three spreading lobes.

A. caudatum is 17.5 cm (7 in.) tall and has 5 to 15 cm (2 to 6 in.) wide leaves. Each of the 2.5 cm (1 in.) wide, brownish-purple flowers opens out into three lobes that develop 5 cm (2 in.) long tails.

A. europaeum bears glossy, 5 to 7.5 cm (2 to 3 in.) wide leaves on 12.5 cm (5 in.) tall stems; it produces greenish-purple flowers which remain tightly cupped and are only 1 cm ($\frac{1}{2}$ in.) in width.

HOW TO GROW. All these gingers are hardy in sheltered parts of Britain. They do best in open to deep shade, in a moist, well-drained, humus-rich soil with a pH of 5.5 to 7.0. Plant rhizomes in spring or autumn, setting them 1 cm ($\frac{1}{2}$ in.) deep, with the tip of the rhizome just at soil level. Space plants about 30 cm (1 ft) apart. Keep the soil moist throughout the growing season by watering during dry spells in spring and summer. Propagate by dividing rhizomes in early spring or autumn, except in frost-free areas, where they can be divided and replanted at any time as long as they are kept moist.

ASPERULA

A. gussonii; *A. odorata*, also called *Galium odoratum* (sweet woodruff); *A. suberosa*. (All also called woodruff)

Woodruffs, commonly considered woodland plants, grow naturally in the rocky soil of moraines and screes, and some species thrive on sunny cliffs; they are well suited to wall gardens out in the open, unshaded by trees. All are perennials, forming dense and sometimes invasive mats of attractive foliage. The flowers are small but profuse, blooming in loose clusters at the ends of square stems.

A. gussonii grows only 7.5 cm (3 in.) tall and has very short, slender stems thickly set with whorls, each composed of four shiny dark green leaves, 1 cm ($\frac{1}{2}$ in.) long. It blooms in early summer, producing pale pink, tubular flowers, 6 mm ($\frac{1}{4}$ in.) across; these are so numerous that they hide the foliage.

A. odorata, a somewhat larger species, forms mounds 15 to 20 cm (6 to 8 in.) tall; its stems are surrounded, pinwheel-fashion, by whorls of eight leaves, 2.5 to 5 cm (1 to 2 in.) long. From early to midsummer, the foliage is capped by dainty clusters of star-shaped, white flowers, 6 mm ($\frac{1}{4}$ in.) across. Both flowers and foliage are sweet-scented; when dried, they smell of new-mown hay and are used to flavour wine and to scent linen.

A. suberosa also forms hummocks, but is only 5 to 7.5 cm (2 to 3 in.) tall and spreads to about 15 cm (6 in.). Its leaves are needle-like, 1 cm ($\frac{1}{2}$ in.) long, and covered with silvery-white hairs. In summer, it bears masses of tiny cross-shaped, pink blooms.

HOW TO GROW. All these woodruffs are hardy in Britain; *A. gussonii* and *A. suberosa* make good scree plants in full sun in a gritty or sandy soil with a pH of 6.0 to 7.5; good drainage is essential. *A. suberosa* is also well suited to an alpine house. *A. odorata* does best in open shade in moist, well-drained soil with an acid pH of 4.5 to 5.5 and enriched with leaf-mould or moss peat. Plant in spring, setting them about 25 to 30 cm (10 to 12 in.) apart. Woodruffs will occasionally seed themselves, but in order to obtain new plants it is easier to divide existing plants in spring, just as growth is beginning.

ASTER
A. alpinus (alpine aster); *A. natalensis*; *A. tibeticus*

These asters are found on steep, rocky slopes and do well in alpine gardens. They are slender, upright perennials with narrow, hairy leaves, 2.5 to 5 cm (1 to 2 in.) long, and daisy-like flowers that usually bloom from midsummer through until autumn.

A. alpinus grows 10 to 15 cm (4 to 6 in.) tall and spreads 30 to 45 cm (1 to 1$\frac{1}{2}$ ft) wide. The species bears blue to violet flowers, 2.5 to 5 cm (1 to 2 in.) wide, with deep yellow centres, but the cultivar 'Albus' has white flowers, 'Beechwood', blue flowers, 'Rosea', pink flowers, and 'Rubra', reddish-purple flowers.

A. natalensis forms mats of grey-green, hairy leaves with other leaves of deep green, and has rich blue flowers on 7.5 cm (3 in.) stems.

A. tibeticus grows to a height of 15 cm (6 in.) and forms a mat, spreading 30 to 38 cm (1 to 1$\frac{1}{4}$ ft) across. Its narrow leaves are sparse, but the single blue flowers, 2.5 to 5 cm (1 to 2 in.) in diameter, which open in summer, are produced in great abundance.

HOW TO GROW. All these asters are hardy in Britain and do well in full sun but will tolerate partial shade. They thrive in a deep, well-drained sandy soil with a pH of 6.0 to 7.5. Sow seeds in spring and thin seedlings to stand 20 cm (8 in.) apart. Flowering begins in the second year. To encourage branching, pinch out growing tips in late spring and again in early summer.

Propagate from seed or by dividing root clumps in autumn or spring; for named cultivars, division is preferable, since plants do not always breed true from seed.

ATRAGENE See *Clematis*

AUBRIETA
A. deltoidea

One of the most charming sights in any rock garden is aubrieta in full bloom, cascading from the crevices of an old stone wall or spreading in patches over the faces of large rocks. In addition, this versatile evergreen may be used as an edging plant at the base of a rocky slope or for herbaceous beds and borders. The plant forms a mound of carpet-like growth, 7.5 to 15 cm (3 to 6 in.) high. Its small, downy, grey-green leaves are hidden under numerous 18 mm ($\frac{3}{4}$ in.) flowers in spring and early summer.

The popularity of aubrietas has prompted plant breeders to develop numerous cultivars in red, violet, blue and mauve as well as different shades of the original purple. Some flower more freely; others have larger or double flowers; there are also cultivars with golden or variegated foliage. Once it has become well established, aubrieta

ALPINE ASTER
Aster alpinus

AUBRIETA
Aubrieta deltoidea

COMMON DAISY
Bellis perennis

SPIKE HEATH
Bruckenthalia spiculifolia

spreads rapidly and may crowd out smaller, less invasive plants if it is not pruned back fairly regularly.

HOW TO GROW. Aubrieta is hardy in northern Europe. It grows best in full sun, but needs some shade in hot, dry areas. It does best in a sandy, well-drained soil with a pH of 6.0 to 8.0. Set plants in the ground in spring or autumn, spacing them 25 cm (10 in.) apart. Water them occasionally during dry periods, but be careful not to overwater; excessive moisture is harmful to the foliage. After flowering, prune plants severely to control their size and to encourage a second flowering in autumn.

Propagate species plants from seeds sown directly in the permanent site in spring or autumn; propagate cultivars from stem cuttings taken before or after flowering or by dividing established plants, preferably in autumn.

B

BELLIS
B. perennis (common daisy); *B. rotundifolia* 'Coerulescens'

The common daisy is a lawn weed in Europe and should never be planted deliberately. There are, however, a number of cultivars with larger, 2.5 to 5 cm (1 to 2 in.) wide, double, pink, white or red flowers commonly used for bedding or for small areas in rock gardens. There are also miniature cultivars with double flowers, 1 to 2.5 cm ($\frac{1}{2}$ to 1 in.) across. Some of the best known are the soft pink and dainty 'Dresden China', red 'Rob Roy' and their white counterpart, 'White Pearl'. The flowers are freely borne from late spring onwards on 10 to 15 cm (4 to 6 in.) stems arising from rosettes of spoon-shaped leaves. They are attractive in sink gardens, between crazy paving or grouped in rock gardens.

B. rotundifolia 'Coerulescens', from North Africa, resembles the common daisy, except that the flowers are blue with yellow centres. All these daisies are short-lived perennials; they are usually treated as biennials and planted out every other year.

HOW TO GROW. These daisies grow throughout Europe. They need full sun or partial shade and do best in a moist, rich soil with a pH of 6.0 to 7.5 Set young plants out in spring or autumn, spacing them 20 cm (8 in.) apart. Plants may also be started from seed, although some of the double-flowered cultivars do not come true from seed; if special forms or colours are required, lift plants and propagate by division.

BRUCKENTHALIA
B. spiculifolia (spike heath)

Spike heath is an evergreen shrub with branches densely covered with tiny needle-like leaves. Tucked among rocks, it spreads to create a low-growing carpet, rarely exceeding 23 cm (9 in.) in height. During summer, spike heath is covered with fragrant, pink, bell-shaped flowers, only 3 mm ($\frac{1}{8}$ in.) in length, blooming along flower spikes 15 cm (6 in.) high. As the plant spreads, its roots penetrate deeply into the ground, and it thrives in stony soil where moisture and nutrients lie well below the surface.

HOW TO GROW. Spike heath is hardy in Britain. It grows best in full sun in a well-drained, gritty or sandy soil with an acid pH between 4.5 and 6.5. Set out plants in spring, placing them where their roots will stay cool during summer, beside a rock or large stone. Work sandy peat into the planting hole to assure a vigorous root system, and water young plants regularly until well rooted. Once established, their deep roots make them drought resistant.

In areas where winter cold is severe, protect spike heath with a cover of pine branches. To encourage thicker foliage, snip off faded flower stalks. Propagate by rooting stem cuttings taken in spring or by detaching and replanting rooted layers in spring or autumn.

C

CALLIRHOË
C. involucrata (wine-cup)

A low-growing perennial suitable for dry soils, wine-cup brightens a rock garden with a continuous display of deep red, saucer-shaped flowers right through the summer. Its sprawling stems, up to 60 cm (2 ft) long, are covered with deeply cut, hairy leaves, and are especially attractive carpeting a rocky slope or trailing over the face of a stone wall. It grows only 15 cm (6 in.) tall, but has a very long taproot and care must be taken to provide soil sufficiently deep to accommodate it. The flowers are 5 cm (2 in.) wide and are borne on 30 cm (1 ft) tall stems that rise from the leaf axils. The plant dies back to the crown each winter.

HOW TO GROW. The wine-cup is hardy in dry sunny areas of northern Europe. It requires a sandy, nearly neutral soil, pH 6.0 to 7.5. Good drainage is essential since the roots may rot in soggy soil. Set out plants in spring, spacing them 45 cm (1½ ft) apart. Propagate by sowing seeds directly in their permanent site in spring, when the danger of frost has passed, or by rooting stem cuttings taken in early summer. Except as a seedling, this plant is difficult to transplant because of its deep taproot.

CALLUNA
C. vulgaris (heather or ling)

Heather conjures up images of Scottish moors and is a rewarding plant for rock gardens with similar settings of bare slopes and open ground. This evergreen shrub forms neat mounds of upright stems sheathed in minute, clasping leaves 3 mm (⅛ in.) long. Some cultivars are only 10 cm (4 in.) tall; others rise to a height of 90 cm (3 ft). Through summer and autumn, 15 to 25 cm (6 to 10 in.) flower spikes of red, pink or white cover the plants.

Although there is only one species, numerous different cultivars have been developed. Among them are 'Alba', white; 'Alba Plena', double white; 'Aurea', with purple flowers and golden foliage; and 'Foxii Nana', a dwarf cultivar with purple flowers which grows only 10 cm (4 in.) high. Two popular pink-flowered cultivars are 'H. E. Beale', which reaches a height of 60 cm (3 ft) and 'J. H. Hamilton', a double-flowered form 23 cm (9 in.) tall. 'Joan Sparkes' has double purple flowers on plants that grow 23 cm (9 in.) tall.

HOW TO GROW. Callunas are fully hardy in northern and temperate Europe, less successful in hot Mediterranean climates. They do best in full sun in a well-drained soil, moist but never soggy, with an acid pH of 4.5 to 6.0. A soil rich in moss peat but not in nutrients is recommended; heathers grow best in rather poor soil, often becoming leggy in fertile soils. Set out plants in early spring, spacing them 30 to 60 cm (1 to 2 ft) apart, depending on their ultimate size. Water newly planted heathers during dry periods for the first year; once established, they are fairly drought resistant. Prune the plants every spring to strengthen them and force new growth. Apply a mixture of equal parts of sand and moss peat round them each year to encourage and renew root growth, but do not cultivate round the plants as their roots are very shallow. Where winters are very cold, protect plants with a winter mulch of evergreen branches. Propagate heathers by detaching and replanting rooted layers in spring or by taking stem cuttings in late autumn.

WINE-CUP
Callirhoë involucrata

HEATHER
Calluna vulgaris

CARPATHIAN BELL FLOWER
Campanula carpatica

SNOW-IN-SUMMER
Cerastium tomentosum

CAMPANULA

C. carpatica (Carpathian bell flower); *C. cochleariifolia*, also called *C. pusilla*; *C. garganica*; *C. rotundifolia* (harebell, bluebell of Scotland); *C. zoysii*

The huge family of campanulas includes many low-growing perennials suitable for planting in rock gardens and in the crevices of stone walls and paving. Although some are difficult to grow, most are prized for their easy culture and profusion of richly coloured, usually blue flowers, which begin to bloom in early summer and continue until autumn.

C. carpatica produces neat clumps of oval leaves 10 to 15 cm (4 to 6 in.) high. Cup-shaped flowers, 4 to 5 cm (1½ to 2 in.) across, are borne singly on wiry stems 15 to 20 cm (6 to 8 in.) high. Among the most favoured cultivars are 'Turbinata', which is extremely dwarf, carries only one upturned bell on each stem and has grey, hairy leaves; 'Isobel', violet-blue, 23 cm (9 in.) high; 'White Star', 30 cm (1 ft) tall and clear white; and 'Ditton Blue', 15 cm (6 in.) tall with indigo-blue flowers.

C. cochleariifolia is a creeping species that spreads from underground runners to form tufted mats 30 cm (1 ft) wide and 10 to 15 cm (4 to 6 in.) high. It has shiny oval leaves, 2.5 cm (1 in.) long, and is often grown in the alpine garden as ground cover. Dainty, bright blue, bell-shaped flowers, 1 cm (½ in.) long, dangle above the foliage on 7.5 cm (3 in.) stems; there is also a pure white cultivar, 'Alba'. *C. garganica* is 12.5 to 15 cm (5 to 6 in.) high, and spreads to 30 cm (1 ft). It bears blue, star-shaped flowers in large panicles throughout the summer.

Harebell produces clumps 15 to 30 cm (6 to 12 in.) high and spreads 23 to 45 cm (9 to 18 in.). It has heart-shaped lower leaves, 2.5 cm (1 in.) long, and slender upper leaves, 7.5 cm (3 in.) long. Loose clusters of drooping, 2.5 cm (1 in.) long, bright blue flowers rise above the foliage on 30 cm (1 ft) wiry stems. This widespread campanula comes in several shades of blue, as well as a white cultivar, 'Alba'.

Another notable species is *C. zoysii*, 7.5 cm (3 in.) high with round basal leaves and narrow stem leaves. It has most unusual blue flowers, about 1 cm (½ in.) long, bell shaped, but pinched in at the mouth. *C. zoysii* is only hardy in favoured situations.

HOW TO GROW. All these campanulas are hardy in Britain and similar climates, except for *C. zoysii*, which must be neither wet nor cold in winter, and is better grown in a cool greenhouse. All do best in full sun but will tolerate partial shade. As a group, campanulas thrive in moist, well-drained but fairly rich sandy or gritty soil. *C. cochleariifolia* benefits from a soil with a pH of 6.0 to 7.0; the others will grow in a more acid soil, pH 5.0 to 7.0. Set out plants in spring, spacing them 30 to 45 cm (1 to 1½ ft) apart, and water well during the growing season.

Campanulas may be propagated from seed sown in late spring for flowers the following year or from stem cuttings of new growth taken in summer. But additional plants are customarily started by dividing clumps in early spring, since the plants often benefit from division every three or four years to prevent them from becoming overcrowded.

CAMPANULA SERPYLLIFOLIA See *Edraianthus*

CERASTIUM

C. tomentosum (snow-in-summer)

Although snow-in-summer is a strong grower and can become rampant, encroaching on other plants, it is an ideal plant for certain situations where quick-spreading cover can be useful, such as steep banks or large rock gardens. It forms a dense mat of silvery, narrowly oblong, rather woolly leaves, spangled in summer with myriads of white, cup-shaped flowers, each nearly 2.5 cm (1 in.) across and with several to a stem. The overall height of snow-in-summer is 10 to 15 cm (4 to 6 in.), but it spreads rapidly to 60 cm (2 ft) or more.

HOW TO GROW. Snow-in-summer is hardy in Britain. Plant in any well-drained and gritty soil, preferably in full sun. Feeding is not necessary. Propagate by dividing clumps in spring and immediately replanting the sections about 60 cm (2 ft) apart.

CERATOSTIGMA

C. plumbaginoides, also called *Plumbago larpentae* (leadwort)

With its deep blue flowers and glossy green leaves, leadwort is unexcelled as ground cover for rock gardens. But it is equally attractive as an accent plant, grown between stones over which its branching stems can trail. It reaches a height of 23 to 30 cm (9 to 12 in.), its wiry stems forming tufted mounds as much as 38 cm (15 in.) in diameter. The flowers are about 2.5 cm (1 in.) across and appear singly or in clusters at the ends of the many branches; they bloom from late summer until frost, when few other plants provide colour. Leadwort's ornamental value is also extended in autumn by its oval 9 cm (3½ in.) leaves, which turn reddish-bronze.

HOW TO GROW. Leadwort is hardy in Britain and sheltered areas of northern Europe, as well as in southern regions. It will survive in shade but flowers more freely in a sunny, open position. A sandy, well-drained soil is essential, preferably one to which moss peat or leaf-mould has been added; dormant plants cannot tolerate soggy soil. Set out plants in early spring, spacing them 45 to 60 cm (1½ to 2 ft) apart. Propagate by dividing plants in spring, just as growth is beginning, or from stem cuttings taken in summer.

CHAMAECYPARIS

C. lawsoniana 'Minima Aurea' (false cypress); *C. obtusa* 'Nana'; *C. obtusa* 'Nana Gracilis'; *C. obtusa* 'Pygmaea' (all called Hinoki false cypress); *C. pisifera* 'Compacta'; *C. pisifera* 'Plumosa Compacta' (both called Sawara false cypress)

Of more than 40 cultivars of the false cypresses, the following are recommended for rock and sink gardens, being slow-growing, easily cultivated and readily available. Since these plants are often listed under different names in catalogues, it may be better to select specimens by their appearance rather than by their labels. Like all false cypresses, they are distinguished by flattened fan-shaped leaf sprays, with leaves that are either overlapping and scale-like or thin and needle-like. Cones are seldom more than 1 cm (½ in.) across, and plants may be conical, rounded or spreading, with foliage of varying colours.

C. lawsoniana 'Minima Aurea' is a dwarf and very slow-growing cultivar, reaching only 30 cm (1 ft) in height after 10 years. Its bright golden foliage lends colour to the rock garden all year round.

C. obtusa 'Nana' is an extremely slow-growing, flat-topped plant; it may reach no more than 15 cm (6 in.) in height and 20 cm (8 in.) in width in 10 years. The foliage of this cultivar is a dark, dull green, forming dense, upward-curving horizontal layers; the shrub is rounded to slightly conical in shape.

C. obtusa 'Nana Gracilis' is an exceptionally sturdy plant with shiny, bright green leaves and an upright

LEADWORT
Ceratostigma plumbaginoides

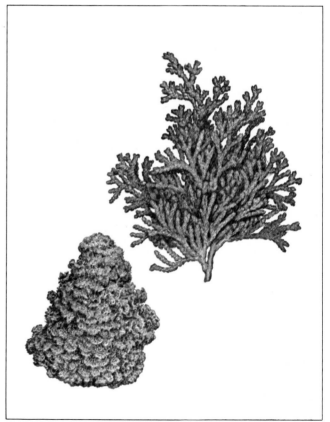

HINOKI FALSE CYPRESS
Chamaecyparis obtusa 'Nana Gracilis'

Chrysogonum virginianum

pyramidal shape. It may reach a height of 60 cm (2 ft) and a spread of 45 cm (1½ ft) in 10 years.

C. obtusa 'Pygmaea' is a flattened, spreading specimen with large, closely spaced horizontal leaf fans. Green in summer, the plant often turns bronze in autumn and winter. After 10 years, it may be 23 cm (9 in.) tall with a spread of 45 cm (1½ ft).

C. pisifera 'Compacta' forms a dense, rounded bush with closely packed leaf sprays that curve downwards. The foliage is blue-green or grey-green in summer, turning brownish-green in winter. It grows very slowly, reaching a height of only 60 cm (2 ft) and a spread of 90 cm (3 ft) in about 20 years.

C. pisifera 'Plumosa Compacta' forms a neat, close bush of bright blue-green, mossy leaf sprays; in 10 years it may reach a height and spread of 30 cm (1 ft).

HOW TO GROW. False cypresses are hardy in cool and temperate regions of Europe. They tolerate shade but do best in sun, protected from drying winds. A moist, well-drained acid soil, pH 5.5 to 6.5, is ideal. Plant in spring or autumn. Keep plants evenly moist until they are well established—about two years. Mulch dwarf plants in winter and, if winds are severe, build shelters round them. False cypresses are damaged by air pollution. Propagate additional plants from stem cuttings which should be taken in autumn.

CHRYSOGONUM
C. virginianum

C. virginianum is an herbaceous, mat-forming plant which grows wild in the woodlands of North America. Five-petalled, yellow, daisy-like flowers, 4 cm (1½ in.) across, bloom in early summer on 12.5 to 15 cm (5 to 6 in.) stems. Its coarse, hairy leaves, 2.5 to 7.5 cm (1 to 3 in.) long, are toothed and oval-shaped.

HOW TO GROW. In northern Europe, this plant needs a protected position with light shade and watering during dry periods. It thrives in a soil rich in leaf-mould but tolerates and will flower well in any well-drained soil with a pH of 6.0 to 7.5. Set out new plants in spring, spacing them 45 cm (1½ ft) apart. Propagate *Chrysogonum* species by dividing the clumps in spring.

CLEMATIS
C. alpina also called *Atragene alpina* (alpine clematis)

This weak-stemmed but handsome climbing plant can either be trained up supports to a height of 1.8 metres (6 ft), or it can be allowed to sprawl over rocks or banks, or to clamber over and hide an old bush or tree stump. Its large, four-sepalled, powder-blue or violet flowers, each 2.5 to 4 cm (1 to 1½ in.) wide, appear in late spring and early summer. They are borne singly on short stems among the compound leaves which are divided into nine coarsely serrated, oblong leaflets.

HOW TO GROW. Like other better-known clematis, this plant requires "cool feet and a hot head", and although it can be sited in an open position, make sure that its roots are shaded by planting it near a rock, for example. The plant likes a limy soil, although this is not essential. Top-dress the soil in spring with a little rotted garden compost or leaf-mould. Set out plants in spring.

Propagate from stem cuttings, 10 to 12.5 cm (4 to 5 in.) long, taken in midsummer. Each cutting should have two buds at its base and be rooted in equal parts of sand and peat in a frame with bottom heat. Alternatively, the stems can be layered into pots of sandy soil in spring. They take about a year to root.

ALPINE CLEMATIS
Clematis alpina

CORYDALIS
C. cashmeriana; *C. lutea*; *C. solida*, also called *C. bulbosa*

Valued for their feathery foliage and curiously shaped flowers, similar to those of *Dicentra*, the perennial forms of corydalis are often found growing naturally in old rock walls and are suitable for both sunny and shaded areas.

C. cashmeriana is the beauty of the genus with clusters of brilliant blue flowers borne on 15 cm (6 in.) stems in spring and early summer. Its blue-green dissected foliage may form clumps up to 23 cm (9 in.) across.

C. lutea has fibrous roots and numerous stems and produces a mound of grey-green foliage 30 to 45 cm (1 to 1½ ft) high. Its 18 mm (¾ in.) yellow flowers bloom in loose clusters all summer long, beginning in late spring. The plant seeds itself and may become invasive if dead flowers or seedlings are not removed.

C. solida grows from a fleshy tuber and blooms in early spring, producing flower spikes of 10 to 20 rose, purple or white flowers, 18 mm (¾ in.) long, on 20 cm (8 in.) stems. The blue-green foliage forms a compact rosette at the base of the plant, 20 to 25 cm (8 to 10 in.) across.

HOW TO GROW. *C. lutea* and *C. solida* are hardy in temperate northern Europe. They grow best in a moist, well-drained sandy or gritty soil with a pH of 6.0 to 8.0. *C. cashmeriana* is more difficult, needing a cool, leafy, lime-free soil. It does well in the north of England but often fails in the south. Set out new plants in spring, spacing them 20 to 25 cm (8 to 10 in.) apart. To keep the roots of *C. cashmeriana* cool during summer, plant where the roots will grow beneath or beside a rock or large stones. All can be propagated from seed, or by division of clumps in spring.

Corydalis lutea

CROCUS
C. chrysanthus; *C. speciosus*; *C. tomasinianus*

All crocuses are suitable rock-garden plants and many naturalize readily if the corms are left undisturbed. Those included here are particularly adaptable. All of them are small plants whose leaves and flowers rise directly from a swollen underground stem, the corm. Because their foliage dies back when the plants become dormant, they are frequently planted among such dwarf alpine plants as saxifrages, whose dense foliage hides the withering leaves of the crocuses.

C. chrysanthus blooms in early spring, its narrow, grey-green leaves appearing at the same time as the golden-yellow flowers. The leaves are about 25 cm (10 in.) long with prominent mid-ribs; the flowers are cup-shaped and 7.5 cm (3 in.) tall. It is the parent of numerous cultivars and hybrids with other species. In some cultivars, the flowers are deep orange, almost brown; in others, the colours range from pale to purple-blue, and there are also cultivars that are speckled and veined with brown and reddish-purple.

C. speciosus flowers in autumn, with large goblet-shaped flowers that are bright blue and 10 cm (4 in.) or more high. In some cultivars, the flowers are pure white and streaked with contrasting lines. Leaves are produced after flowering.

C. tomasinianus blooms in early spring, its leaves appearing after the flowers have opened. Its blooms are pale mauve on the outside, lilac within, and when fully open are star-shaped and 7.5 cm (3 in.) wide. The narrow leaves are dark green with white mid-ribs. Some cultivars of this species are reddish-purple, and there is also a pure white form.

In addition to these species are numerous large-flowered Dutch cultivars, spanning the full colour range.

HOW TO GROW. These crocuses are hardy in northern and temperate Europe, and they need cold winters to complete

Crocus tomasinianus

DWARF JAPANESE CEDAR
Cryptomeria japonica 'Globosa Nana'

KEW BROOM
Cytisus x *kewensis*

their growth cycle. They do best in full sun but will tolerate partial shade and thrive in a light, well-drained sandy soil enriched with leaf-mould or garden compost. Plant corms in early autumn in groups of five or more, setting them 5 to 10 cm (2 to 4 in.) deep and 5 to 15 cm (2 to 6 in.) apart. Crocuses may be lifted and separated every three or four years if desired. *C. tomasinianus* seeds itself readily. All species and cultivars may be propagated by separating and replanting offsets of the corms after the foliage begins to turn yellow.

CRYPTOMERIA
C. japonica 'Globosa Nana'; *C. japonica* 'Lobbii Nana'; *C. japonica* 'Vilmoriniana'. (All called dwarf Japanese cedar)

The dwarf Japanese cedars are slow-growing, coniferous shrubs, useful in the rock garden as specimen plants or for providing a framework against which to display small plants. Their distinguishing characteristics include thin, curving needles, 6 mm ($\frac{1}{4}$ in.) long, clasped in spirals along the stems, and peeling, reddish-brown bark.

C. japonica 'Globosa Nana' is cone-shaped when young, but as it matures its silhouette becomes more rounded. Growing at the rate of less than 5 cm (2 in.) a year, it will reach a height of 45 cm ($1\frac{1}{2}$ ft) in 15 years and ultimately becomes 0.9 to 1.8 metres (3 to 6 ft) high with a spread of 0.6 to 1.5 metres (2 to 5 ft). The drooping, spreading branches are covered with yellow-green needles that become slightly blue in winter.

C. japonica 'Lobbii Nana' forms a small cone-shaped bush, reaching a height of 60 cm (2 ft) in 10 years. It has short, compact branches with tight knots of foliage that form along the stems. The needles of this cultivar, straighter than those on other dwarf Japanese cedars, are light green in summer and bronze in winter.

C. japonica 'Vilmoriniana' reaches 30 cm (1 ft) in height and 38 cm ($1\frac{1}{4}$ ft) across in 10 years. It forms a compact mound with a slightly irregular appearance from the clumpy nature of the new growth. The closely packed leaves are light green in summer, turning reddish-purple to bronze in winter.

HOW TO GROW. Dwarf Japanese cedars are hardy in temperate regions; the foliage may turn brownish in winter and should be shielded from winter sun. A deep, sandy soil with a pH of 5.5 to 6.5 is recommended, and the soil should be kept evenly and constantly moist, especially when the plants are young. Plant in spring or autumn, preferably from container-grown plants. Mulch winter and summer with a 5 cm (2 in.) layer of organic material such as garden compost or leaf-mould. Pruning is seldom needed. Dwarf Japanese cedars can only be transplanted successfully when young; they do not grow well in a polluted atmosphere.

CYTISUS
C. decumbens (prostrate broom); *C.* x *kewensis* (Kew broom)

Dwarf brooms are interesting shrubs that flourish in poor, dry soils where few other plants will grow. In the rock garden, they are used to best advantage above a large rock face over which their trailing branches can sprawl. They flower profusely in spring or summer, depending on the species. Though the flowers are small, the effect is spectacular, for they bloom singly or in clusters all along the branches, and each tiny flower resembles a yellow sweet pea. The slender leaves are decorative as well, giving the plant a fine-textured appearance. Even after the leaves fall, the thicket of green twigs on the plants provides colour throughout the winter.

C. decumbens produces a thick mat of foliage, 20 cm (8 in.) high. Its grey-green leaflets are 18 mm ($\frac{3}{4}$ in.) long and its flowers, which bloom in summer, are bright yellow.

C. x kewensis has creamy-white or soft yellow flowers in spring, and soft, hairy, grey-green leaflets, 18 mm ($\frac{3}{4}$ in.) long. The plant is only 30 cm (1 ft) high but may cover an area 1.8 metres (6 ft) in diameter.

HOW TO GROW. Both brooms are hardy in Europe and grow best in full sun in dry, open sites. Since these plants require perfect drainage, a soil with a high content of sand or gravel is recommended. The soil pH is of no consequence. Set out plants from pots to avoid breaking the soil ball, as brooms resent root damage. It is necessary for newly planted shrubs to be watered during dry periods in the first year, though once established they are drought-resistant. Immediately after flowers have faded, prune plants to prevent them from becoming leggy or straggly but never cut into the old wood or the plants will die. Propagate additional plants from stem cuttings taken in summer or autumn.

D

DAPHNE
D. arbuscula; *D. blagayana*; *D. cneorum* (garland flower); *D. petraea*, also called *D. rupestris*; *D. retusa*. (All also called daphne)

Daphnes grow wild on rocky hillsides, making them a natural choice for alpine gardens. Many are small trees but those described here are shrubs; some of them are useful as creeping ground covers. These daphnes are not care-free plants, having rather exacting cultural requirements, but they reward gardeners with masses of sweetly scented spring flowers and handsome evergreen foliage. Keep in mind that all parts of the plants are poisonous if eaten.

The diminutive *D. arbuscula*, a creeping species, reaches only 15 cm (6 in.) in height with a spread of 60 cm (2 ft); its glossy dark green leaves are 18 to 25 mm ($\frac{3}{4}$ to 1 in.) long, and its tiny, rose-pink flowers bloom in clusters 2.5 to 4 cm (1 to 1$\frac{1}{2}$ in.) across. *D. blagayana* comes from the limestone areas of south-eastern Europe and spreads its bare woody stems to a distance of 90 cm (3 ft). At the branch tips are small oval, evergreen leaves and crowded heads of very fragrant, tubular, creamy-white flowers. *D. cneorum*, one of the most popular of all the daphnes, produces mounds of trailing branches up to 30 cm (1 ft) high and 60 cm (2 ft) across. The branches are densely clothed with narrow, grey-green leaves, 2.5 cm (1 in.) long, and an abundance of extremely fragrant pink flowers borne in 2.5 cm (1 in.) clusters at the branch tips. The cultivar 'Eximia' produces larger flowers in deeper shades of pink; another, 'Alba', has white flowers.

D. petraea is considered by many gardeners to be the most beautiful of alpine shrubs. It is slow growing, about 10 cm (4 in.) high and 20 cm (8 in.) across, with pink, fragrant flowers and small, dark green, shiny leaves. It is often sold grafted on to the taller *D. mezereum*. *D. retusa* is a compact alpine shrub, growing 90 cm (3 ft) high, with a spread of 45 to 90 cm (1$\frac{1}{2}$ to 3 ft). Its pink flowers, purple inside, bloom in dense, 5 to 7.5 cm (2 to 3 in.) clusters and are followed by red oval berries. The leaves are shiny above, dull beneath, and are 2.5 to 7.5 cm (1 to 3 in.) long.

HOW TO GROW. All these daphnes are hardy in Britain and temperate areas of Europe. Most do best in full sun but will tolerate partial shade and need a sandy, well-drained soil, rich in leaf-mould, with a pH of 5.5 to 7.5. *D. petraea*, however, favours a limy, peaty soil, which must

GARLAND FLOWER
Daphne cneorum

ALPINE PINK
Dianthus alpinus

FRINGED BLEEDING HEART
Dicentra eximia

never dry out. Set out plants in spring, spacing them 45 cm (1½ ft) apart. Choose a sheltered position, protected from winter winds and beside rocks where their roots will stay cool and moist throughout summer. Prune plants lightly after flowering to keep them neat and compact. Mulch in late autumn for winter protection, especially in northern areas. Mulch again in spring with a mixture of leaf-mould and sand, to renew the plants' vigour, but do not disturb their roots. Daphnes have few roots, and may easily be harmed if moved. For this reason, mature plants should not be transplanted.

Propagate *Daphne* species by means of layers pinned down into good leafy soil.

DIANTHUS
D. alpinus (alpine pink)

There are countless dianthus suitable for rock-garden pockets, drystone walls and sink gardens. Most of the species are variable, as is this dwarf species from the Austrian Alps. The colour of the flowers varies from pale pink to purple, usually with white eyes and purple spots; there is also a white form, 'Albus'. The neat, narrow, silvery-grey leaves form compact cushions, about 10 cm (4 in.) high, which are attractive at all seasons. The flowering period extends from late spring until late summer.

HOW TO GROW. Alpine pinks like an alkaline, well-drained soil, although lime is not an essential. They do, however, need sun, but are tolerant of industrial pollution and even salt sprays. Plant them in spring, 15 cm (6 in.) apart, and renew frequently from cuttings taken in summer or from seeds sown in late spring or early summer.

DICENTRA, also called DIELYTRA
D. canadensis (squirrel corn); *D. cucullaria* (Dutchman's-breeches); *D. eximia* (fringed bleeding heart); *D. formosa*

Dicentras belong to the poppy family, but are quite distinctive with their pendulous, locket-shaped flowers and feathery foliage.

Squirrel corn grows from tiny yellow tubers that look like grains of corn. Clusters of green-tinged, white flowers 1 cm (½ in.) long, bloom in spring on 15 to 25 cm (6 to 10 in.) mounds of grey-green leaves. After flowering, the plants become dormant and lose their leaves. Therefore, they should be planted among companions that retain their foliage throughout the summer.

Dutchman's-breeches is similar to squirrel corn in foliage, size and habit of growth. The flowers, however, are different. They are white with yellow tips and resemble tiny riding jodhpurs hanging upside down. Like squirrel corn, Dutchman's-breeches grows from tubers and becomes dormant after flowering.

Fringed bleeding heart is a sturdier plant, up to 30 cm (1 ft) tall, blooming in May, in sun or partial shade. It bears its pink-purple flowers, 12 to 18 mm (½ to ¾ in.) long, in drooping clusters above grey-green foliage. This species is occasionally found with pure white flowers. *D. formosa* reaches a height of 30 to 45 cm (1 to 1½ ft) and bears rose-pink flowers, 1 cm (½ in.) long, from late spring onwards. These two species both grow from plump underground stems known as rhizomes.

HOW TO GROW. Dicentras are hardy in temperate Europe and all are woodland plants, growing best in partial shade such as that found beneath high-branching trees or tall shrubs. However, they will tolerate full sun if the soil is kept evenly and consistently moist. They are not suitable for the hotter regions of France and the Mediterranean area. Ideally, the soil should be well drained, with a pH of 5.5 to 7.5, and should be rich in leaf-mould. Set out plants in the spring, spacing them 30 cm (1 ft) apart. Water during dry periods. Propagate by dividing the tubers or rhizomes after the plants have flowered.

DIELYTRA See *Dicentra*

DRABA

D. mollissima; *D. rigida*, also called *D. dicranoides*; *D. sibirica*, also called *D. repens*

Drabas are diminutive plants whose natural habitats are open rocky meadows or rock crevices on high mountains, and several of them merit a place in a scree, moraine or pockets of a rock garden. Most of them are characterized by neat rosettes of tiny leaves that grow in tufts along ground-hugging stems, by massed flowers that bloom in dome-shaped, yellow or white clusters in spring, and by deep taproots. They are members of the mustard family and are frequently found in alpine collections. They do, however, need a place of their own, isolated from other plants, because they can easily be crowded out by plants that are larger and more vigorous. A few are annuals, but the three described are perennials.

D. mollissima grows 2.5 to 5 cm (1 to 2 in.) high and spreads 15 cm (6 in.) or more. In late spring, it bears bright yellow, cross-shaped flowers, each 8 to 12 mm ($\frac{1}{3}$ to $\frac{1}{2}$ in.) wide, with up to 18 blooms on a spike. *D. rigida* forms a moss-like mound 7.5 to 15 cm (3 to 6 in.) across. Its 6 mm ($\frac{1}{4}$ in.) leaves are shiny and stiff, giving the plant a bristly appearance. The flowers are deep golden-yellow and appear in small clusters of five to 20 blooms; the wiry stalks are 2.5 to 7.5 cm (1 to 3 in.) tall.

D. sibirica is the easiest to grow. It bears loosely spaced rosettes of hairy leaves, 2.5 to 7.5 cm (1 to 3 in.) high, along slender, trailing stems up to 30 cm (1 ft) long. Its bright yellow spring flowers bloom in drooping clusters of eight to 20 flowers on stalks 15 cm (6 in.) tall. It sometimes blooms a second time in the autumn.

HOW TO GROW. All these drabas are hardy and do best in full sun. They thrive in a well-drained gritty soil, pH 6.0 to 7.5. Set plants out in spring, choosing a position deep enough to accommodate their long taproots; space plants 15 cm (6 in.) apart. To encourage new growth, add a top layer of gritty soil annually. Propagate from seed sown in spring.

DRYAS

D. octopetala (mountain avens); *D. x suendermannii*

These members of the rose family are dwarf evergreen shrubs that usually grow wild in the mountains above the tree line. In a rock garden, they adapt to any sunny situation and are especially useful where a year-round mat of green is desired. Their shiny dark green leaves, which look like miniature oak leaves, grow densely along prostrate trailing stems that spread rapidly to cover rock contours. In spring, they produce an abundance of white saucer-shaped flowers similar in appearance to wild roses, followed by decorative seed heads that are covered with silvery silken hairs.

The mountain avens is the more familiar species. Its crinkled, scalloped leaves, green above and silvery beneath, are 2 to 2.5 cm ($\frac{3}{4}$ to 1 in.) long, and its white flowers with yellow centres, 4 cm ($1\frac{1}{2}$ in.) wide, rise above the foliage on 5 to 10 cm (2 to 4 in.) stalks. The cultivar 'Minor' is even more compact, with leaves and flowers half the size of the species plant. *D. x suendermannii*, a

Draba mollissima

MOUNTAIN AVENS
Dryas octopetala

107

Edraianthus pumilio

BISHOP'S HAT
Epimedium grandiflorum

hybrid, is almost identical to the mountain avens except that the flower buds are yellow until they open white and that the flowers nod on their stems.

HOW TO GROW. Both plants are hardy in northern Europe. They normally grow best in full sun, though strong direct sun in winter may burn the foliage. They will also grow in partial shade. They need a light, well-drained soil, with a pH of 6.0 to 7.5, preferably one with a high content of leaf-mould. Water during dry periods. Propagate from ripe stem cuttings taken in summer, or by separating small plants that grow where stems touch the ground and put down roots.

E

EDRAIANTHUS
E. pumilio; *E. serpyllifolius*, also called *Campanula serpyllifolia*; *E. tenuifolius*

Edraianthus species are members of the *Campanula* family and are closely related to *Wahlenbergia*, with which they are frequently confused. They are low-growing, deep-rooted perennials, well suited to dry rock gardens and stone walls. They have open, blue, bell-shaped flowers and form tufted clumps, 15 to 30 cm (6 to 12 in.) across, with long, trailing stems that curl up at the tips to lift the flowers above the foliage. They bloom in late spring and early summer.

E. pumilio has slightly hairy, silvery leaves that grow in a clump 5 to 7.5 cm (2 to 3 in.) high. The deep purple flowers are 2.5 cm (1 in.) wide. *E. serpyllifolius* has smooth green, lance-shaped leaves, 2.5 cm (1 in.) long, that form a mat up to 15 cm (6 in.) high. The flowers bloom round the edges of the mat and are violet-blue with white centres; they are usually about 5 cm (2 in.) across; the cultivar 'Major', however, has larger flowers.

E. tenuifolius produces a mat 10 to 15 cm (4 to 6 in.) high. Its leaves are narrow, up to 10 cm (4 in.) long, with bristly edges, and its small, violet-blue flowers, each 2.5 cm (1 in.) long, bloom in dense clusters of six to 10 flowers each.

HOW TO GROW. The plants are hardy, but sometimes short lived, and grow best in full sun in a deep, well-drained, gritty soil, pH 6.0 to 7.5. Set plants out in the spring, spacing them 15 cm (6 in.) apart. Choose a site where moisture will not collect round their roots; these plants do not tolerate consistently wet soil during the winter months. Water during dry periods throughout the growing season. Propagate from seed or cuttings of non-flowering shoots.

EPIMEDIUM
E. grandiflorum, also called *E. macranthum* (bishop's hat, barrenwort)

Epimediums are excellent plants for shady rock gardens, providing colourful foliage almost all year round and in late spring and early summer, delightful flowers. They spread from underground runners and are therefore used as ground cover, but they may also be tucked into crevices between rocks or between the stones of a drystone wall.

There are species and cultivars with plain green leaves as well as variegated and with yellow, white, pink, red or violet flowers. Perhaps the sturdiest is *E. grandiflorum*, which grows 23 to 45 cm (9 to 18 in.) high and has compound leaves made up of two or three light green, heart-shaped leaflets. In the spring, when the new leaves emerge, each leaf is rimmed with a narrow margin of red; in autumn, the entire leaf turns reddish-bronze. Where winter temperatures are not extreme, this colourful foliage remains on the plant all winter. The flowers appear in loose clusters on wiry stems; they are unusual in form, having four outer sepals topped by four petal-shaped inner sepals and finally by four true petals that end in spurs 2.5 cm (1 in.) long. In this species, each of these flower parts is a different colour—the outer sepals are reddish, the inner ones purplish, the petals white. But in named cultivars, the coloration is different: on 'Rose Queen', a popular cultivar, the entire flower is crimson with white-tipped spurs; 'Album' is pure white; 'Violaceum' has lavender flowers.

HOW TO GROW. Bishop's hat is hardy in Britain and temperate northern Europe and grows best in shade, thriving under the protective covering of tall shrubs or high-branched trees. However, if the soil is kept moist throughout the growing season, this plant will tolerate full sun. Ideally, it should have a sandy, well-drained woodland soil, rich in moss peat or leaf-mould, but it will also grow in soil with a high clay content. Propagate by dividing and replanting clumps in early summer.

ERICA
E. carnea, also called *E. herbacea*; *E. tetralix* (cross-leaved heath); *E. vagans* (Cornish heath). (All also called heath)

With careful selection, a rock garden can have heaths in bloom almost all year round. These compact woody perennials have needle-like, evergreen foliage, long-lasting flowers and masses of fibrous roots that are effective in preventing soil erosion. They spread slowly and are tolerant of both wind and salt spray. In the rock garden, they are useful either as specimen plants or in massed displays, their bell-shaped blooms of white, red, pink or purple rising in tight clusters on thin, wiry stems.

E. carnea has 6 mm ($\frac{1}{4}$ in.) leaves that may be green, bronze or yellow, depending on the cultivar. The creeping stems fill an area 60 to 90 cm (2 to 3 ft) across, forming a carpet 30 cm (1 ft) high. The 6 mm ($\frac{1}{4}$ in.) flowers often cluster on one side of the stems. In Britain and temperate Europe, flowers open in winter as well as at other seasons. Among cultivars of special interest are 'Aurea', with golden-yellow leaves and pink flowers; 'Eileen Porter', a long-flowering carmine cultivar; and 'King George', with rose to crimson flowers that bloom very early. Dwarf cultivars that grow less than 20 cm (8 in.) tall include 'Vivellii', with vivid red flowers and leaves that turn reddish-green in winter; 'Springwood White', with white flowers; and 'Springwood Pink', clear pink.

E. tetralix has fuzzy grey-green leaves only 3 mm ($\frac{1}{8}$ in.) long and grows up to 30 cm (1 ft) tall with a spread of up to 60 cm (2 ft). The 2.5 to 5 cm (1 to 2 in.) long clusters of 6 mm ($\frac{1}{4}$ in.) pink flowers are borne throughout summer.

E. vagans forms rounded masses 45 to 60 cm (1$\frac{1}{2}$ to 2 ft) tall and equally wide. It has 9 mm ($\frac{3}{8}$ in.) bright green leaves, and sprays, 12.5 to 23 cm (5 to 9 in.) long, of tiny flowers that bloom from summer until autumn. Cultivars of this species have white, rose pink or cerise flowers.

HOW TO GROW. Heaths are hardy in northern and temperate Europe. For abundant flowers, they require full sun, but heaths will tolerate partial shade. They do best in a moist, well-drained, sandy soil enriched with plenty of moss peat or leaf-mould. An acid pH of 4.5 to 5.5 is recommended, although cultivars of *E. carnea* tolerate alkaline soil conditions. Plant in spring or autumn, without breaking the soil ball. Mass plants in groups, spacing them 45 cm (1$\frac{1}{2}$ ft) apart. Keep the soil evenly moist while the plants are young, and mulch with peat in spring. Propagate from stem cuttings taken in summer or autumn and kept over the winter in a cold frame. Or start new plants by layering prostrate stems in spring.

CROSS-LEAVED HEATH
Erica tetralix

FLEABANE
Erigeron compositus

FAWN LILY
Erythronium americanum

ERIGERON

E. aureus; *E. compositus*; *E. uniflorus*. (All called fleabane)

Found growing in the rocky terrain of mountains in North America and Europe, these low-growing fleabanes are choice plants for a sunny rock garden, in a sink garden, alpine house, on a slope, moraine, or tucked into a rock wall. All are perennial, producing daisy-like flowers in spring or summer.

E. aureus is a creeping plant with fibrous roots, sending up 5 to 15 cm (2 to 6 in.) tall tufts of hairy, 7.5 cm (3 in.) leaves to form clumps 23 cm (9 in.) across. The leaves are almost round and spoon shaped, and they often have violet-coloured stems. From spring until midsummer, the mat of green foliage is dotted with 18 mm ($\frac{3}{4}$ in.) wide yellow-orange flowers that are borne individually on 5 cm (2 in.) long stems.

E. compositus forms dense, 7.5 to 15 cm (3 to 6 in.) tall mounds of finely divided, fuzzy, grey-green leaves and spreads into clumps 20 cm (8 in.) across. Growing from a thick taproot, this species bears white, pale blue or pink flowers with yellow centres from early summer until frost; the flowers, up to 18 mm ($\frac{3}{4}$ in.) across, top 7.5 to 15 cm (3 to 6 in.) flower stems.

E. uniflorus grows only 5 to 7.5 cm (2 to 3 in.) high and spreads to form dense clumps 23 cm (9 in.) across. The leaves have woolly surfaces and stems, and the flowers, appearing from spring until frost, are 1 cm ($\frac{1}{2}$ in.) across; they open white but change to lavender-blue with age.

HOW TO GROW. These fleabanes are hardy in sheltered parts of northern Europe, although *E. aureus* is best left in a moraine or alpine house. They generally require a hot, dry, sunny site and well-drained, sandy, gritty or gravelly soil with a pH of 6.0 to 7.5. Plant in spring, spacing them 15 to 23 cm (6 to 9 in.) apart. Propagate from seed sown in the spring.

ERYTHRONIUM

E. americanum (fawn lily, adder's tongue); *E. dens-canis* (dog's-tooth violet); *E. hendersonii*; *E. revolutum*

The nodding flowers of erythroniums may be used to decorate woodland areas in spring and are also excellent naturalized in small clumps in rock gardens. The 2.5 to 7.5 cm (1 to 3 in.) lily-like flowers bloom on slender stems up to 30 cm (1 ft) tall. They have six flaring petals that curve back like cyclamen petals, in colours ranging from white to pink, rose, purple or yellow. At the base of each flower stalk are two strap-shaped leaves, which may be plain green or mottled with grey or maroon. The deciduous foliage dies back to the ground by midsummer.

E. americanum grows up to 25 cm (10 in.) high. Its leaves, up to 15 cm (6 in.) in length, are dappled with grey or brownish-purple markings; its flowers, 4 to 5 cm (1$\frac{1}{2}$ to 2 in.) long, are bright yellow suffused on the outside with reddish-brown.

E. dens-canis has 10 to 15 cm (4 to 6 in.) long leaves mottled with grey or reddish-brown. The slightly fragrant 2.5 to 7.5 cm (1 to 3 in.) flowers are red, rose or purple with red markings at the base of each petal. There are a number of named cultivars, including 'Rose Beauty', which has deep rosy-pink flowers.

E. hendersonii bears 10 to 20 cm (4 to 8 in.) long mottled leaves with wavy edges, and its flowers, 4 cm (1$\frac{1}{2}$ in.) long, are lavender-purple with dark purple centre markings. As many as four flowers may develop on one stalk.

E. revolutum has 20 cm (8 in.) long leaves with similar wavy edges; they are mottled with light brown or white. The flowers, up to 5 cm (2 in.) long, may be white, rose-pink or lavender in colour and are distinguished by darker markings but as they age they become purple. Several flowers are borne on each flower stalk.

HOW TO GROW. Erythroniums should be planted in moist, leafy soil in light shade, for example beneath deciduous shrubs. Ideally, the soil should be enriched with moss peat or leaf-mould and have an acid to neutral pH of 5.0 to 7.0. Set them out in late summer or early autumn 7.5 to 12.5 cm (3 to 5 in.) deep and space them 10 to 15 cm (4 to 6 in.) apart. Feed annually in spring with a light sprinkling of bone-meal. In very cold regions, protect in winter with a mulch of coarse moss peat, chopped leaves, well-rotted manure or leaf-mould.

Erythroniums will last for many years but do not survive transplanting well. Plants can be propagated from seeds sown when ripe. They germinate readily but take a couple of years to reach flowering size.

G

GALIUM See *Asperula*

GENTIANA
G. acaulis; *G. farreri*; *G. septemfida*; *G. sino-ornata*; *G. verna* (spring gentian)

One of the most coveted of rock-garden plants, the gentian comes in hundreds of species and hybrids, most having intensely blue, trumpet-shaped flowers. The blues vary in shade from light to dark and may be turquoise or almost purple. In addition, there are gentians with white, yellow, gold or red flowers. Some bloom in spring, others in summer or autumn, and they range from low creepers to tall, open plants with arching stems. There is also considerable difference in their cultivation: some are easy to grow, others extremely difficult. The species described here are alpine plants, suitable for use on shaded, stony slopes or between the slabs of drystone walls or paving; they can also be grown in a cool alpine greenhouse. All are perennial and form dense clumps.

G. acaulis is a group name covering a number of species such as *G. clusii* and *G. kochiana*. Mostly these have upward-facing, deep blue flowers, 5 to 7.5 cm (2 to 3 in.) long with green or white-marked throats. The shiny leaves are 2.5 cm (1 in.) long and 1 cm (½ in.) wide; the plants spread from underground stems to form thick mats up to 45 cm (1½ ft) across. There are many cultivars, some with white flowers. Sometimes these gentians will not bloom, or bloom once and never again, for an unknown reason.

G. farreri is a superb species, its upturned trumpets a clear luminous blue spotted with greenish-blue and violet, with white throats. Thought by many gardeners to be the finest gentian in cultivation, it grows 15 cm (6 in.) high and flowers in early autumn.

G. septemfida is one of the easiest gentians to grow and, in summer, bears small clusters of 2.5 to 5 cm (1 to 2 in.) long, bell-shaped, blue flowers with white throats. The leafy stems grow 23 to 45 cm (9 to 18 in.) tall and form clumps 30 cm (1 ft) across; the leaves are oval, 2.5 to 4 cm (1 to 1½ in.) long. The variety *lagodechiana* has deep blue flowers on 12.5 to 15 cm (5 to 6 in.) stems and is one of the best low-growing varieties. In autumn, *G. sino-ornata* bears large flowers, more than 5 cm (2 in.) long, that are bright blue striped with deep blue and greenish-yellow.

G. verna is a variable, short-lived species with rich blue flowers that are borne in spring; *G.v.* 'Angulosa' is one of the best cultivars; it grows 7.5 cm (3 in.) high and has intensely blue flowers that are borne in late spring.

HOW TO GROW. Gentians are temperamental plants, and do better in some gardens than others. In the main, they

DOG'S-TOOTH VIOLET
Erythronium dens-canis

Gentiana acaulis

CRANE'S-BILL
Geranium sanguineum

AVENS
Geum reptans

do best where summers are cool and moist. They generally need partial shade, but tolerate full sun in cool summers, provided the soil is kept constantly moist. The ideal soil is a moist, gritty, well-drained loam enriched with moss peat or leaf-mould, with a slightly acid to neutral pH of 5.5 to 7.0. Plant gentians in spring; be sure to firm the roots in the soil. Propagate from seed sown when ripe; those that have thong-like roots, such as *G. sino-ornata*, can be divided when they are dormant.

GERANIUM
G. dalmaticum; *G. renardii*; *G. sanguineum*; *G. sanguineum* var. *prostatum*, also called *G. lancastriense*. (All called crane's-bill)

Not to be confused with the common geranium, *Pelargonium*, crane's-bills belong to a different genus, with hundreds of species, ranging from 10 cm (4 in.) to 75 cm (2½ ft) tall. The four listed here can be grown in rock pockets, among the slabs of a drystone wall or paving, as ground cover in a moraine bed, or in containers in an alpine house. All are perennials that die back to the ground in winter; they have divided leaves and bowl-shaped, five-petalled flowers that bloom throughout summer.

G. dalmaticum forms low, dense carpets, 7.5 to 10 cm (3 to 4 in.) tall, with a spread of 20 to 30 cm (8 to 12 in.). The dark, glossy leaves are divided into five leaflets. In autumn the foliage turns red. The flowers, pink with red veins and 2.5 cm (1 in.) wide, are borne in delicate sprays on 15 cm (6 in.) stems. There is also a white cultivar. *G. renardii* grows in clumps 23 to 30 cm (9 to 12 in.) tall and 30 to 38 cm (12 to 15 in.) wide. The hairy, rounded, grey-green leaves have bumpy surfaces and scalloped edges. Open clusters of 2.5 cm (1 in.) wide flowers are lavender with prominent reddish-violet veins.

G. sanguineum, a favourite garden perennial, forms dense mounds 30 cm (1 ft) tall and 60 cm (2 ft) across. The finely divided foliage turns red in autumn. The reddish-purple flowers are 2.5 to 5 cm (1 to 2 in.) wide. There is also a white form.

G. sanguineum var. *prostatum*, only 10 to 15 cm (4 to 6 in.) tall, spreads to a width of 45 cm (1½ ft). Its trailing stems form a thick mat on the ground. The finely textured leaves also turn red in autumn; the 2.5 cm (1 in.) wide flowers are pale pink with red veins.

HOW TO GROW. Crane's-bills are all hardy in Britain and similar temperate climates; they grow best in full sun but will tolerate very light shade. A well-drained, sandy or gritty soil with poor to average fertility is best; plants tend to become rampant if the soil is too rich. A pH of 6.0 to 7.5 is preferable. They can be planted in autumn or spring. Once established, they need little attention and should not be disturbed; divide them only if the plants seem to be deteriorating.

G. sanguineum should be trimmed back to half its height after the first main flowering period to encourage branching. Propagate all these species by means of seed sown in spring or by dividing the clumps in early spring. Crane's-bills will often seed themselves.

GEUM
G. coccineum, also called *G. borisii*; *G. reptans*. (Both called avens or geum)

Forming neat mounds of foliage and bearing large flowers that resemble strawberry blossoms, these avens can be planted anywhere in open, sunny positions, in raised beds or among the stones of a retaining wall. Their brightly coloured flowers appear from spring to midsummer. The foliage of *G. coccineum* is green and of a coarse texture. Each heart-shaped leaf is deeply indented. The nodding, yellow to orange-red flowers are 4 cm (1½ in.) across and are borne on 20 to 25 cm (8 to 10 in.) stalks. Toothed leaflets give the foliage of *G. reptans* a delicate, fern-like texture. This plant grows 10 to 15 cm (4 to 6 in.) tall and may spread to 38 cm (1¼ ft) by long, red runners. The flowers are golden-yellow and 4 cm (1½ in.) wide.

HOW TO GROW. Both these avens are hardy. In hot climates, midday shade is necessary; elsewhere full sun is tolerated. The soil should be a deep, well-drained, gritty loam enriched with moss peat or leaf-mould, with an acid-to-neutral pH of 5.5 to 7.0. Soil must not be allowed to become dry. Plant avens in spring or autumn, spacing them 25 to 30 cm (10 to 12 in.) apart. Sprinkle bone-meal lightly round the plants in spring. To prolong the flowering period, remove flowers as they fade. A light mulch of leaves or bracken will protect plants in severe winters. Propagate by sowing seed in spring; transplant the seedlings to their permanent sites in autumn. Established clumps can also be lifted and divided in early spring or autumn; plants grow best when divided every two or three years. The small plantlets on runners of *G. reptans* can be detached during the summer and transplanted.

GYPSOPHILA
G. cerastioides; *G. repens*; *G. tenuifolia*

Although much smaller than the usual gypsophilas found in herbaceous borders, these rock-garden species have the same delicate cloud-like quality with tiny white or pink flowers. Hardy perennials, they can be planted in rock-garden pockets, used as an edging or allowed to trail over ledges, steps or rocks. The roots, thick and fleshy, run deep into the soil. Stems that creep above ground form spreading mats.

G. cerastioides has small, rounded leaves that are soft and grey. The foliage rosettes grow 5 to 7.5 cm (2 to 3 in.) tall with a spread of 30 to 45 cm (1 to 1½ ft). From early summer until autumn, clusters of flowers are borne on 7.5 cm (3 in.) stems above the foliage. The tiny flowers, up to 1 cm (½ in.) wide, are white with red-purple veins.

The thin, wire-like stems of *G. repens* branch and rebranch to form mounds 7.5 to 15 cm (3 to 6 in.) tall and up to 60 cm (2 ft) across. Its narrow leaves are less than 2.5 cm (1 in.) long and are a soft grey-green colour. Fast-growing, it is best used in clumps cascading over rocks or walls. Graceful, open flower clusters appear throughout the summer. Only 8 mm (⅓ in.) wide, the flowers may be white or pink. Named cultivars include 'Fratensis', dwarf with pink flowers, and 'Rosea', with double, rose-pink flowers. Fine-textured *G. tenuifolia* has smooth leaves and pink flowers on 10 cm (4 in.) stems.

HOW TO GROW. Gypsophilas are hardy in Britain and sheltered temperate areas of northern Europe. They grow best in full sun. Set plants in a deep, well-drained, gritty soil. Being chalk-lovers, they will also do well in limy soils. Plant young gypsophilas in early spring, spacing them 30 to 38 cm (12 to 15 in.) apart. Clip plants lightly after the first major period of bloom to encourage more blooms later. Propagate from cuttings in spring or from seed gathered and sown when ripe.

H

HELIANTHEMUM
H. nummularium, also called *H. chamaecistus* (rock rose)

Grown for the brilliantly coloured, buttercup-like flowers that cover trailing, hairy foliage throughout

Gypsophila repens

ROCK ROSE
Helianthemum nummularium

late spring and summer, helianthemums can be used to trail over a retaining wall, to cover banks or to form an edging along a raised bed. These shrubby perennials are semi-evergreen to evergreen and do particularly well in sheltered coastal gardens.

Rock roses grow up to 23 cm (9 in.) tall and spread up to 45 cm (1½ ft) wide. The narrow, oval leaves are 2.5 cm (1 in.) long and glossy dark green or grey-green, depending on the cultivar. The underside is grey and hairy. Clusters of 2.5 cm (1 in.), paper-thin flowers appear at the end of each trailing stem. Although each flower is short-lived, hundreds are produced. There are many named cultivars in a multitude of colours, with single or double flowers, including 'Ben Hope', carmine-red with an orange-yellow eye; 'Jubilee', double, bright yellow; and 'The Bride', which is pure white.

HOW TO GROW. Helianthemums are hardy in northern Europe but must have full sun to thrive. They grow best in poor, dry, gritty or sandy soil that is deep and has a pH of 7.5 to 8.5. They are difficult to transplant, so purchase young plants grown in containers. Plant in early spring, spacing them 30 to 45 cm (1 to 1½ ft) apart. Prune rock roses back to two-thirds of the original height after the first heavy flowering to stimulate repeated bloom and also to encourage young shoots to use for cuttings.

Propagate helianthemums from cuttings of new growth rooted in late summer; grow these in individual pots over winter in a cold frame, setting them out in the garden the following spring.

HELIOSPERMA See *Silene*

HEPATICA
H. nobilis, also called *H. triloba*; *H. transsylvanica*. (Both called hepatica)

A harbinger of spring, *H. nobilis* may be planted along the edges of rockeries or in semi-shaded pockets. The semi-evergreen foliage remains attractive into the winter months. The three-lobed leaves form dense clumps, up to 10 cm (4 in.) high, spreading to 30 cm (1 ft). The bowl-shaped, anemone-like flowers may be white, blue, pink or purple and double-flowered cultivars are available in the same colours. The flowers, 1 to 4 cm (½ to 1½ in.) wide, appear in early spring. *H. transsylvanica* grows 10 to 15 cm (4 to 6 in.) tall and has a spread of 25 cm (10 in.). The leaves have scalloped, toothed edges. This species is very similar to *H. nobilis* but is slightly more delicate in growth habit. The blue flowers may be up to 4 cm (1½ in.) across.

HOW TO GROW. Hepaticas are hardy throughout Britain and temperate northern Europe. Provide open shade with some direct sun. The soil should be a gritty, woodland loam enriched with moss peat or leaf-mould and having a pH of 6.0 to 7.0; hepaticas also like lime. The soil must be kept constantly moist. In early spring, set out plants 20 to 30 cm (8 to 12 in.) apart. In very cold districts, provide winter protection by lightly mulching with leaves before the first frost; remove the mulch early the following spring. Propagate from seeds which should be sown as soon as they are ripe while they are still green.

HUTCHINSIA
H. alpina

A plant for an alpine rock garden, stone sink or the crevices in a drystone wall, *H. alpina* is a tufted evergreen perennial, 5 to 10 cm (2 to 4 in.) tall, with a spread of 20 cm (8 in.). The finely divided leaves grow in a rosette; the

Hutchinsia alpina

flowers bloom in early summer, covering the entire plant with 2.5 cm (1 in.) clustering masses of small, pure white, four-petalled flowers.

HOW TO GROW. *H. alpina* is hardy. It does best in partial shade but tolerates full sun provided temperatures are cool. Ideally, it should have a well-drained gritty or gravelly soil with a pH of 6.0 to 7.5. The soil should be kept constantly moist. Plant in autumn at 7.5 to 15 cm (3 to 6 in.) intervals. Propagate from seeds, which should be sown as soon as they are ripe.

IBERIS
I. saxatilis; *I. sempervirens*. (Both called candytuft)

The ground-hugging candytufts are mainstays of a rock garden. They are easy to grow, generally stay green all year round, and at their peak, in late spring, they are covered with dazzling white flowers. They can be used in the crevices of walls, among paving stones or in drifts over and around rocks. In addition, *I. saxatilis* can be grown in pots in an alpine greenhouse.

I. saxatilis forms a 7.5 to 15 cm (3 to 6 in.) high carpet of twisted, contorted branches that spread over an area 20 to 30 cm (8 to 12 in.) wide. It is covered with tiny, cylindrical leaves, 18 mm ($\frac{3}{4}$ in.) long, that are a dull, dark green. The small white flowers, sometimes purple-tinged, bloom in flat-topped clusters 5 cm (2 in.) across.

I. sempervirens spreads slowly to form a dense, compact carpet, 60 cm (2 ft) across, its stems rooting where they touch moist soil. It grows 15 to 23 cm (6 to 9 in.) tall and has shiny, dark green leaves, 2.5 to 5 cm (1 to 2 in.) long. Blooming profusely into early summer, the small, pure white flowers are borne in flat clusters 5 cm (2 in.) across. In warmer regions, blooms may appear again in autumn. There are numerous cultivars, including 'Little Gem', which is only 10 cm (4 in.) tall, and 'Snowflake', 25 cm (10 in.) tall, both with larger white flowers. There is also a cultivar with double flowers, 'Plena'.

HOW TO GROW. These candytufts are hardy in northern Europe. In areas with cold winters and little snow cover, the leaves may turn brown, but fresh new growth is produced when the plants are trimmed back. Both species do best in a site with full sun or very light shade. Candytufts thrive in a well-drained, sandy loam with a pH of 6.0 to 7.5. Although both plants suffer if moisture collects round their roots, especially in winter, they should be watered regularly during prolonged droughts in summer.

Set new plants out in spring. To encourage continuous new growth, prune off one third to one half of the old flower stems after the flowers fade. Renew the soil every spring by working equal parts of leaf-mould or moss peat, fresh soil and sand into the topsoil round the plants. Propagate from cuttings taken in the summer.

IRIS
I. cristata; *I. gracilipes*; *I. pumila*; *I. verna*

With hundreds of forms and cultivars to choose from, there are irises suitable for rock gardens of every kind and size. Some thrive in sun, others in shade. All are perennial, blooming in late spring or early summer. They grow from bulbs or fleshy rhizomes and have sword-shaped foliage. The clear, vivid colours of iris blooms include pink, lilac, purple, white, cream, yellow, brown, maroon, orange, near-black and blue; the flowers of many cultivars are bicoloured.

I. cristata, one of the most beautiful irises, grows up to 15 cm (6 in.) tall. It will spread to cover a large area, its

CANDYTUFT
Iberis sempervirens

IRIS
Iris verna

rhizomes forming a mat over the surface of the ground. Its flowers are lavender, 5 to 6 cm (2 to 2½ in.) across, with white crests marked with orange tips. The bright green, broad, arching leaves die to the ground in winter.

I. gracilipes grows 15 to 25 cm (6 to 10 in.) tall and its small fans of leaves die back in winter. Its slender, branched stems bear several pinkish-lilac, flat-petalled flowers, 2.5 to 5 cm (1 to 2 in.) across, in late spring.

I. pumila, suitable for a cool alpine greenhouse as well as a rock garden, grows up to 10 cm (4 in.) tall, and some cultivars have stemless blooms. It has blue-grey leaves and dark red-purple flowers, 5 to 7.5 cm (2 to 3 in.) wide.

I. verna forms spreading clumps of shiny evergreen foliage, 7.5 to 25 cm (3 to 10 in.) tall. Because the flower stems are so short, the blooms seem to nestle among the foliage. The fragrant flowers, up to 7.5 cm (3 in.) across, are lilac-blue or white with an orange band on the falls.

HOW TO GROW. All these irises are rhizomatous and hardy in sheltered places in northern temperate climates. They do best in a moist, acid soil, pH 5.0 to 6.5, enriched with moss peat or compost except for *I. pumila* which prefers neutral soil, pH 7.0. All four species grow well in the high, open shade of deciduous trees, but *I. pumila* is also recommended for full sun. Plant irises in spring or autumn, spacing smaller-growing species 15 to 23 cm (6 to 9 in.) apart, larger-growing species 30 to 45 cm (1 to 1½ ft) apart. To prevent rotting, rhizomes of *I. cristata* and *I. pumila* should be only half buried, with tips facing out from the centre. Keep the soil moist round the rhizomes for several weeks. Irises are most often propagated by dividing the rhizomes, making sure each division has one, and preferably two, growth buds. Divide after flowering.

J

JUNIPERUS
J. communis 'Compressa'; *J. communis* 'Depressa Aurea'; *J. horizontalis* 'Bar Harbor'; *J. horizontalis* 'Wiltonii', also called 'Blue Rug'; *J. x media* 'Old Gold'; *J. sabina* 'Tamariscifolia'. (All called dwarf juniper)

Dwarf junipers are probably the most popular and attractive conifers for rock-garden plantings. Some, while remaining low in stature, spread to form gracefully arching mats that are outstanding in rock landscapes or as evergreen ground cover; others are slow-growing, slender and upright and ideal for raised beds and sink gardens.

J. communis 'Compressa' is a miniature of the pencil-slim Irish juniper; it grows slowly to 60 cm (2 ft) high and rarely exceeds 10 cm (4 in.) in width. It is ideal for window boxes, sink and container gardens and as an accent plant in a small-scale rock garden. The closely packed needles are bluish-green. *J. communis* 'Depressa Aurea' makes good ground cover, growing up to 30 cm (1 ft) high and spreading to 90 cm (3 ft), with shoots and leaves that are yellow in summer, maturing to bronze-gold in winter.

J. horizontalis 'Bar Harbor' is almost prostrate in the early years, its branches clothed with narrow, blue-grey needles that turn purple in winter. It spreads to form a carpet 1.2 metres (4 ft) or more wide and 15 cm (6 in.) high. *J. horizontalis* 'Wiltonii' is completely prostrate, growing to 10 cm (4 in.) high, and forms silvery-blue mats.

J. x media 'Old Gold' is most suitable for a large rock garden; although of compact habit, with arching branches, it eventually grows 90 cm (3 ft) high and as much wide. It is, however, an outstanding specimen plant with foliage that remains golden throughout the year.

J. sabina 'Tamariscifolia' is one of the loveliest of the dwarf junipers, equally handsome in large rock gardens, draping low walls or rocky slopes or as a feature plant

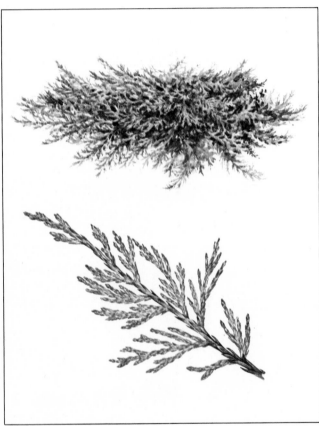

DWARF JUNIPER
Juniperus horizontalis 'Bar Harbor'

on paved terraces. The horizontal branches, which spread to 90 cm (3 ft), are arranged in tiers and form a low mound up to 30 cm (1 ft) high; the foliage is bluish-green.

HOW TO GROW. Dwarf junipers are fully hardy in northern and temperate Europe. They are extremely tough and do well in well-drained, ordinary, even poor and dry soils. *J. communis* cultivars thrive on chalky ground, but none of those described object to either acid or alkaline conditions. All are best planted in full sun, particularly those with coloured foliage. Plant in spring.

L

LEONTOPODIUM
L. alpinum (edelweiss)

This famous but modest flower, covered with woolly white hairs, forms bushy mounds about 20 cm (8 in.) high and 23 cm (9 in.) wide. The narrow, grey-green leaves grow mainly near the base of the stem, which bears star-shaped flowers in summer. The flannel-like flowers are made up of tight clusters of round yellow heads, 6 mm ($\frac{1}{4}$ in.) in diameter, surrounded by five to 15 velvety white, petal-like bracts, 1 to 2.5 cm ($\frac{1}{2}$ to 1 in.) long. The roots of edelweiss are far-ranging, but short-lived; though a perennial, the plant normally does not survive more than two or three years. There are several cultivars with shorter stems or whiter flowers.

HOW TO GROW. Edelweiss is hardy in sunny, protected rock pockets in well-drained, sandy soil with a pH of 6.5 to 7.5. Sand, gravel or gritty lime should be worked into the soil to lighten it, as edelweiss cannot stand much moisture. Seeds may not ripen in wet summers, and roots rot in wet winters. Named cultivars are best grown in an alpine house to protect them from winter wet and rain. Plant edelweiss in spring, setting the plants 15 cm (6 in.) apart. Propagate from seed, sown as soon as it ripens or early in spring. Plants that are started from seed will flower in the second year.

LEWISIA
L. cotyledon; *L. rediviva* (bitter-root); *L. tweedyi*

In mountains of the western United States, lewisias can be found growing in the crevices of bare rock, making them ideal for an alpine scree or the crevices of drystone walls and paving stones. Growing from carrot-like tap-roots, they spread by forming rosettes on these roots; each new rosette develops its own fleshy root. Lewisias bloom in late spring and summer.

L. cotyledon is a variable species with evergreen tongue-shaped leaves, 7.5 cm (3 in.) long, sometimes with wavy edges. It forms rosettes 15 cm (6 in.) wide, and its flowers bloom in clusters on stems 10 to 30 cm (4 to 12 in.) high. Each flower, up to 4 cm ($1\frac{1}{2}$ in.) wide, is salmon-pink striped with pink or white. There are also pink, clear white and yellow forms of this species.

The bitter-root, a deciduous plant, produces clumps of narrow, stemless, succulent leaves, 2.5 to 10 cm (1 to 4 in.) long, in late summer. This foliage lasts through the winter and into the following summer, when the almost stemless flowers appear. These are pink or white, 2.5 to 5 cm (1 to 2 in.) across. As the flowers fade, the plant becomes dormant, disappearing until late summer when new leaves emerge.

L. tweedyi, another evergreen, bears one to three apricot-pink flowers, about 6 cm ($2\frac{1}{2}$ in.) wide, on 15 cm (6 in.) stems. A single plant may produce more than 50 flowers during its blooming season. The broad, light-green leaves, often tinged with red, form rosettes 23 cm (9 in.) wide.

EDELWEISS
Leontopodium alpinum

BITTER-ROOT
Lewisia rediviva

Lithodora diffusa 'Heavenly Blue'

COMMON GRAPE HYACINTH
Muscari botryoides

HOW TO GROW. These three lewisias are hardy in Britain provided they are left fairly dry in winter, have full sun and are planted in well-drained, sandy soil with an acid pH of 5.5 to 6.5. A mixture of 1 part fine stone chips, 1 part sand and 1 part acid leaf-mould is recommended.

Plant lewisias in spring, setting the root crown about 2.5 cm (1 in.) above the soil, so that moisture will drain away from the crown, minimizing the danger of rot; crown rot will cause the plants to die after flowering. The best method of avoiding excess moisture is to plant lewisias on a slope between rocks, covering them with a cloche or a pane of glass raised on bricks in winter. Lewisias need to have some moisture during spring and summer, but wetness in winter will kill them. Pot-grown plants need frequent repotting and must be rested after flowering.

Propagate all lewisias from seed or by cutting off rosettes in spring and rooting them in sand. Seeds require several months of cold weather to germinate, so refrigerate them over winter and sow in spring. Transplant the seedlings to individual containers and keep them in a cold frame for one or two full seasons before setting them in the garden. Plants that are grown from seed will usually flower within three years.

LITHODORA
L. diffusa, also called *Lithospermum diffusum*

L. diffusa is one of the loveliest blue-flowered, summer-blooming plants for the rock garden, where its mat-forming habit makes good ground cover; it can also be allowed to trail over rocks or the edges of sink gardens. Two selected colour forms, 'Grace Ward', with the larger, intensely blue flowers, and the highly floriferous 'Heavenly Blue', are the kinds usually cultivated. Both have small, rough, oval, dark green leaves, and 12 to 18 mm ($\frac{1}{2}$ to $\frac{3}{4}$ in.) wide flowers, with five spreading lobes. They bloom from early summer until early autumn.

HOW TO GROW. *L. diffusa* and its cultivars are fully hardy, but will not tolerate lime and can therefore not be grown on chalky soils. Their chief requirements are full sun and sandy soil with a little added moss peat or leaf-mould. In dry weather, water to keep the stems from flagging, and once or twice during the growing season give the plants a foliar feed. Increase by means of cuttings taken in summer from side shoots, preferably with a heel of the old woody stem attached. Make these 5 cm (2 in.) long and root in pans of equal parts by volume of sand and peat in a cold frame.

LITHOSPERMUM See *Lithodora*

LYCHNIS
L. viscaria 'Splendens Plena', also called *Viscaria vulgaris* (double-flowered campion)

The true campion, *L. viscaria*, is native to Europe. It is excellent for rock-garden planting but superseded by the outstanding double cultivar, 'Splendens Plena'. It grows about 23 cm (9 in.) tall and spreads to 15 cm (6 in.) with small, narrow and pale green stems. In early summer, spikes of rich carmine flowers are borne on 30 to 45 cm (1 to 1$\frac{1}{2}$ ft) high stalks.

HOW TO GROW. The double-flowered campion needs good, well-drained garden soil, a sunny position and a sheltered rock pocket. It is not a long-lived plant but can easily be propagated from basal cuttings, 5 to 7.5 cm (2 to 3 in.) long, which should be taken in early spring and rooted in a frame with bottom heat.

M

MUSCARI

M. aucheri, also called *M. tubergenianum*; *M. botryoides* (common grape hyacinth); *M. latifolium*

Among the heralds of spring, grape hyacinths are ideally suited for massed plantings in sunny rock gardens and alpine meadows. These tiny bulbs form clumps of grass-like leaves 15 to 30 cm (6 to 12 in.) tall; they push up through the soil in late autumn, last through the winter, then die down to the ground by summer. Their fragrant, urn-shaped flowers, each less than 6 mm ($\frac{1}{4}$ in.) wide, appear in grape-like clusters on 15 to 23 cm (6 to 9 in.) flower spikes in spring.

M. aucheri has flowers that shade from light blue at the bottom of the spike to dark blue at the top.

The common grape hyacinth produces blue flowers with white tips, but there is also a cultivar, 'Album', with white flowers. *M. latifolium* bears dark purple flowers.

All grape hyacinths spread moderately fast by developing small bulbs round the larger ones and by seeding themselves. These hardy perennials can even grow through the dense root system of grass and are therefore suitable for naturalizing.

HOW TO GROW. Grape hyacinths are hardy in northern and temperate Europe. They do best in full sun but will tolerate light shade; in deep shade, plants produce more leaves than flowers. They thrive in moist, rich, well-drained soil with a pH of 5.5 to 7.0. Set bulbs in the ground as soon as they are available, in late summer or early autumn. Place them 7.5 cm (3 in.) deep and 7.5 to 10 cm (3 to 4 in.) apart. Keep moist during the growing season. These bulbs do not need any winter protection or fertilizer, and may be left in the ground indefinitely. Divide plants in midsummer, when they are dormant. Propagate by division of the clumps every three years, at the same time separating the small bulbils from the parents.

O

OENOTHERA

O. missouriensis (Ozark sundrops)

O. missouriensis fits well in a rocky meadow setting and stages a splendid show in wall pockets or on the surface of scree. The plants have dark trailing stems, up to 38 cm (15 in.) long, which turn upright to form broad mounds, 15 to 30 cm (6 to 12 in.) high. The narrow oval leaves, 7.5 to 12.5 cm (3 to 5 in.) long, are covered with silvery hairs. From summer to late autumn, satiny, trumpet-shaped, yellow flowers, up to 12.5 cm (5 in.) wide, provide a spectacular display. They open late in the day, stay open until dawn and are faintly fragrant. The plants are perennials and die back to the ground in winter.

HOW TO GROW. The plants are hardy in Britain and grow best in a dry, sandy or gritty, lime-enriched soil with a pH of 7.0 to 8.0. Good drainage is important, as the plants are susceptible to rot. Set them out in the garden in spring, spacing them 30 to 38 cm (12 to 15 in.) apart. Propagate by division or from seeds sown outdoors as soon as they ripen, or in a cold frame or greenhouse.

OMPHALODES

O. verna (blue-eyed Mary)

Blue-eyed Mary, reputed to be the favourite flower of Marie Antoinette, is a creeping deciduous perennial for shady, woodland rock gardens. It spreads on horizontal, jointed stems to form 10 to 12.5 cm (4 to 5 in.) high tufts of dark green, heart-shaped leaves, 2.5 to 10 cm (1 to 4 in.) long. In spring, 1 cm ($\frac{1}{2}$ in.) wide, bright blue flowers with

OZARK SUNDROPS
Oenothera missouriensis

BLUE-EYED MARY
Omphalodes verna

Onosma alborosea

white throats bloom in pairs on erect flower stalks that rise above the foliage.

HOW TO GROW. Blue-eyed Mary is hardy in Britain and temperate northern Europe. It grows best in light shade, in moist, sandy or gritty soil with a pH of 6.0 to 7.5. Once established, blue-eyed Mary requires little care. Propagate from seed or by dividing rooted stems in spring.

ONOSMA
O. alborosea; O. taurica

Onosmas are southern European plants, suitable for sunny, well-drained and sheltered rock pockets or the alpine house. *O. alborosea* has rough, hairy, evergreen leaves, grey-green in colour and narrowly spoon-shaped. It forms mats about 15 cm (6 in.) high and as wide across; from mid-spring until late summer, it bears pendent clusters of white, tubular flowers, flushed with pink or red, up to 2.5 cm (1 in.) long. *O. taurica* is similar in all respects, except that the flowers are smaller, each about 18 mm ($\frac{3}{4}$ in.) long and deep yellow; they are similar in appearance to drop ear-rings.

HOW TO GROW. Onosmas resent winter wet, which leads to rotting. Grow them in very well-drained, light soil, and prevent excess moisture by mulching the topsoil with granite chippings. They need a site in full sun. They may also be planted in a drystone wall which never retains moisture, or they can be covered with cloches in winter. Propagation is best carried out from 5 cm (2 in.) long soft cuttings taken in late summer and rooted in moss peat and sand in a cold frame. They can also be increased from seed sown in spring in pans or boxes, and germinated in a cold frame, then potted on and kept in the frame until the following spring.

P
PHLOX
P. adsurgens; P. amoena; P. douglasii; P. stolonifera (creeping phlox); P. subulata (moss phlox)

With but one exception, all species of phlox are native to North America. Those listed here are low-growing species suitable for carpeting rock walls and banks with sheets of lavish spring colour. On most of them, the flowers bloom in loose clusters. *P. adsurgens* forms tufts, up to 30 cm (12 in.) wide and 10 cm (4 in.) high, of shiny oval leaves with creeping stems which root down into the surrounding soil. The flowers are variable, but usually salmon-pink, and open in midsummer.

P. amoena, a mat-forming species, 15 cm (6 in.) high, spreading to 30 cm (1 ft), bears glossy, lanceolate leaves. The 20 cm (8 in.) creeping stems are covered with rose-pink to purple flowers. *P. douglasii* is lower growing, to 7.5 cm (3 in.) high, forming 45 cm ($1\frac{1}{2}$ ft) wide mats of small, linear leaves. The almost stemless flowers are lilac.

P. stolonifera spreads rapidly on stems that root wherever nodes touch the ground, forming broad mats of foliage. It grows 15 to 23 cm (6 to 9 in.) high and is commonly used as ground cover. Its broad, oval leaves, about 4 cm ($1\frac{1}{2}$ in.) across, are covered with downy hairs and lie flat on the ground, forming a dense carpet. The flowers, 2.5 cm (1 in.) across, are usually blue or purple but may occasionally be pink or white.

P. subulata stays green all year round in mild climates. It forms dense mats of foliage, 15 cm (6 in.) high, by sending out rooting stems and is often used as ground cover. Tiny needle-like leaves cover its stems, and it flowers profusely. The many cultivars of moss phlox offer a wide choice of flowers with round, narrow, notched or star-like petals

MOSS PHLOX
Phlox subulata

in a range of colours including white, lilac, lavender, pink, rose, magenta and mauve. In many of the cultivars, the flowers are fragrant.

HOW TO GROW. These species of phlox are hardy in Britain and temperate northern Europe. *P. adsurgens*, *P. amoena* and *P. stolonifera* grow best in dappled sunlight in soil enriched with leaf-mould, pH 5.5 to 7.0. *P. subulata*, the easiest to grow, and *P. douglasii* thrive in full sun in any well-drained soil. Phlox may be grown from seed sown in spring or from nursery plants set out in the spring or autumn and spaced about 25 cm (10 in.) apart. To stimulate fresh growth and sometimes renew blooming, clip the plants back after flowering.

Propagation of phlox depends on their root structure and growing habits. Established clumps may often be divided in spring after flowering. New plants may also be started from seed but, if definite colours or named cultivars are wanted, propagate from tip cuttings taken in summer and rooted in sandy soil in a cold frame.

PICEA
P. abies 'Nidiformis'; *P. abies* 'Pumila' (both called dwarf Norway spruce); *P. glauca* 'Conica' (dwarf Alberta spruce); *P. mariana* 'Nana' (dwarf black spruce)

Useful as small coniferous accent shrubs in a rock garden, the dwarf spruces, like their full-sized counterparts, are notable for their tolerance of high winds and low temperatures. They may grow as rounded globes or as spreading mounds, much wider than they are high. The sharp, stiff needles are usually dark green. The fast-growing fibrous root system is wide and deep, adapting to a variety of sites.

P. abies 'Nidiformis', one of the most popular of the dwarf Norway spruces, is spreading in habit, with a flattened top that has a slight bird's-nest depression in the centre. It is a formal, tidy plant with tiny, dark green needles; it is vigorous but rarely becomes more than 30 cm (1 ft) high and 60 cm (2 ft) wide.

P. abies 'Pumila' forms a dense bush of globose shape that ultimately reaches 60 cm (2 ft) high and across, with a flattened top. The small, thick needles are bright green and borne on branchlets arranged in tiers.

The dwarf Alberta spruce is a compact, conical tree with dense, dark green foliage. It grows slowly, reaching a height of 90 cm (3 ft) and a spread of 30 cm (1 ft) in 10 years. *P. mariana* 'Nana' forms a dense, rounded shrub, eventually 30 cm (1 ft) high and 60 cm (2 ft) wide. The branches are sub-divided into smaller and smaller sideshoots, all covered with flattened, blue-green needles.

HOW TO GROW. These dwarf spruces grow well in northern and temperate Europe; they do best in full sun, although partial shade is tolerated. Ideally, they should have a moist, well-drained soil enriched with moss peat or leaf-mould and having a slightly acid pH of 5.5 to 6.5, but they will survive in dry soil. Plant spruces in late spring or autumn. Mulch young plants with moss peat or garden compost and water well during periods of drought.

PLUMBAGO See *Ceratostigma*

POTENTILLA
P. alba (white cinquefoil); *P. tridentata*. (Both called cinquefoil)

Mixed with heathers in an alpine garden, where growing conditions approximate to the rocky outcrops of high mountains, these low-growing cinquefoils offer small size,

DWARF ALBERTA SPRUCE
Picea glauca 'Conica'

CINQUEFOIL
Potentilla tridentata

121

AURICULA
Primula auricula

DRUMSTICK PRIMROSE
Primula denticulata

hardiness and interesting foliage. The name cinquefoil refers to their finger-like leaflets, which typically occur in groups of five, although there are also three and seven-fingered forms. Flowers, too, are five petalled, and tend to be saucer-shaped like the flowers of a wild rose.

White cinquefoil forms low, spreading mounds 12.5 to 20 cm (5 to 8 in.) high. Its five-part leaves are smooth and green on the upper side but are covered with silky white hairs beneath, giving the foliage a glistening appearance. Sprays of white, 2.5 cm (1 in.) flowers bloom on 15 cm (6 in.) stems throughout most of the summer.

P. tridentata grows 15 to 30 cm (6 to 12 in.) high and is open enough for bulbs to grow beneath it. It bears sprays of 6 mm ($\frac{1}{4}$ in.) wide, white flowers which resemble strawberry blossoms, but its chief ornament is its foliage. The shiny, dark green leaves are made up of three 1 to 2.5 cm ($\frac{1}{2}$ to 1 in.) leaflets, each tipped at the end with three teeth. This cinquefoil is evergreen in the warmer parts of Europe, but in cooler regions it becomes brilliant red in the autumn. Both of these species spread by means of creeping underground stems.

HOW TO GROW. Both species require full sun and thrive in a well-drained garden soil, though the foliage of *P. tridentata* will colour more deeply if the soil is acid, pH 5.0 to 6.0. Neither species requires much water. Set plants out in spring, spacing them 25 cm (10 in.) apart. Once established, cinquefoils require little care except pruning to remove dead wood. Propagate by dividing roots in spring or autumn or from cuttings of ripe shoots taken in autumn.

PRIMULA

P. auricula (auricula); *P. denticulata* (drumstick primrose); *P. juliae*; *P. sieboldii*; *P. veris*, also called *P. officinalis* (cowslip); *P. vulgaris*, also called *P. acaulis* (primrose)

Treasured for their brilliant spring flowers, primroses play many roles in the rock garden. Most are suited to moist, partially shaded environments, some even grow in bogs. Others, the more succulent types, need good drainage and bright light, as is found on alpine moraines. The following are recommended for colour and ease of growth.

P. auricula is an alpine species suitable for use in a moraine, raised bed or alpine house. Its thick, oval, green or grey-green leaves, often covered with a mealy farina, form rosettes 15 cm (6 in.) high that persist all year round. The species bears fragrant, clear yellow or sometimes purple flowers in mid-spring. Cultivars come in almost every colour, usually with contrasting centres. A hybrid between this species and *P. hirsuta*, *P.* x *pubescens*, needs similar growing conditions. It forms 10 cm (4 in.) high rosettes of grey-green leaves and bears rose-crimson flowers with white centres.

P. denticulata, also with powdery foliage, produces many sturdy flower stalks, 20 to 30 cm (8 to 12 in.) tall, bearing 5 cm (2 in.) globes of white, purple, deep rose or, more commonly, mauve flowers when grown in moist soil.

P. juliae is a dwarf species only 7.5 cm (3 in.) high. Its creeping stems bear tufts of heart-shaped leaves and 2.5 cm (1 in.) wide, reddish-purple flowers with yellow eyes. The flowers, on 5 cm (2 in.) stalks, are so profuse that they hide the foliage. More common are its cultivars, particularly 'Wanda', with bright claret flowers, often in mid-winter; and 'Garryarde', which has long, wrinkled, reddish-bronze leaves and large, frilled flowers, soft pink in 'Garryarde Guinevere' or purple in 'Victory'.

P. sieboldii, a Japanese species, is 15 to 20 cm (6 to 8 in.) high and has toothed leaves that die down in late summer and reappear the following spring. The flowers on this plant are 5 cm (2 in.) wide and have white, pink or purple petals and coloured centres.

P. veris, the cowslip, is about 20 cm (8 in.) tall. It blooms in mid-spring, normally bearing tubular cream to yellow flowers in drooping clusters.

P. vulgaris, the primrose, a hardy perennial that grows 15 cm (6 in.) high, bears fragrant, 2.5 cm (1 in.) wide, yellow flowers that bloom one to a stem. Hybrids from this species include the well-known polyanthus primroses which are evergreen and form clumps of rosettes up to 30 cm (1 ft) tall. Their flower stalks bear clusters of single or double flowers up to 4 cm (1½ in.) wide in a broad range of colours that includes pastels as well as striped and blended forms.

HOW TO GROW. All these primroses are hardy in northern Europe. A cool, moist climate in summer suits them best. Auriculas require well-drained neutral soil, pH 6.0 to 7.5, and moderate sun. Plant this species so that moisture will drain away from the crowns; otherwise they may rot. Other species require an acid soil, pH 5.5 to 6.5, enriched with leaf-mould or garden compost, and grow best in the partial shade of deciduous trees. *P. denticulata* thrives in rock pockets or bog conditions, and *P. sieboldii* adapts to deep shade or moderate sun as well as light shade.

Set plants out in spring, 15 to 30 cm (6 to 12 in.) apart. Keep the soil moist during the growing season. Dig up and divide crowded clumps, particularly of polyanthus, after flowering and keep them in a shady, damp place all summer. In autumn, they can be moved to more open sunny places to flower.

Primroses, which spread by forming side rosettes, can be propagated by rooting these offsets after flowering. Many species seed themselves, but the seedlings may not breed true to form, and are often not worth keeping.

PTILOTRICHUM See *Alyssum*

PULSATILLA

P. vernalis; *P. vulgaris*, also called *Anemone pulsatilla*. (Both called pasque flower)

Pasque flowers take their name from the fact that they bloom early in spring, around Easter-time. They bear large flowers that open almost flat when the stems have barely pushed through the soil, even before the silvery leaves have fully unfolded. After the flowers fade, the stems grow taller and feathery mops of silvery seed clusters develop. All parts of these plants are coated with silky hairs that glisten in the sunlight.

P. vernalis grows as deep green tufts that are 15 cm (6 in.) high and wide; the cup-shaped flowers, 5 cm (2 in.) across, are pearly-white.

P. vulgaris grows 15 to 30 cm (6 to 12 in.) tall and bears blue to reddish-purple blooms that are up to 6 cm (2½ in.) wide. The leaves of this plant are finely cut into numerous segments. There are cultivars of this beautiful wild plant, which was formerly known as *Anemone pulsatilla*, with purple, white or pink flowers.

HOW TO GROW. Pasque flowers are native to European mountains and hardy in Britain and northern Europe. They do best in pockets in the rock garden, in full sun and in soil which is moist at the time of flowering. A scattering of leaf-mould on the soil from time to time benefits the plants. As pasque flowers have long taproots, they do not transplant readily; propagation is best effected by sowing freshly gathered seeds. Sow in seed trays, pot up the seedlings individually and plant out the following spring. They will not flower until the third season.

COWSLIP
Primula veris

PASQUE FLOWER
Pulsatilla vernalis

Ramonda myconi

R

RAMONDA

R. myconi, also called *R. pyrenaica*

This, as the name implies, is a southern-European plant from the Pyrenees which forms flat rosettes of dark green, deeply toothed, corrugated leaves, oval-oblong in shape. It usually grows 10 to 15 cm (4 to 6 in.) high, with a spread of 23 cm (9 in.). The five-petalled flowers appear in late spring, several to a stem. They vary in colour from lavender to deep purple, and each bloom is 2.5 to 4 cm (1 to 1½ in.) across with a prominent yellow eye. White and pink cultivars are also known.

HOW TO GROW. Ramondas resent both wet and sunny conditions. If the plants sit in water they will rot and die, but they do well in a shady north-facing position, perched sideways between rocks so that drainage is effective at all times. They thrive in a humus-rich soil containing rotted leaf-mould, and benefit from a mulch with this material each spring. In very dry weather, water well, with lime-free water if possible.

Ramondas can be propagated from seed sown in boxes in early autumn, or from leaf cuttings taken in midsummer. These leaves should be pulled from the plants so that the dormant bud at the base of each is retained. Insert them obliquely in peat and sand in boxes or pans, burying only 2.5 cm (1 in.) of each leaf. Keep them in a cold frame. They should root in about six weeks and can then be potted up.

RANUNCULUS

R. montanus, also called *R. geraniifolius* (mountain buttercup)

The mountain buttercups are a divergent group found in various places on European mountains. They are suitable for growing in gardens that simulate rocky outcrops and scree conditions, where they form 15 cm (6 in.) high mats of dense, dark green foliage, the lower leaves being nearly round while the upper ones are divided into three to five parts. In spring, shiny-petalled, bright yellow flowers, 2.5 cm (1 in.) wide, bloom on 15 cm (6 in.) stems; 'Molten Gold' is a particularly good form.

HOW TO GROW. Mountain buttercups are hardy over most of the cooler parts of Europe. They grow in either partial shade or full sun and adapt to any ordinary garden soil, but grow best in a moist, well-drained, gritty, acid loam with a pH of 5.0 to 6.5, enriched with leaf-mould or garden compost. Water during dry spells, as the roots are close to the surface. Mountain buttercup seeds, unless very fresh, may not germinate. It is better to propagate plants by dividing the underground stolons after flowering.

RHODOHYPOXIS

R. baurii

These are tiny perennials from the Drakensberg mountains of South Africa. Growing from corm-like roots to a mere 7.5 cm (3 in.) in height, with a spread of 7.5 to 10 cm (3 to 4 in.), they have tufts of narrow, hairy leaves, literally smothered under masses of six-petalled, rosy-red flowers from late spring until early autumn. Pink, rose and white cultivars are available. Their small size and profuse flowering habit make them ideal plants for sink gardens and similar small containers, as well as for rockery pockets and the alpine house.

HOW TO GROW. Rhodohypoxis are hardy only in sheltered parts of the British Isles and northern Europe, in moist but well-drained, lime-free soil. They do better in southern France provided the soil can be kept moist and cool. Excess moisture round the crowns frequently leads to

MOUNTAIN BUTTERCUP
Ranunculus montanus

rotting, and it is a good idea to top-dress the soil round the crowns with granite chippings. The plants can be protected from winter wet by covering them with cloches or by putting a pane of glass raised on bricks over the plants. Those in alpine houses should be repotted every autumn, after flowering is finished. Propagate by removing offsets from the old corms in autumn. These should flower the following season.

S
SAPONARIA
S. x 'Bressingham'; *S. ocymoides*. (Both called soapwort)

S. x 'Bressingham', a garden hybrid, grows only 7.5 cm (3 in.) high and spreads very slowly; it is covered with rich pink, white-eyed flowers in early summer.

S. ocymoides forms trails of multi-branched stems thickly clad with downy leaves, 1 to 2.5 cm ($\frac{1}{2}$ to 1 in.) long. The 1 cm ($\frac{1}{2}$ in.) flowers, borne in summer in loose clusters, have bright pink petals, deeper pink, tubular bases and purple throats. There is also a pure white cultivar. This vigorous plant is ideal for trailing over rocks, the edges of sink gardens and similar situations. It grows 15 to 23 cm (6 to 9 in.) high, but spreads in a few years to form mats 60 cm (2 ft) or more wide.

HOW TO GROW. Soapworts are mainly hardy in Britain and are exceptionally easy to grow. They do well in any open, sunny situation and in ordinary garden soil, though a light, gritty soil with a pH of 6.0 to 7.5 is best; they do not need much moisture. Sow seeds or set out nursery plants in spring or autumn, setting *S.* x 'Bressingham' 15 cm (6 in.) and *S. ocymoides* 30 cm (1 ft) apart. When the plants have flowered, cut the largest stems back almost to the ground to keep the plants neat and compact. Additional plants may be started from stem cuttings taken in summer or by division of the rhizomes in early spring.

SAXIFRAGA
S. cochlearis; *S. cotyledon*; *S.* Kabschia hybrids; *S. marginata*; *S. paniculata*, also called *S. aizoon*; *S. stolonifera*, also called *S. sarmentosa*. (All called saxifrage)

The saxifrages are alpine plants *par excellence*; there are more than 300 different species growing in the crevices of rocks all over the world. In fact, the Latin word *saxifraga* means rock breaker. Most of them are low-growing perennials that spread on creeping stems, sending up rosettes or clumps of foliage to form thick mats. Often the leaves are thick and fleshy, and many of them are edged with silvery deposits of lime that make them appear translucent. The flowers are usually star shaped and in many species are borne in loose sprays on tall stalks that rise above the foliage. Most *Saxifraga* species bloom in spring or early summer.

S. cochlearis has lime-encrusted, 2.5 cm (1 in.) long, spoon-shaped leaves with toothed margins, which form rosettes of foliage 5 to 7.5 cm (2 to 3 in.) high and 23 to 30 cm (9 to 12 in.) wide. The white flowers, up to 18 mm ($\frac{3}{4}$ in.) across, bloom in late spring on 20 cm (8 in.) stalks.

S. cotyledon forms 10 cm (4 in.) wide, pyramid-shaped rosettes of tongue-shaped leaves with lime-beaded edges. The branched flower stalks rise like plumes as much as 60 cm (2 ft) high, bearing 18 mm ($\frac{3}{4}$ in.), white flowers that may be speckled with red or purple spots and which bloom in early summer.

The Kabschia saxifrages are a group with grey-green or silver, lime-encrusted leaves, 1 cm ($\frac{1}{2}$ in.) long, that create small, dense hummocks 15 to 20 cm (6 to 8 in.) across. The 1 cm ($\frac{1}{2}$ in.) wide, saucer-shaped flowers are yellow in

Rhodohypoxis baurii

SOAPWORT
Saponaria ocymoides

125

S. burseriana, but there are a multiplicity of hybrids and cultivars with white, pink and yellow flowers, all on 7.5 cm (3 in.) stalks.

S. marginata grows in 7.5 cm (3 in.) high tufts of blunt-tipped, lime-encrusted leaves 1 cm ($\frac{1}{2}$ in.) long. Its 7.5 cm (3 in.) flower stalks bear white or pale pink flowers, 1 cm ($\frac{1}{2}$ in.) wide, in late spring and summer.

S. paniculata forms dense, 15 cm (6 in.) wide rosettes of narrow, spoon-shaped leaves, 4 cm (1$\frac{1}{2}$ in.) long, with toothed and lime-encrusted margins. The 1 cm ($\frac{1}{2}$ in.) wide flowers are cream-white with purple dots and bloom in summer. The many cultivars offer different flower colours and leaf forms.

S. stolonifera forms tufts of foliage 10 to 12.5 cm (4 to 5 in.) high and spreads on thin, thread-like runners, similar to those of the strawberry plant, extending out from the base of the plant 60 cm (2 ft) or more. The 7.5 cm (3 in.) wide leaves are round, green on top and red beneath, with silvery veins. In summer, sprays of white flowers, 2.5 to 4 cm (1 to 1$\frac{1}{2}$ in.) wide, bloom on 15 to 20 cm (6 to 8 in.) stalks. It is also a popular house plant.

HOW TO GROW. The saxifrages are hardy in northern Europe and grow best in partial shade or dappled sunlight. They thrive among rocks in a well-drained, gritty soil with a pH of 6.5 to 7.5. Set plants out in autumn or spring, spacing them 30 cm (1 ft) apart. Propagate from seed or by separating offsets after flowering, treating them as cuttings. To stimulate the growth of new rosettes on old plants, spread a thin layer of sifted loam, leaf-mould and sand over the top of the plants.

SEDUM
S. cauticolum; *S. ewersii*; *S. reflexum*, also called *S. rupestre*; *S. sieboldii*; *S. spathulifolium*; *S. spurium*. (All called stonecrop)

The sedums are creeping succulents that are easy to grow and ideal for draping rock walls and carpeting poor, dry soil. These six species also bear outstanding flowers. The foliage is usually evergreen or semi-evergreen, depending on the severity of the winter, and often turns purple in autumn. All are perennials spreading on rooting stems.

S. cauticolum, 7.5 cm (3 in.) high, has 20 cm (8 in.) stems laden with pairs of roundish, blue-green leaves with red edges. Rose-red flowers, 1 cm ($\frac{1}{2}$ in.) across, bloom in flat clusters up to 10 cm (4 in.) wide in late summer and early autumn. *S. ewersii* has stems 15 to 30 cm (6 to 12 in.) long, which appear to pass through the centres of roundish, blue-grey leaves about 18 mm ($\frac{3}{4}$ in.) wide. Its rosy-pink flowers bloom in late summer in clusters 5 cm (2 in.) across.

S. reflexum is 20 to 30 cm (8 to 12 in.) high; its narrow, 1 cm ($\frac{1}{2}$ in.) long, blue-green leaves grow thickly along its 25 cm (10 in.) stems. It blooms in late spring and early summer in flattened 5 cm (2 in.) clusters of golden-yellow flowers. *S. sieboldii*, up to 30 cm (1 ft) high, has arching, purple-tinged stems bearing whorls of three round leaves, 2.5 cm (1 in.) across, with wavy pink edges. Flat clusters of small pink flowers bloom in October. The entire plant dies down in winter. *S. spathulifolium*, 7.5 to 15 cm (3 to 6 in.) high, has rosettes of 2.5 cm (1 in.) long, blue-green leaves that are often tinged with red. The 1 cm ($\frac{1}{2}$ in.) yellow flowers bloom in flat clusters, 5 to 7.5 cm (2 to 3 in.) wide, in late spring. *S. spurium*, 23 cm (9 in.) high, has oval leaves, 2.5 cm (1 in.) long, with wavy edges. Its flowers are white, pink or red, up to 1 cm ($\frac{1}{2}$ in.) across, and bloom in summer in flat, 5 to 7.5 cm (2 to 3 in.) clusters.

HOW TO GROW. These sedums are hardy over most of Europe and grow well in full sun or light shade. Plant

SAXIFRAGE
Saxifraga cotyledon

SAXIFRAGE
Saxifraga Kabschia hybrid

SAXIFRAGE
Saxifraga paniculata

STONECROP
Sedum reflexum

STONECROP
Sedum sieboldii

127

COMMON HOUSELEEK
Sempervivum tectorum

S. *spathulifolium* in light, moist humus; the other sedums will tolerate almost any well-drained soil, and even periods of drought. They spread rampantly in fertile soil, slowly in poor soil. Set out plants at any time during the growing season. Sedums do not need fertilizing. Propagate by division or from stem cuttings, which are quick to root.

SEMPERVIVUM

S. *arachnoideum* (cobweb houseleek); S. *tectorum* (common houseleek); S. hybrids.

The houseleeks are alpine perennials that grow in only a trace of soil, covering rocks and drystone walls in almost any dry, well-drained situation. Their succulent-leaved rosettes multiply almost as you watch; the mother plant is soon surrounded by numerous offshoots, giving rise to one popular name, hen-and-chickens. Houseleeks bloom in summer, but their main attraction is the colour, texture and pattern of their foliage. After flowering, the mother rosette usually dies, but the offsets continue to spread. A single rosette may form a metre-wide colony of several hundred houseleeks in only a few years. There are about 20 species and large numbers of hybrids and cultivars.

Cobweb houseleek forms a 6 to 18 mm ($\frac{1}{4}$ to $\frac{3}{4}$ in.) ball of some 50 pointed leaves draped with cobweb-like strands of white hair. The outer leaves are tinged with red. The flowers are rose-coloured and bloom in sprays of nine to 12 flowers, about 2.5 cm (1 in.) wide, on a 7.5 to 10 cm (3 to 4 in.) high stalk. The common houseleek forms 7.5 to 10 cm (3 to 4 in.) wide, flattened rosettes of wedge-shaped leaves ending in a sharp point; they are pale green tipped with purple. The 23 cm (9 in.) tall, hairy flower stalks bear sprays of star-shaped, rose-coloured flowers, 2.5 cm (1 in.) wide. Common houseleek is one of the fastest spreading species. In Europe, it is often planted on thatched or tiled roofs for insulation and as a charm against lightning. The many hybrid forms of sempervivum offer a wide range of leaf shapes, sizes and colours, including bronze-green, silver, pale green-tinted violet and jade-green.

HOW TO GROW. Houseleeks are hardy in temperate northern Europe. They grow well in full sun or partial shade. Almost any well-drained soil with a pH of 5.5 to 7.5 suits them, so long as it is not too wet. Plant them in spring, spacing them 15 to 23 cm (6 to 9 in.) apart; they will quickly fill in the gaps. Do not fertilize houseleeks. Propagate by separating offsets at any time.

SILENE

S. *alpestris*, also called *Heliosperma alpestre* (alpine catchfly); S. *maritima* (sea campion); S. *schafta*

Thriving in dry, sandy soils in open woodlands and alpine meadows, these plants provide dependable summer colour on stone walls, rocky slopes or gravelly moraines. They are perennials with soft, hairy, lance-shaped leaves and blunt-tipped flowers similar to those of the garden pink. They spread slowly from deep, fleshy roots.

Alpine catchfly is creeping in habit and forms dense mats, 15 to 30 cm (6 to 12 in.) high. It has slightly sticky leaves and stems and star-shaped, white flowers, 6 mm ($\frac{1}{4}$ in.) across, with fringed edges. These bloom in loose clusters for about a month in summer.

Sea campion forms tufts, up to 30 cm (1 ft) across, of grey-green leaves. It grows wild on rocks and cliffs by the sea and is ideal for a rock garden. Its white flowers open in late summer and autumn on 15 cm (6 in.) stems. One cultivar, 'Florepleno', has double white flowers.

S. *schafta* grows in rosettes, forming dense, 15 cm (6 in.) high tufts of light green leaves. The 2.5 to 5 cm (1 to 2 in.)

Silene schafta

wide flowers, in shades of rose and purple, appear either singly or in pairs and bloom profusely from late summer through into autumn.

HOW TO GROW. These silenes are hardy in temperate northern Europe and grow in soil with a pH of 5.5 to 7.0. Alpine catchfly grows best in sun and thrives in a deep, moist, well-drained soil. *S. schafta* and *S. maritima* will grow in sun or partial shade and prefer a deep, moist well-drained soil. All are easily grown from seed. Sow seeds in a cold frame in early spring, barely covering them with soil. Transplant seedlings when they are large enough to handle, spacing them 15 to 20 cm (6 to 8 in.) apart; or divide plants in spring. *S. schafta* may also be propagated from cuttings of young shoots, taken in summer and rooted in a cold frame in sandy soil.

T

THALICTRUM See *Anemonella*

THYMUS
T. x *citriodorus* (lemon-scented thyme); *T. praecox*, also called *T. drucei* (thyme)

The evergreen thymes are invaluable for all kinds of rock-work, in drystone walls, in pockets of the rock garden, in sink gardens and planted between paving stones in terraces and paths. They are prized for their aromatic foliage, and some, notably the lemon-scented thyme, *T.* x *citriodorus*, are classic kitchen herbs.

T. x *citriodorus* is a shrubby species, usually 23 cm (9 in.) high and spreading to 45 cm (1½ ft), with wiry stems lined with tiny, broadly ovate and dark green leaves, heavy with lemon scent. Pale lilac flower heads, composed of minute blooms, appear in profusion during the summer months. One cultivar, 'Aureus', has golden-yellow leaves and grows only 10 cm (4 in.) high. Both are suitable as ground cover.

T. praecox is probably in part evolved from the wild thyme, *T. serpyllum*. In cultivation it is represented by named cultivars, all of which grow 2.5 to 7.5 cm (1 to 3 in.) high and spread to form mats of narrow, grey-green leaves on creeping stems. In summer, terminal flowers, 1 cm (½ in.) across, are freely produced. 'Annie Hall' is pale pink; 'Coccineus', deep crimson; 'Snowdrift', pure white with lemon-scented leaves; and 'Lanuginosus' has silvery-grey, densely hairy leaves.

HOW TO GROW. Thymes are hardy in northern and temperate Europe and are among the easiest plants to grow. They thrive in full sun, preferably in a light, well-drained soil, pH 5.5 to 7.0. Plant in autumn or spring, setting plants about 30 cm (1 ft) apart. Feed once a year, in spring, with a little bone-meal scattered round the plants, and cut them back by about half annually in spring to encourage compactness and to prevent the plants from becoming leggy.

Propagate *Thymus* species by division of plants in spring or autumn or from heel cuttings taken in midsummer and rooted in a cold frame.

TRILLIUM
T. erectum; *T. grandiflorum* (wake robin); *T. ovatum*. (All called wood lily)

Trilliums are spring-blooming, moisture-loving plants native to North America. Of more than 30 species, these three are recommended for large, shady rock gardens. All trilliums grow from thick rhizomes that spread laterally just below the soil level; some produce offsets to form clumps of plants. Leaves and flowers grow from a

THYME
Thymus praecox

WOOD LILY
Trillium erectum

single stem and, as the name implies, there are three leaves per stem and each flower has three petals, three sepals and a three-celled berry.

T. erectum grows 23 to 30 cm (9 to 12 in.) high and bears reddish-brown, nodding flowers, 2.5 to 7.5 cm (1 to 3 in.) across, that look purple in some lighting but more often are closer in colour to maroon. *T. grandiflorum*, the largest of the trilliums and the easiest to grow, has pure white flowers, 7.5 cm (3 in.) across; they turn pale pink as they mature. It is somewhat taller than *T. erectum*, growing 20 to 40 cm (8 to 16 in.) high, and a single rhizome may produce up to eight stems. Its leaves are a clear deep green; in some rare forms, the flowers are double. *T. ovatum* is a smaller version of *T. grandiflorum*, up to 23 cm (9 in.) high. The pure white flowers, in early spring, are half the size and the petals are narrower; they change to pink as they age.

HOW TO GROW. Trilliums are hardy in northern and temperate Europe and thrive in a moist, well-drained, slightly acid soil that is rich in humus. For *T. erectum*, the acidity can range from pH 4.5 to 6.0; the others do best in a range of pH 6.0 to 7.0. Plant them in early autumn, setting the rhizomes 12.5 to 20 cm (5 to 8 in.) apart and 5 to 10 cm (2 to 4 in.) deep. Propagate *Trillium* species by division of the rhizomes in autumn.

TSUGA

T. canadensis 'Armistice Dwarf'; *T. canadensis* 'Cole'; *T. canadensis* 'Jervis'; *T. canadensis* 'Minima'. (All called dwarf eastern hemlock)

The dwarf eastern hemlocks include numerous named cultivars, among them some of the smallest conifers known. Eastern hemlocks are often found growing in marshy bogs, and the dwarf cultivars are suitable for similarly cool, moist, rock-garden situations. All of them have graceful, curving branches and flat, glossy, dark green needles, 9 mm ($\frac{3}{8}$ in.) long, with white bands on the underside. *T.c.* 'Armistice Dwarf' is very slow growing, eventually forming a 90 cm (3 ft) high, flat-topped mound.

T.c. 'Cole' is completely prostrate. When it is planted near a rock, the slender stems drape over and round the rough terrain, forming a broad mat 5 to 15 cm (2 to 6 in.) tall and 60 to 90 cm (2 to 3 ft) wide. In a year, its branches will spread 10 to 20 cm (4 to 8 in.) and, with age, the main branches at the centre will become bare.

T.c. 'Jervis' is a compact shrub with gnarled, short branches and needles clustered densely and irregularly along the branches, giving the plant an asymmetrical silhouette. It grows less than 2.5 cm (1 in.) a year, reaching 30 to 38 cm (1 to 1$\frac{1}{4}$ ft) in 10 years.

T.c. 'Minima' is a low, spreading shrub with tiered branches that droop at the tips so that the plant forms a softly rounded mound. It has the advantage of holding its needles for many years and thus its shape as it ages. With a maximum height of 90 cm (3 ft) and a spread of 3 metres (10 ft), it is best suited to large rock gardens.

HOW TO GROW. Dwarf eastern hemlocks are hardy in northern and temperate Europe. They grow best in light shade but will tolerate sun, and they thrive in a cool, moist, well-drained acid soil with a pH of 5.5 to 6.5. They are susceptible to damage from polluted air, summer heat and drying winter winds. Water plants deeply during droughts. Plant hemlocks in autumn or spring, preferably in a position protected from winter winds.

V

VISCARIA See *Lychnis*

DWARF EASTERN HEMLOCK
Tsuga canadensis 'Cole'

Bog and water plants

A

ACORUS

A. calamus 'Variegatus' (variegated sweet flag); *A. gramineus*

Every pool should contain a specimen of *A. calamus* 'Variegatus' for the pleasure of its green and cream variegated, iris-like foliage. The species, *A. calamus*, with plain green leaves, belongs to the arum family and has a wide distribution in Asia and Europe, including Britain. Growing 60 to 75 cm (2 to 2½ ft) high, it does best and will only flower satisfactorily in shallow water. The blooms resemble arums without the wrap-around spathes, indeed they resemble nothing as much as small cow's-horns protruding from the tops of the stems. Commonly known as sweet flag or sweet rush, the aromatic foliage was once used for strewing in churches on special occasions; the candied root was a popular sweetmeat in the 19th century. A favourite medicinal herb of the Greeks and Romans, it was at one time greatly esteemed for flavouring, and as a cure for toothache, while the powdered root is still used in tooth powders, hair tonics, and as a moth repellant. An aromatic oil distilled from the rhizomes is still used in perfumery and medicine.

A. gramineus has fine leaves like a stiff grass and grows only 20 to 30 cm (8 to 12 in.) tall. The cultivar 'Variegatus' has green and white leaves; and *A.g.* 'Pusillus' forms fans of foliage only 5 to 7.5 cm (2 to 3 in.) high. Neither of these flowers in Britain.

HOW TO GROW. All *Acorus* species and cultivars are hardy in Britain except *A. g.* 'Pusillus', which is normally used in cold-water aquaria. The other plants like a heavy loam soil, plenty of sun and shallow water.

All *Acorus* species can be propagated by dividing the plants; this should be done in spring.

ANACHARIS See *Elodea*

APONOGETON

A. distachyus (water hawthorn)

Water hawthorn is excellent for mild and temperate-climate ponds and pools with still water. Its bright green, oblong leaves, 10 cm (4 in.) or more long, float on the surface, supported by long underwater leaf stalks that rise from a fat, rounded tuber; in bright sun the leaves sometimes have maroon or purple markings. From late spring through summer, waxy, almond-scented flowers burst into bloom on V-shaped flower spikes, each fork of which is 5 to 10 cm (2 to 4 in.) long. The flowers continue to appear well into autumn and sometimes into the winter. They are normally white when they first open, with jet-black anthers, gradually turning green as they age. In shallow water, 5 to 10 cm (2 to 4 in.) deep, white flowers become tinged with red. In very mild climates, the foliage stays green all year. The plant is a perennial; it spreads moderately fast from seed in warm water, but slowly in northern Europe and may eventually cover an area 60 to 90 cm (2 to 3 ft) in diameter.

HOW TO GROW. Water hawthorn is hardy in Britain and temperate parts of northern Europe and does well in full sun. It grows best in neutral or slightly acid soil with a pH of 5.0 to 7.0. Plant the tubers in spring, setting them directly in the bottom of a pool, 15 cm (6 in.) apart, or in containers; if the pool is small, containers are preferable. Ideally, tubers should be barely covered with water

WATER HAWTHORN
Aponogeton distachyus

FLOWERING RUSH
Butomus umbellatus

WATER ARUM
Calla palustris

at the start but should eventually be 15 to 30 cm (6 to 12 in.) below the surface.

Propagate by separating offsets from the tubers or by sowing seeds as soon as they are ripe. Scatter seeds on top of 5 to 7.5 cm (2 to 3 in.) of compost in a container that will hold water, then cover the compost with 10 to 15 cm (4 to 6 in.) of water. Keep at temperatures of 13° to 16°C (55° to 60°F) until seedlings germinate. When the tubers are about pea-sized, plant them outdoors for flowering the following year. Water hawthorn can also be started by dividing old tubers but they grow very slowly.

ASTILBOIDES See *Rodgersia*

B

BUTOMUS
B. umbellatus (flowering rush)

The flowering rush is a European plant, frequently found along streams and rivers and growing in wet marshland. It has triangular, long and narrow, daffodil-like leaves, 45 to 60 cm (1½ to 2 ft) high, which are reddish when young but become mid-green with age. In summer, smooth leafless stems, 0.9 to 1.2 metres (3 to 4 ft) high, carry umbels of rosy-pink, three-petalled flowers. Each bloom is about 2.5 cm (1 in.) across. Flowering rush associates pleasingly with the blue pickerel weed, *Pontederia cordata*, and flowers about the same time. It grows from a rhizomatous rootstock and increases slowly.

HOW TO GROW. Plant the flowering rush in good loamy soil, with 5 to 10 cm (2 to 4 in.) of water above the crowns. Plants should be set about 23 cm (9 in.) apart, in early spring. In late autumn, cut back the old stems to within 15 cm (6 in.) of the base. Propagation is by dividing and replanting the rhizomes in early spring.

C

CALLA
C. palustris (water arum)

The water arum flourishes in bog gardens and shallow pools, and is a useful plant for hiding unsightly pool edges of concrete or mud. These aquatic perennials creep in and out of the water, their glossy heart-shaped leaves, up to 15 cm (6 in.) long, rising on 20 to 30 cm (8 to 12 in.) stems from long underwater rhizomes. Beginning in the second summer, numerous 5 cm (2 in.) long flowers bloom just above the leaves; each looks like a miniature calla lily, with a white, petal-like spathe surrounding a yellow, knob-shaped spadix. The latter contains the true flowers. In autumn, bright red berries cover the spadix. The water arum multiplies fairly rapidly and is often pollinated by snails that laboriously crawl up and down the stems of one flower after another, attracted by an unpleasant smell.

HOW TO GROW. Water arum is hardy in northern Europe, where it seeds naturally in certain areas. It does best in full sun, in most soil types. It needs still water; running water disturbs its roots. Set out plants in spring, in 5 to 15 cm (2 to 6 in.) of water with leaves above water level.

CALTHA
C. palustris, also called *C. polypetala* (marsh marigold, kingcup)

A good plant for stream banks and wet bog gardens, marsh marigold will also thrive in shallow water. Its hollow stems, 20 to 30 cm (8 to 12 in.) tall, bear heart-shaped leaves, 5 to 17.5 cm (2 to 7 in.) wide. In spring, clusters of cup-shaped, waxy-yellow flowers, 2.5 to 5 cm (1 to 2 in.) wide, bloom on separate stalks along the stems. One cultivar, 'Alba', has white flowers, while another, C. palustris 'Plena', bears large double flowers and is the showiest of the group. Marsh marigolds spread moderately fast and are perennial, but the entire plant dies to the ground by midsummer. Because they need wet soil only during active growth, they are excellent for gardens that are soggy in spring but dry in summer.

HOW TO GROW. Calthas are hardy in northern Europe and do best in full sun but will tolerate open shade. They thrive in moist, humus-rich, acid soil with a pH of 5.0 to 7.0. Plant in spring, spacing them 23 to 30 cm (9 to 12 in.) apart in wet ground or in 7.5 to 10 cm (3 to 4 in.) of water. During spring, keep the soil wet. Propagate by dividing root clumps in early spring or after flowering.

CRASSULA
C. recurva, also called *Tillaea recurva*

Most crassulas are fleshy succulents which appreciate warm, well-drained conditions, but there are also several true aquatic species, such as *C. recurva*. This is an excellent oxygenator and is equally useful for aquaria, shallow water and wet mud. It is perennial, with many-branched stems packed with small needle-shaped, opposite leaves. In summer, small, rather insignificant white flowers appear near the tops of the stems.

HOW TO GROW. *C. recurva* is hardy in southern England and places with a similar climate. In very cold areas, lift small portions of the plant in autumn and overwinter them in a bowl indoors. It thrives in moist soil, in full sun or light shade, and is readily propagated by dividing the fibrous-rooted clumps in spring, summer or early autumn.

CYPERUS
C. alternifolius (umbrella grass); C. haspan; C. longus; C. papyrus (papyrus, Egyptian paper rush)

The umbrella grass and papyrus are semi-aquatic plants, growing either in water or at the water's edge. Both species are tall, the umbrella grass up to 90 cm (3 ft), papyrus sometimes rising to a height of 3 metres (10 ft). There is a variegated cultivar of the umbrella grass, 'Variegatus', which is about 30 cm (1 ft) tall, and a finer-leaved cultivar, 'Gracilis', which grows 30 to 45 cm (1 to 1½ ft) tall. C. haspan looks like a miniature papyrus, growing to 60 cm (2 ft). The plants have leafless stems at the tops of which are wide-spreading clusters of leaf-like sepals and inconspicuous spikelets of flowers that change from yellow or green to light brown. C. longus, sometimes called sweet galingale, is a European species which can be invasive. The wide leaves are olive-green and ribbed and reach a height of 45 to 60 cm (1½ to 2 ft).

HOW TO GROW. *C. longus* is the only species hardy in northern Europe and may be grown in or at the edges of outdoor pools. Grow the others in pots or indoor pools in a frost-free situation in sun or partial shade. Provide water temperatures of 10° to 16°C (50° to 60°F) and depth of 7.5 cm (3 in.). Plant in heavy topsoil; in containers, use pots or tubs with widths and depths of 20 to 30 cm (8 to 12 in.).

E
EICHHORNIA
E. crassipes, also called *E. speciosa* (water hyacinth)

Decorative, ornamental floaters, water hyacinths grow in dense mats. In parts of the world, they become a menace to navigation and block tropical waterways. However,

MARSH MARIGOLD
Caltha palustris

UMBRELLA GRASS
Cyperus alternifolius

WATER HYACINTH
Eichhornia crassipes

CANADIAN PONDWEED
Elodea canadensis

one frost is sufficient to kill them, and in Britain and northern Europe, they must be kept under glass for most of the time. In warm summers only, they may be moved to an outside pool. When grown in a warm-water pool where they can be controlled, these attractive aquatic plants offer an intriguing display of lovely flowers and strange foliage. The water hyacinth grows 15 to 23 cm (6 to 9 in.) tall and ranges from 15 to 30 cm (6 to 12 in.) in diameter. The shiny, light green, oval leaves, 5 to 12.5 cm (2 to 5 in.) wide, have curiously swollen, spongy leaf stalks filled with air pockets that give the plants buoyancy; the leaves rise from a common source, in rosette formation. Delicate clusters of pale lavender flowers, 7.5 to 10 cm (3 to 4 in.) long, bloom at the ends of 15 cm (6 in.) stalks that grow from the centre of each rosette. The uppermost petal of each flower bears a distinctive, deep purple and yellow patch. The water hyacinth's feathery, purple-white roots, usually 30 to 45 cm (1 to 1½ ft) long, trail in the water and provide spawning grounds for fish.

HOW TO GROW. Water hyacinths need full sun and plenty of space. Provide 5 cm (2 in.) of rich bottom soil, a water depth of 15 to 45 cm (6 to 18 in.) and temperature of 13° to 16°C (55° to 60°F). Simply float water hyacinths on the water. Most gardeners purchase new plants each spring, but if they are packed tightly in a bowl of wet soil and kept just moist in a greenhouse for the winter, some usually survive and may be planted out the following year.

ELODEA
E. canadensis, also called *Anacharis canadensis* (Canadian pondweed); *E. crispa*, also called *Lagarosiphon major*

These plants, although rather insignificant, are nevertheless essential if garden pools are to be kept clear and fish healthy. They oxygenate the water, use up animal manures from fish, provide nesting areas for them and protect the young after their eggs hatch. Plant growth is soft, with long trails of branching, leafy and brittle stems, which are curled in the case of *E. crispa* and straight in the Canadian pondweed.

HOW TO GROW. Place two or three stems together and carefully wrap the basal ends with a strip of lead. Throw the bunches into the pool, with a water depth of 30 to 90 cm (1 to 3 ft), according to conditions, and leave the plants to adapt and increase. Remove surplus plants if necessary with a garden rake.

ERIOPHORUM
E. angustifolium; *E. latifolium*; *E. scheuchzeri*. (All called cotton grass)

Cotton grasses are plants for the bog garden or for very shallow water. All have narrow, slightly rough, grassy leaves, and in summer bear terminal heads of white, fluffy seed heads.

In *E. angustifolium* and *E. scheuchzeri*, the flower heads are compact and solitary in a single "mop head", while those of *E. latifolium* are composed of individual drooping spikelets of cotton whiteness, each set off by dark purplish-green scales. Most cotton grasses grow 30 to 45 cm (1 to 1½ ft) tall and should be grouped for maximum effect. The downy flower heads have been used for stuffing pillows and cushions.

HOW TO GROW. Provided the soil is always damp, cotton grasses will grow in shallow pools and bogs anywhere in northern Europe; they do best in slightly acid conditions.

Propagation is carried out by division of the clumps in spring, or from seed sown in pans of loam topped with 1 cm (½ in.) of water.

H

HOTTONIA

H. palustris (water violet)

The water violet is not only an efficient oxygenator which will assist in keeping pools clean but is also an attractive plant in itself. In early spring, it bears spikes of handsome, pale mauve flowers on 10 to 12.5 cm (4 to 5 in.) stems held above the water surface. These flowers are very like the wild lady's smock, *Cardamine pratensis*. After flowering, the deeply divided leaves and stems sink lower in the water, and in autumn the plants form dormant turons for overwintering as does *Stratiotes aloides*.

HOW TO GROW. Water violets have few roots and need only have their stems pushed into the mud of a shallow pool or stream. The stems can also be weighted with a strip of lead as for *Elodea*. Increase by division in spring.

HYDROCHARIS

H. morsus-ranae (frogbit)

The frogbit is a charming little European floating plant which helps to destroy algae in ornamental pools by depriving them of light. It forms rosettes of several kidney-shaped, dark green leaves, each about 4 cm (1½ in.) across, white beneath, with adhering spongy tissue which causes them to float. The small, white, three-petalled flowers appear in spring and are pollinated by insects.

HOW TO GROW. Cultivation is simple; merely drop the plants on to the surface of the pool in spring. In autumn, terminal buds appear and drop into the mud where they overwinter, and the old foliage disintegrates.

I

IRIS

I. kaempferi (Japanese iris); I. laevigata

These irises, similar in appearance, are suited to slightly different areas of the water garden. The Japanese iris thrives in bogs and does well in sites that are wet in spring and summer but dry in winter. *I. laevigata* flourishes in shallow water and is a useful plant for the edges of pools and streams. Both of these hardy perennials bloom in summer and grow up to 60 cm (2 ft) tall, with sword-like leaves that are almost identical except for the conspicuous centre rib of the Japanese iris leaf. Branching sprays of two or three large flowers dance above the foliage in summer and sometimes again in autumn. These distinctive flowers have three erect petals, called standards, and three large, outer, petal-like sepals called falls. Neither of these moisture-loving species is bearded.

Japanese iris has large flowers, 10 to 25 cm (4 to 10 in.) wide, with short standards and broad falls that resemble butterfly wings. The species has reddish-purple flowers with yellow blotches but named cultivars come with single or double flowers in blue, purple, pink and white, veined in contrasting colours. 'Hugo' is an excellent strain with 20 to 25 cm (8 to 10 in.) wide blooms whose petals are remarkably resistant to strong wind.

I. laevigata has 10 to 15 cm (4 to 6 in.) wide flowers with standards and falls of equal size. While the species has deep blue flowers with white or yellow blotches, cultivars may have all-white, rose or purple flowers, and one variegated form, 'Colchesteri', bears white-edged, blue flowers. Both these irises form clumps from fibrous roots.

HOW TO GROW. Both species are hardy in Britain. They grow best in full sun and a moist or wet, acid soil with a pH of 5.5 to 6.5; however, the roots of Japanese iris must be dry in winter. Set plants out in spring, spacing them 30 to 45 cm (1 to 1½ ft) apart. Japanese iris roots should

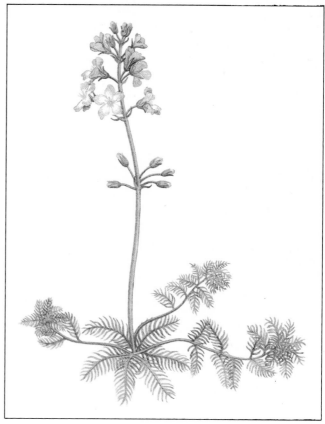

WATER VIOLET
Hottonia palustris

FROGBIT
Hydrocharis morsus-ranae

JAPANESE IRIS
Iris kaempferi

CARDINAL FLOWER
Lobelia cardinalis

be set so that their tops are 5 to 7.5 cm (2 to 3 in.) below the soil level, *I. laevigata* roots so that their tops are 5 to 7.5 cm (2 to 3 in.) below water level. Sprinkle moss peat or garden compost round the base of Japanese iris and fertilize it once a year in early spring with liquid manure. Do not fertilize *I. laevigata*. Divide plants every three or four years to prevent crowding. Propagate by dividing established plants in spring.

J

JUNCUS
J. effusus 'Spiralis' (corkscrew rush)

Rushes make up a very large plant group with round, green, pith-filled stems, usually topped with green or brown insignificant inflorescences in summer. Few are garden-worthy, but the evergreen corkscrew rush is an interesting plant with 45 cm (1½ ft) tall stems that spiral in corkscrew fashion.

HOW TO GROW. Plant the corkscrew rush in shallow water, 2.5 to 5 cm (1 to 2 in.) deep, or in wet mud, in spring. Remove any straight stems which may appear or these will take over and crowd out the twisting shoots. A heavy loam soil is ideal and fertilization is not necessary. Increase the plants by dividing the roots in early spring. They will grow in sun or shade.

L

LAGAROSIPHON See *Elodea*
LIMNANTHEMUM See *Nymphoides*

LOBELIA
L. cardinalis (cardinal flower); *L. siphilitica* (blue cardinal)

Both of these perennial *Lobelia* species grow naturally in marshy ground and are especially useful for banks of brooks and streams. They are usually 30 to 90 cm (1 to 3 ft) tall, with stiff stems and thin, serrated leaves, 5 to 10 cm (2 to 4 in.) long. Their flower spikes carry tiny tubular flowers with five lobes each; the two top lobes flare outwards like rabbit ears, while the bottom three lobes resemble a hanging lip. Cardinal flower produces 5 cm (2 in.) long, scarlet blooms from midsummer to autumn; blue cardinal bears 2.5 cm (1 in.) long, white-tipped, blue-violet flowers in midsummer. Occasionally, both species produce white-flowered forms, and one cultivar of blue cardinal has burgundy flowers.

HOW TO GROW. *L. cardinalis* is short-lived but is easily renewed each autumn from cuttings kept in a cold frame all winter. *L. siphilitica* is hardy in Britain and sheltered parts of northern Europe and may be kept all year round in shallow water. Both species do well in full sun or open shade. They do best in wet, humus-rich soil with a pH of 5.5 to 7.0. Set plants out in late spring, spacing them 20 to 30 cm (8 to 12 in.) apart. During dry periods, mulch plants to keep them moist. Propagate by dividing roots in spring or from stem cuttings.

LYSICHITUM
L. americanum, also called *L. japonicum* (yellow arum); *L. camtschatcense*

These large-flowered arums always attract attention as the blooms appear very early in spring and are bright enough to be seen from a long distance. Unfortunately, the leaves which follow are so large—60 to 90 cm (2 to 3 ft) long and 90 to 120 cm (3 to 4 ft) high—that the plants are only suitable for larger water gardens. *L. americanum* is the easier to grow. The smooth, elongated oval leaves are mid-green; its deep yellow flower spathes, up to 45 cm (1½ ft) high, enclose a green spadix. *L. camtschatcense* is similar but the blooms are white, and the overall habit smaller; it grows to a height of 60 to 90 cm (2 to 3 ft).

HOW TO GROW. These are long-lived perennials with fleshy rootstocks and need deep, humus-rich soil with plenty of moisture, such as at the edge of pools, ponds and streams. They will grow in full sun or partial shade. Plant the roots in spring, 60 cm (2 ft) apart, and fertilize occasionally if the flowers become scarce or small. Increase from seed sown as soon as it is ripe in boxes of good potting compost in shallow water, or divide the tubers in spring.

M

MENYANTHES
M. trifoliata (bogbean, buckbean)

The bogbean is a hardy perennial aquatic of creeping habit, spreading from pencil-thick, trailing rhizomes with large, smooth, trifoliate, clover-like leaves. Spikes of heavily fringed, white flowers are borne in early summer, opening from pink buds. The usual height is 23 to 30 cm (9 to 12 in.) and the plant's rambling habit makes it invaluable for masking the edges of man-made pools, as it scrambles over mud, bog or shallow water with impunity.

HOW TO GROW. The bogbean must always be kept moist, otherwise it will shrivel and die. Plant portions of rhizome 30 cm (1 ft) apart in early spring, preferably in shallow water. No fertilization is necessary. Propagate by dividing rhizomes, with a terminal or side shoot in each portion.

MIMULUS
M. cupreus; *M. luteus* (monkey musk); *M. ringens* (lavender water musk); *M. variegatus*

The monkey musk and lavender water musk are two moisture-loving, short-lived perennials, but are easily reproduced and ideal for the water garden. Blooming in mid to late summer, they provide colour at a time when the first burst of seasonal bloom is over. The monkey musk takes its name from the simian-like flowers, each 2.5 to 5 cm (1 to 2 in.) across, rich yellow and variously spotted or patterned with crimson-brown markings. It varies in height from 15 to 60 cm (6 to 24 in.), according to the warmth of the weather, and has smooth, oblong-ovate leaves. The lavender water musk grows 45 to 60 cm (1½ to 2 ft) high, the leafy stems bearing axillary, lavender-blue, tubular flowers about 18 mm (¾ in.) long.

M. cupreus, a Chilean species, allied to and, by some authorities, referred to as *M. luteus*, has a more tufted habit and makes a good rock plant for a damp situation or can be grown by the banks of a stream. It is usually represented in cultivation by such cultivars as 'Whitecroft Scarlet', 10 cm (4 in.) high and brilliant red; 'Bee's Dazzler', scarlet, 10 cm (4 in.); and 'Fireflame', red.

M. variegatus grows 30 cm (1 ft) high and is similar to *M. luteus*, but has larger, 5 cm (2 in.) flowers, particularly in cultivars such as 'Queen's Prize', gold and scarlet, and 'Bonfire', orange and scarlet.

HOW TO GROW. The monkey musk is hardy—and indeed naturalized—in Britain, requiring a damp site, such as a bog, and good loamy soil. It does best in full sun or very light shade. The lavender water musk is a true aquatic and should be planted in shallow water, 5 to 12.5 cm (2 to 5 in.) deep; it will also grow in boggy ground.

M. cupreus and *M. variegatus* will grow in light shade or full sun provided the soil is always damp. They are less hardy than the other species and it is a good idea to

YELLOW ARUM
Lysichitum americanum

BOGBEAN
Menyanthes trifoliata

137

Mimulus variegatus

LOTUS
Nelumbo nucifera

WATER LILY
Nymphaea alba

WATER LILY
Nymphaea 'Attraction'

138

overwinter a few rooted cuttings under glass or raise them from seed annually. Musks can be propagated by division of the roots in spring or from soft cuttings taken in spring and rooted in sand and peat in a cold frame.

NELUMBIUM See *Nelumbo*

N

NELUMBO

N. nucifera, also called *Nelumbium nelumbo* and *N. speciosum* (lotus, sacred lotus, Hindu lotus, sacred bean)

The stately lotus is the most exotic of all water-garden plants. It produces huge, hauntingly aromatic, 30 cm (1 ft) wide, pink, rose, yellow or white flowers, occasionally double, that open from elegantly pointed buds in mid to late summer on top of 0.9 to 2.4 metre (3 to 8 ft) stems. Each flower takes three days to open fully, opening each morning and closing each afternoon. When its petals fall, an unusual, brown, bowl-shaped seed pod is revealed, flat-topped and pierced with holes, like the nozzle of a watering can. Silvery blue-green, parasol-shaped leaves, 30 to 90 cm (1 to 3 ft) in diameter, float on the water or flare out 0.9 to 1.8 metres (3 to 6 ft) above the surface. Their waxy coating causes raindrops to slide off like quicksilver. Lotuses grow from brittle, banana-shaped tubers that send out lateral runners when grown in warm climates. Unless they are planted in large pools, lotuses should be confined to containers.

HOW TO GROW. Lotuses are not hardy in northern Europe but may be grown in tubs moved indoors for the winter or in heated indoor pools; they will only survive the winter outdoors where their roots do not freeze. The plants do best in full sun and for good bloom require water temperatures of 16° to 21°C (60° to 70°F). For container-grown plants, use large tubs filled with heavy garden soil preferably mixed with ¼ part clay and commercial fertilizer recommended for aquatic plants. Moisten the soil thoroughly, make a shallow depression, and place the tuber in it, taking care not to touch the growing tip. Cover it with about 2.5 cm (1 in.) of soil, leaving about 1 cm (½ in.) of the growing tip exposed. Top with 2.5 cm (1 in.) of sand. Submerge the container in 5 cm (2 in.) of water; as the plant grows, gradually lower it to a depth of 15 to 30 cm (6 to 12 in.).

Feed lotuses with aquatic fertilizer every month during the growing season. During the winter, protect lotuses by bringing them indoors to a well-ventilated spot where the temperature remains between 2° and 7°C (35° and 45°F), keeping the soil thoroughly moist. Alternatively, cover the tubs with wood or canvas, topped with a 7.5 cm (3 in.) layer of straw or leaves, when conditions are cold. Every two years, dig up container-grown plants in spring; cut away old sections and replant healthy portions with several growing tips attached.

WATER LILY
Nymphaea 'Director George T. Moore'

NYMPHAEA

N. alba; *N. colorata*, also called *N. polychroma*; *N.* hardy hybrids; *N.* tropical hybrids. (All called water lily)

There are hardy water lilies and tender water lilies, the former generally frost-hardy in the British Isles and over most of northern Europe, the latter frost-tender and accordingly less common in Europe. Both groups have been hybridized into many forms, sizes and colours. There are pygmy water lilies 5 cm (2 in.) across, and giant types with 35 cm (14 in.) flowers. The blooms, which are cup-shaped or star-shaped, usually last for three or four days

WATER LILY
Nymphaea 'Comanche'

WATER LILY
Nymphaea 'Emily Grant Hutchings'

and come in shades and combinations of pink, yellow, apricot, red, lavender, purple, blue and white. The leaves, called lily pads, range in width from 5 to 45 cm (2 to 18 in.) and may be round, indented or heart-shaped. Though normally green, they may in some cultivars be reddish-brown or purple, and they are often streaked or speckled with contrasting colours.

Hardy lilies bloom only in the daytime. The most common European species is *N. alba*, a fine white water lily capable of growing in very deep water, 1.5 metres (5 ft) or more. The best depth for most of the hybrids is 45 to 60 cm (1½ to 2 ft), for this rarely freezes solid in British winters. There are countless kinds for such depths, including a double cream, 'Gloire de Temple-sur-Lot', semi-doubles such as the white 'Gonnère', as well as others in pink, red, vermilion, yellow, orange-red and cream. All hardy lilies are perennial and will last for several years without need for division. There are also smaller hybrids, such as the *N.* x *laydekeri* group, suitable for tub culture or 30 cm (1 ft) deep pools; these may have to be protected with boards covered with sacking or straw in very severe winters. The pygmy hybrids, from 7.5 to 23 cm (3 to 9 in.), should be overwintered indoors.

Among the best of the hardy lilies are 'Attraction', the largest of all red water lilies, with flowers up to 25 cm (10 in.) across; 'Chromatella' and 'Moorei', both with 10 to 12.5 cm (4 to 5 in.) chrome-yellow flowers; 'Comanche', the largest of what are often called the changeables; i.e. its 12.5 cm (5 in.) blooms open as apricot-rose and gradually darken to a deep coppery-bronze; 'Paul Hariot', whose 10 cm (4 in.) blooms open as light yellow with pink overtones and darken to reddish-orange; 'Sunrise', with 20 to 23 cm (8 to 9 in.), sulphur-yellow flowers and olive-green leaves marked for two days with maroon; 'Rose Arey', rose pink and very prolific; 'James Brydon', red and free-flowering with cup-shaped flowers; 'Virginalis', white; and 'Escarboucle', ruby-red. The smaller types include *N.* x *laydekeri* 'Fulgens', dark crimson; *N.* x *laydekeri* 'Lilacea', rosy-crimson; *N. odorata*, white; and *N. odorata* 'Sulphurea', soft yellow. The pygmies may be pure white with plain green leaves or soft yellow with chocolate-blotched foliage.

Tropical lilies are sub-divided into day-blooming and night-blooming types. The petals of the latter are often fewer and much broader than those of the day bloomers. They are generally grown as annuals and replaced each year. Hardy lilies bloom throughout the summer, bearing the flowers at water level on short stalks or just above the surface. Tropical lilies bloom from summer well into the autumn, bearing their flowers on stalks that rise 15 to 45 cm (6 to 18 in.) above the surface of the water. Their flowers tend to be more waxy than those of hardy lilies, and their leaves are more prominently marked. Even when they are grown in containers, they spread rapidly to cover wider areas than the hardy lilies.

In the category of tropical day-blooming lilies, the most popular cultivars include 'Director George T. Moore', whose deep blue-purple flowers, 20 to 25 cm (8 to 10 in.) across, are remarkable for the rarity of their colour, and 'General Pershing', a very fragrant lily with 20 to 25 cm (8 to 10 in.) wide pale pink flowers. Other day-blooming tropicals with large blooms are 'Mrs G. H. Pring', pure white; 'Pink Platter', lilac; 'Aviator Pring', rich yellow; 'Blue Beauty', deep blue; and 'Panama Pacific', a changeable type which opens wine-blue and develops to royal purple. Among smaller versions is *N. colorata*, whose 10 cm (4 in.) flowers are bright blue tinged with mauve.

Night-blooming tropical water lilies, which open at dusk and tend to remain open until the following noon, are as a group larger than their day-blooming relatives. Among recommended cultivars, all with 23 to 30 cm (9 to 12 in.) flowers, are 'Emily Grant Hutchings', a pink lily; 'H. C. Haarstick', vivid red shading to pink with bronze-red leaves; 'Missouri', a very large white; and 'Evelyn Randig', fire-engine red.

HOW TO GROW. In Mediterranean Europe, hardy and tropical water lilies can be grown together in the same pool. Hardy lilies survive the winter in such climates, while tropical lilies are considered annuals. They all need five to eight hours of sun a day and grow best with a southern exposure. Still water is essential and, for tropical water lilies, water temperatures should not drop below 21°C (70°F); hardy lilies will flower at temperatures somewhat lower, about 16°C (60°F). The best planting medium is a heavy fibre-free topsoil enriched with one-sixth of its bulk of well-decayed manure or two handfuls of bone-meal.

Set out hardy lilies in April or May when water temperatures are between 10° and 13°C (50° and 55°F); for tropical lilies, wait until water temperatures have risen to 21°C (70°F). Plant them in aquatic baskets with holes round the sides, setting the rhizomes or rootstocks just beneath the surface of the soil, with their bud tips exposed. Allow enough space between plants to accommodate their eventual sizes. A medium-sized water lily is about 90 cm (3 ft) in diameter; giant water lilies spread to fill an area 1.8 to 2.7 metres (6 to 9 ft) across. Cover the newly planted stock with water appropriate to its stage of growth. If growth has barely begun, the plants should be covered with only a few centimetres of water so that sunlight can reach the young buds. Once growth is established, lower the plant to its normal growing depth. Some types of water lilies do well in very shallow or very deep water, but hardy lilies in general need 30 to 45 cm (1 to 1½ ft) of water above them and tropical lilies need 15 to 30 cm (6 to 12 in.).

Remove decaying foliage regularly and trim off faded flowers. In areas where winters are severe, cover the pool with a framework of laths and plastic netting or boards and a layer of sacking, leaving an air space on the south edge if there are fish in the pool. Or move shallow-water plants and their containers indoors, wrapping the containers in moist sacking and then plastic film to retain moisture. Store in a cool place.

To propagate hardy lilies, wash soil off the roots to locate the growing tips; cut roots into 15 to 20 cm (6 to 8 in.) sections and replant. Most gardeners divide roots in spring or late summer. Propagating tropical lilies generally requires a greenhouse and plants are usually purchased new each season.

WATER FRINGE
Nymphoides peltata

NYMPHOIDES

N. peltata, also called *Limnanthemum peltatum* and *L. nymphoides* (water fringe, floating heart)

The water fringe is hardy and can be grown outdoors in Britain and over most of northern Europe. The leaves are dainty, crinkly-edged and heavily mottled with chocolate brown so that they look slightly like pygmy water lily leaves. The golden flowers have fringed petals and appear in small clusters in the leaf axils. Under good conditions, this is a vigorous plant, producing long stems that snake their way along the top of the water. It is easily kept in check by raking out unwanted growth.

HOW TO GROW. Push small pieces of rooted growth down into the soil in spring and let nature do the rest. Slightly acid water suits the plant best, in full sun or light shade. It is a good subject for casting shade, thereby keeping down algae growth and protecting fish in hot weather.

GOLDEN CLUB
Orontium aquaticum

PICKEREL WEED
Pontederia cordata

O

ORONTIUM
O. aquaticum (golden club)

The golden club is a handsome member of the arum family which can be grown under two entirely different conditions. In deep water, 30 cm (1 ft) or more, it produces oblong floating leaves with a waxy upper surface which repels water. When grown in shallow water, a few centimetres deep, the golden club produces much larger, bluish-green leaves on 45 cm (1½ ft) high stems. It has small yellow flowers closely packed at the tops of white, pencil-like stems, which bear a close resemblance to the interior of a calla lily without the white spathe wrapping.

HOW TO GROW. The golden club is hardy in Britain and over much of northern Europe. It does best in a sunny situation planted in rich loamy soil. It can be propagated by division of the tubers in spring.

P

PISTIA
P. stratiotes (water lettuce)

Water lettuce is a tender, free-floating, aquatic perennial. In the wild, these heat-loving plants are found in quiet ponds and streams, but they will also flourish in warm-water indoor pools. Water lettuce is grown for its iridescent blue-green foliage rather than for its inconspicuous green flowers. The velvety, heavily veined leaves form rosettes 15 cm (6 in.) wide, from which long, slender, hair-like roots dangle in the water. When restricted, the plants will take root in soil, but as a rule they stay on the surface and spread lateral runners.

HOW TO GROW. Water lettuce requires water temperatures of 21° to 27°C (70° to 80°F) and thus grows permanently only in Mediterranean outdoor pools or in aquaria in northern Europe. The plants grow best when they are shaded from direct sun at midday. To plant, simply float water lettuce on the surface of the water at a temperature around 21°C (70°F). The plants require no further attention. To propagate, detach and float the small plants on the lateral runners.

PONTEDERIA
P. cordata (pickerel weed)

In shallow streams throughout the eastern half of the United States of America, pickerel weed grows wild, its forest of sturdy stems providing a hiding place for young pike (pickerels), the fish that give it its common name. In the garden, pickerel weed is suitable for similar situations but it will also grow in boggy soil at the water's edge. One of the most handsome of aquatic plants, its dark green, heart-shaped leaves, 25 cm (10 in.) long and 15 cm (6 in.) wide, sheathe stems that rise 30 to 120 cm (1 to 4 ft) tall. In summer and autumn, it bears dense, 7.5 to 10 cm (3 to 4 in.) spikes of orchid-like, blue-violet flowers. The plant spreads by means of rhizomes and in Europe rarely becomes a nuisance.

HOW TO GROW. Pickerel weed is hardy in Britain and over most of northern Europe. It needs slow-moving or still, shallow water, 15 cm (6 in.) deep. In spring, plant rhizomes on the surface of the soil; cover them with a stone until they have rooted. To propagate, divide rhizomes at any time during the growing season.

PRIMULA
P. beesiana; *P. bulleyana*; *P. florindae*; *P. frondosa*; *P. japonica* (Japanese primrose); *P. pulverulenta*

All primulas need moisture to some degree but the species described here have a special affinity for it and are widely used along the waterside. *P. frondosa*, an alpine plant, is also suitable for scree gardens. All are alike in being perennial, with oval, coarse-textured leaves and flowers that bloom in clusters, 5 to 15 cm (2 to 6 in.) wide. Most have light green leaves and produce their flower clusters in candelabra-like tiers along tall stems, but the low-growing *P. frondosa*'s blooms rest against its rosette of ground-hugging, grey-green foliage. *P. beesiana* grows 45 to 60 cm (1½ to 2 ft) tall, with 20 cm (8 in.) long leaves; its 18 mm (¾ in.) flowers are rose-lilac with yellow centres and bloom in early summer. *P. bulleyana* also flowers in early summer and is 45 to 60 cm (1½ to 2 ft) tall; its leaves are up to 30 cm (1 ft) long and its 18 mm (¾ in.) flowers come in hues of pink, white, purple, orange and red. *P. florindae* is like a giant yellow cowslip, with umbels of nodding fragrant flowers on 30 to 38 cm (1 to 1¼ ft) stems. *P. frondosa* grows only 5 to 12.5 cm (2 to 5 in.) tall with 10 cm (4 in.) leaves and 1 cm (½ in.) rose-purple flowers with yellow centres. It blooms in spring. *P. japonica* reaches a height of 75 cm (2½ ft) and bears several whorls of 2.5 cm (1 in.) white, pink, red or blue flowers from late spring until early summer. *P. pulverulenta* has flowers of fairy-like daintiness on 60 to 90 cm (2 to 3 ft) stems; they are borne in whorls, with particularly fine shades of pink in *P. p.* 'Bartley Strain'. Primulas have deep taproots, spread rapidly and often seed themselves.

HOW TO GROW. These primulas are hardy in temperate areas of northern Europe. All do best in areas with cool, moist summers and prefer partial shade, but *P. japonica* can also tolerate some sun. They need a wet, well-drained, gritty, acid soil with a pH of 5.0 to 6.0, supplemented with moss peat or leaf-mould. Set out plants in spring, spacing them 15 to 30 cm (6 to 12 in.) apart. Keep moist at all times. In late autumn, cover plants in doubtfully hardy areas with a light mulch of dry leaves or straw. Propagate by dividing plant clumps after flowering or by removing and planting offshoots. New plants are also easily started from seed sown in autumn as soon as they are ripe and kept over winter in a cold frame. Transplant to the garden the following spring. In mild climates, *P. japonica* may act as a biennial, dying after two years; for a constant supply of flowers, sow seed every year. All primulas need to be divided every two or three years to prevent overcrowding.

R

RODGERSIA
R. aesculifolia; *R. pinnata*; *R. tabularis*, also called *Astilboides tabularis*

Rodgersias are hardy herbaceous plants with plumes of spiraea-like flowers and striking foliage. In *R. aesculifolia* the leaves are divided like those of a huge horse-chestnut, and have a glossy bronze finish. Pink and white flowers, in 30 to 45 cm (1 to 1½ ft) plumes, are borne in summer. The plant grows about 90 cm (3 ft) or more high. *R. pinnata* is slightly smaller, but also with deeply cut, bronzed leaves. Many-branched sprays, up to 30 cm (1 ft) long, of white, pink or red blooms occur in midsummer. *R. tabularis*, 90 cm (3 ft) tall, has round, umbrella-shaped leaves, up to 90 cm (3 ft) across; creamy-white flowers in 20 cm (8 in.) long panicles are produced in summer.

HOW TO GROW. Rodgersias should be planted where they can be sheltered from hot sun and strong winds, both of which ruin the foliage. They are suitable for semi-shaded positions in the bog garden. Plant in spring, about 75 cm (2½ ft) apart, in moist, loamy soil, with added decayed garden compost or leaf-mould. Propagate by divi-

JAPANESE PRIMROSE
Primula japonica

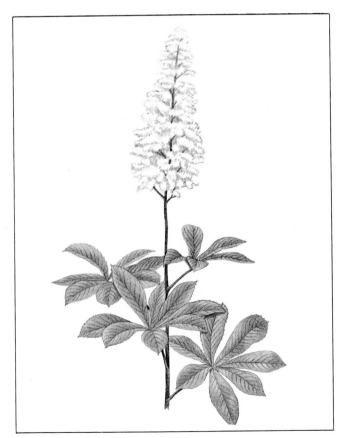

Rodgersia aesculifolia

ARROWHEAD
Sagittaria sagittifolia

sion in spring, or from seed sown in spring and kept in a cold frame to germinate. Pot the seedlings as necessary, but keep them in a frame until the second season before planting them out.

S

SAGITTARIA
S. sagittifolia (arrowhead)

This tall, aquatic perennial derives its name from the distinctive shape of the above-water leaves. (At water level, the leaves are oval, and foliage growing under water is slender and ribbon-like.) The species grows in ponds and slow-moving streams in Europe, including Britain. It reaches a height of 45 to 60 cm (1½ to 2 ft), with 5 to 20 cm (2 to 8 in.) aerial leaves. Its whorls of 2.5 cm (1 in.) wide, white flowers with green or yellow centres bloom in late summer. Because of its invasive hold, the species is less popular in gardens than the subspecies *S. s. leucopetala*, often sold as *S. japonica*, which has flowers up to 5 cm (2 in.) across and bolder foliage. The cultivar 'Flore Pleno' is particularly outstanding with large, double white flowers in spikes that resemble double stocks.

HOW TO GROW. Arrowheads require full sun and should be planted in early spring. Push the tuberous roots 5 to 7.5 cm (2 to 3 in.) deep into the mud at the edge of the pond or into the bottom soil of the pool, spacing them 30 to 38 cm (1 to 1¼ ft) apart. In containers, plant them 5 to 7.5 cm (2 to 3 in.) deep in 15 to 20 cm (6 to 8 in.) of heavy garden loam topped with 2.5 cm (1 in.) of sand; submerge them in 5 to 15 cm (2 to 6 in.) of water.

If arrowheads become invasive or crowded, lift tubers and trim them. Propagate by division in early spring.

STRATIOTES
S. aloides (water soldier)

The water soldier spends its life hovering between various depths of water, but is normally completely submerged. In late summer, when the three-petalled white flowers appear, the plant rises to the top of the water and the blooms and tips of its leaves become visible. The blooms are pollinated by insects, male and female flowers, identical in shape, being carried on separate plants. Overall, the plant looks like the top of a pineapple with rosettes of spiky leaves spreading almost 30 cm (1 ft) across. Later, as summer advances, the leaves tend to silt up with dust and other debris and sink to the bottom of the pool, where they disintegrate. Small winter buds, called turons, develop and remain in the mud until the next spring, when they start to grow into new plants.

HOW TO GROW. Simply drop the plant on the surface of the pool. It is hardy in Britain and over most of northern Europe, the turons ensuring its survival through winter. Small plantlets develop at the sides of mature specimens and can be detached if new stock is required; left alone they increase naturally.

T

TILLAEA See *Crassula*

TROLLIUS
T. europaeus; *T. laxus*, also called *T. americanus*. (All called globe flower)

Trollius are hardy perennials for moist sites, such as borders of water gardens or damp herbaceous borders.

WATER SOLDIER
Stratiotes aloides

T. europaeus grows wild as far north as arctic Lapland and is fully hardy in northern Europe. Its flowers resemble those of the buttercup, but are larger, 2.5 to 4 cm (1 to 1½ in.) across. Each flower is composed of five or six spreading, yellow or yellow-green sepals, surrounding a cluster of much more numerous petals that form a globe-shaped centre. There are many hybrids with pale to deep yellow-orange flowers, popular cultivars being 'Canary Bird', 'Orange Princess' and 'Golden Wonder'; all have buttercup-like blooms. *T. laxus* grows up to 60 cm (2 ft) high from a thick, fibrous root and has deeply cut leaves, 7.5 to 12.5 cm (3 to 5 in.) wide, with serrated edges. It blooms in spring with yellow flowers similar to those of *T. europaeus*.

HOW TO GROW. Globe flowers need a constantly moist, humus-enriched soil with a pH of 6.0 to 7.0. Plant sections of root 30 cm (1 ft) apart in spring or autumn. Propagate in spring by dividing roots of established plants, or start new plants from seed in a shady seedbed, transplanting them to the garden when they are large enough to handle.

TYPHA

T. angustifolia; *T. minima*, also called *T. gracilis*. (Both called reedmace)

Reedmaces, often but erroneously known in Britain as bulrushes, with their rigid, poker-shaped heads much used in dried arrangements, grow freely in swamps, marshes and bogs. The wild plant is *T. latifolia*, an invasive species which should never be planted in ornamental pools. One species, *T. minima*, which grows about 60 cm (2 ft) high, is suitable for tub culture or small pools. The best, however, is *T. angustifolia*, which has very narrow leaves. It is suitable for large ponds and lakes and usually becomes 0.6 to 1.5 metres (2 to 5 ft) tall. It develops stiff, green, strap-like leaves, 45 to 60 cm (1½ to 2 ft) in length and about 1 cm (½ in.) in width. They are frequently used in chair caning and basket weaving. The cylindrical, brown flower heads, borne in summer at the ends of sword-like stalks, measure from 1 to 4 cm (½ to 1½ in.) in diameter and 15 to 20 cm (6 to 8 in.) in length.

HOW TO GROW. Typhas are hardy in northern Europe. To keep them under control, plant short pieces of rhizome with young shoots attached in early spring in tubs or, alternatively, portion off a section of the pool with a retainer to keep them within bounds. They do best submerged in 5 to 12.5 cm (2 to 5 in.) of water. They require no further care except to remove the poker heads prior to ripening to prevent indiscriminate seeding and spreading.

GLOBE FLOWER
Trollius laxus

REEDMACE
Typha angustifolia

Characteristics of 198 rock-garden plants

	PLANT HEIGHT				LIGHT NEEDS			GROWTH HABIT			SPECIAL TRAITS				FLOWER COLOUR				FLOWERING SEASON			SOIL NEEDS		
	Under 15 cm (6 in.)	15 to 30 cm (6 to 12 in.)	30 to 90 cm (1 to 3 ft)	Over 90 cm (3 ft)	Shade	Partial shade	Full sun	Upright	Spreading	Trailing	Flowers	Distinctive foliage	Evergreen	Decorative fruit	White to green	Yellow to orange	Pink to red	Blue to purple	Spring	Summer	Autumn	Acid	Neutral	Alkaline
ACHILLEA CHRYSOCOMA		•				•	•	•			•	•				•				•			•	
ACHILLEA TOMENTOSA (woolly yarrow)		•					•				•		•			•				•			•	
AJUGA PYRAMIDALIS (ajuga)	•					•	•		•		•	•					•	•	•				•	
AJUGA REPTANS (bugle)	•					•	•		•		•	•					•	•	•				•	
ALLIUM BEESIANUM		•				•	•				•						•	•	•			•	•	
ALLIUM MOLY		•				•	•				•					•			•	•			•	
ALLIUM TUBEROSUM		•				•	•				•				•	•	•			•	•		•	
ALYSSUM MONTANUM	•						•		•	•	•					•			•				•	
ALYSSUM SAXATILE (gold dust)		•					•		•	•	•					•			•				•	
ALYSSUM SPINOSUM		•					•		•	•	•		•	•			•		•				•	
ANACYCLUS DEPRESSUS (Atlas daisy)	•						•		•		•	•			•		•		•				•	
ANDROSACE CARNEA (rock jasmine)	•					•	•				•				•		•		•			•	•	
ANDROSACE SARMENTOSA (rock jasmine)	•					•	•	•			•						•		•			•	•	
ANEMONE APENNINA	•					•					•						•	•	•			•	•	
ANEMONE BLANDA	•					•					•						•	•	•			•	•	
ANEMONE NEMOROSA (wood anemone)		•				•					•				•				•			•	•	
ANEMONELLA THALICTROIDES (rue anemone)	•		•		•				•		•	•			•		•		•			•		
AQUILEGIA BERTOLONII (columbine)	•					•					•		•				•	•	•			•	•	
AQUILEGIA CANADENSIS (columbine)		•	•			•					•		•		•	•	•		•			•	•	
AQUILEGIA FLABELLATA (columbine)		•	•			•					•		•	•			•		•			•	•	
AQUILEGIA SCOPULORUM (columbine)	•	•				•					•					•	•		•			•	•	
ARABIS ALPINA		•				•	•	•	•		•	•			•		•		•			•	•	
ARABIS CAUCASICA (wall rock cress)		•				•	•	•	•		•				•		•		•			•	•	
ARABIS FERDINANDI-COBURGII		•				•	•	•	•		•				•				•				•	
ARCTOSTAPHYLOS UVA-URSI (bearberry)	•					•	•		•		•	•	•	•	•		•		•			•		
ARENARIA GRANDIFLORA (sandwort)	•					•	•	•			•				•				•	•		•		
ARENARIA MONTANA (sandwort)	•	•				•			•	•	•				•				•			•		
ARISAEMA CANDIDISSIMUM			•			•		•			•			•	•		•		•			•		
ARISAEMA DRACONTIUM (green dragon)		•				•		•			•			•	•				•			•		
ARISAEMA SIKOKIANUM		•				•		•			•			•			•	•	•			•		
ARISAEMA TRIPHYLLUM (Jack-in-the-pulpit)		•				•		•			•			•	•		•		•			•		
ARMERIA JUNIPERIFOLIA (juniper thrift)	•						•		•		•		•				•		•	•			•	
ARMERIA MARITIMA (thrift)	•	•					•		•		•		•				•	•	•				•	
ARTEMISIA SCHMIDTIANA 'NANA'	•					•	•	•	•		•	•			•	•			•				•	
ASARUM CANADENSE (wild ginger)	•		•		•	•					•				•	•	•		•			•	•	
ASARUM CAUDATUM (wild ginger)		•			•	•				•	•				•	•	•		•			•	•	
ASARUM EUROPAEUM (wild ginger)	•		•		•	•				•	•		•		•	•	•		•			•	•	
ASPERULA GUSSONII (woodruff)	•					•	•				•				•		•		•				•	
ASPERULA ODORATA (sweet woodruff)		•				•	•		•		•		•				•	•				•	
ASPERULA SUBEROSA (woodruff)	•					•	•				•						•		•				•	
ASTER ALPINUS (alpine aster)	•					•	•	•			•						•		•	•			•	
ASTER NATALENSIS	•					•	•	•			•						•	•		•			•	
ASTER TIBETICUS	•					•	•	•			•						•	•		•			•	
AUBRIETA DELTOIDEA	•						•		•	•	•						•	•	•	•				•
BELLIS PERENNIS (common daisy)	•					•	•				•		•		•		•		•	•			•	
BELLIS ROTUNDIFOLIA 'COERULESCENS'	•					•	•				•						•	•	•				•	
BRUCKENTHALIA SPICULIFOLIA (spike heath)		•				•	•		•		•	•	•				•			•		•		
CALLIRHOË INVOLUCRATA (wine-cup)	•						•		•	•	•						•		•	•			•	
CALLUNA VULGARIS (heather)	•	•	•			•	•		•		•	•	•		•		•			•	•	•		
CAMPANULA CARPATICA (Carpathian bell flower)	•	•				•		•			•				•			•		•	•		•	

Species	PLANT HEIGHT				LIGHT NEEDS			GROWTH HABIT			SPECIAL TRAITS				FLOWER COLOUR				FLOWERING SEASON			SOIL NEEDS		
	Under 15 cm (6 in.)	15 to 30 cm (6 to 12 in.)	30 to 90 cm (1 to 3 ft)	Over 90 cm (3 ft)	Shade	Partial shade	Full sun	Upright	Spreading	Trailing	Flowers	Distinctive foliage	Evergreen	Decorative fruit	White to green	Yellow to orange	Pink to red	Blue to purple	Spring	Summer	Autumn	Acid	Neutral	Alkaline
CAMPANULA COCHLEARIIFOLIA	•						•		•		•							•		•	•		•	
CAMPANULA GARGANICA	•						•		•		•							•		•	•	•		
CAMPANULA ROTUNDIFOLIA (harebell)		•					•	•	•		•	•						•		•	•	•		
CAMPANULA ZOYSII	•						•		•		•							•		•	•	•		
CERASTIUM TOMENTOSUM (snow-in-summer)	•					•	•		•		•	•	•		•					•			•	
CERATOSTIGMA PLUMBAGINOIDES (leadwort)		•				•	•		•		•	•	•					•		•	•		•	
CHAMAECYPARIS LAWSONIANA 'MINIMA AUREA' (false cypress)		•				•	•					•	•										•	
CHAMAECYPARIS OBTUSA 'NANA' (Hinoki false cypress)	•					•	•					•	•										•	
CHAMAECYPARIS OBTUSA 'NANA GRACILIS' (Hinoki false cypress)			•				•					•	•										•	
CHAMAECYPARIS OBTUSA 'PYGMAEA' (Hinoki false cypress)		•					•					•	•										•	
CHAMAECYPARIS PISIFERA 'COMPACTA' (Sawara false cypress)			•				•					•	•										•	
CHAMAECYPARIS PISIFERA 'PLUMOSA COMPACTA' (Sawara false cypress)		•					•					•	•										•	
CHRYSOGONUM VIRGINIANUM	•					•			•		•					•			•	•			•	
CLEMATIS ALPINA (alpine clematis)			•			•	•			•	•						•	•	•				•	•
CORYDALIS CASHMERIANA		•				•	•	•			•						•	•	•			•	•	
CORYDALIS LUTEA			•			•	•	•			•					•			•	•			•	•
CORYDALIS SOLIDA		•				•	•	•			•			•			•	•	•				•	•
CROCUS CHRYSANTHUS	•					•	•	•			•	•				•			•			•	•	
CROCUS SPECIOSUS	•					•	•	•			•							•		•	•	•	•	
CROCUS TOMASINIANUS	•					•	•	•			•						•	•				•	•	
CRYPTOMERIA JAPONICA 'GLOBOSA NANA' (dwarf Japanese cedar)		•				•	•					•	•										•	
CRYPTOMERIA JAPONICA 'LOBBII NANA' (dwarf Japanese cedar)		•				•	•					•	•										•	
CRYPTOMERIA JAPONICA 'VILMORINIANA' (dwarf Japanese cedar)		•				•	•					•	•										•	
CYTISUS DECUMBENS (prostrate broom)		•					•		•	•	•		•			•				•		•	•	•
CYTISUS X KEWENSIS (Kew broom)			•				•	•	•	•	•		•			•			•	•		•	•	•
DAPHNE ARBUSCULA (daphne)	•					•	•		•		•		•				•		•				•	
DAPHNE BLAGAYANA (daphne)		•				•	•		•		•		•		•				•				•	
DAPHNE CNEORUM (garland flower)		•				•	•		•		•		•				•		•				•	
DAPHNE PETRAEA (daphne)	•					•	•		•		•		•				•		•				•	•
DAPHNE RETUSA (daphne)		•				•	•		•		•		•				•	•	•				•	
DIANTHUS ALPINUS (alpine pink)	•					•	•	•			•	•					•	•		•			•	•
DICENTRA CANADENSIS (squirrel corn)		•				•		•			•				•			•	•	•			•	
DICENTRA CUCULLARIA (Dutchman's-breeches)		•				•		•			•				•	•		•	•	•			•	
DICENTRA EXIMIA (fringed bleeding heart)		•				•	•		•		•						•	•	•	•			•	
DICENTRA FORMOSA		•				•	•		•		•						•		•	•			•	
DRABA MOLLISSIMA	•						•	•			•					•			•				•	
DRABA RIGIDA	•						•		•	•	•					•			•				•	
DRABA SIBIRICA	•						•		•		•					•			•		•		•	
DRYAS OCTOPETALA (mountain avens)	•					•	•		•		•	•	•		•				•				•	
DRYAS X SUENDERMANNII	•					•	•		•		•	•	•	•	•				•				•	
EDRAIANTHUS PUMILIO	•						•		•	•	•	•					•	•		•			•	
EDRAIANTHUS SERPYLLIFOLIUS	•						•		•	•	•	•						•		•			•	
EDRAIANTHUS TENUIFOLIUS	•						•		•	•	•	•						•		•			•	
EPIMEDIUM GRANDIFLORUM (bishop's hat)		•			•	•		•			•	•			•		•	•	•			•	•	
ERICA CARNEA (heath)		•				•	•	•			•		•				•	•	•	•	•	•	•	
ERICA TETRALIX (cross-leaved heath)		•				•	•	•			•		•				•	•		•	•	•		
ERICA VAGANS (Cornish heath)			•			•	•	•			•		•				•	•		•	•	•		
ERIGERON AUREUS (fleabane)	•						•	•			•					•				•			•	
ERIGERON COMPOSITUS (fleabane)	•						•	•	•		•				•			•	•	•			•	
ERIGERON UNIFLORUS (fleabane)	•						•	•	•		•				•			•	•	•			•	

Column groups: **PLANT HEIGHT** (Under 15 cm / 15 to 30 cm / 30 to 90 cm / Over 90 cm) · **LIGHT NEEDS** (Shade / Partial shade / Full sun) · **GROWTH HABIT** (Upright / Spreading / Trailing) · **SPECIAL TRAITS** (Flowers / Distinctive foliage / Evergreen / Decorative fruit) · **FLOWER COLOUR** (White to green / Yellow to orange / Pink to red / Blue to purple) · **FLOWERING SEASON** (Spring / Summer / Autumn) · **SOIL NEEDS** (Acid / Neutral / Alkaline)

Plant	U15	15-30	30-90	O90	Shade	Part	Sun	Upr	Spr	Trl	Flw	Fol	Evg	Frt	Wht	Yel	Pnk	Blu	Spr	Sum	Aut	Aci	Neu	Alk
ERYTHRONIUM AMERICANUM (fawn lily)		●				●		●			●	●			●			●	●			●	●	
ERYTHRONIUM DENS-CANIS (dog's-tooth violet)		●				●		●			●	●				●	●	●	●			●	●	
ERYTHRONIUM HENDERSONII		●				●		●			●						●	●	●			●	●	
ERYTHRONIUM REVOLUTUM		●				●		●			●	●		●			●	●	●			●	●	
GENTIANA ACAULUS	●					●		●			●							●		●		●	●	
GENTIANA FARRERI	●					●		●					●					●		●	●	●	●	
GENTIANA SEPTEMFIDA			●			●		●					●					●		●		●	●	
GENTIANA SINO-ORNATA	●					●		●					●					●			●	●	●	
GENTIANA VERNA (spring gentian)	●					●		●			●							●	●			●	●	
GERANIUM DALMATICUM (crane's-bill)	●					●	●		●		●						●			●		●	●	
GERANIUM RENARDII (crane's-bill)		●				●	●		●		●						●	●		●		●	●	
GERANIUM SANGUINEUM (crane's-bill)		●				●	●		●		●						●	●		●		●	●	
GERANIUM SANGUINEUM var. PROSTATUM (crane's-bill)	●					●	●		●		●						●			●		●	●	
GEUM COCCINEUM (avens)		●					●	●			●					●	●		●	●		●	●	
GEUM REPTANS (avens)	●						●	●			●				●		●		●	●		●	●	
GYPSOPHILA CERASTIOIDES	●						●		●	●	●				●		●		●	●				●
GYPSOPHILA REPENS	●						●		●	●	●				●		●			●				●
GYPSOPHILA TENUIFOLIA	●						●		●		●						●			●	●			●
HELIANTHEMUM NUMMULARIUM (rock rose)		●					●		●		●		●		●	●	●			●		●	●	
HEPATICA NOBILIS	●				●	●		●			●		●		●		●	●	●			●		
HEPATICA TRANSSYLVANICA	●				●	●		●					●				●	●	●			●		
HUTCHINSIA ALPINA	●					●		●			●		●		●				●	●		●		
IBERIS SAXATILIS (candytuft)	●					●	●		●	●	●		●		●				●			●		
IBERIS SEMPERVIRENS (candytuft)		●				●	●		●	●	●		●		●				●			●		
IRIS CRISTATA	●					●		●			●				●		●	●	●			●		
IRIS GRACILIPES		●				●		●			●					●	●	●	●			●		
IRIS PUMILA	●					●	●	●			●					●	●	●	●			●		
IRIS VERNA		●				●		●			●		●		●		●	●	●			●		
JUNIPERUS COMMUNIS 'COMPRESSA' (juniper)			●			●	●						●									●	●	●
JUNIPERUS COMMUNIS 'DEPRESSA AUREA' (juniper)		●				●			●				●									●	●	●
JUNIPERUS HORIZONTALIS 'BAR HARBOR' (juniper)	●					●			●				●									●	●	●
JUNIPERUS HORIZONTALIS 'WILTONII' (juniper)	●					●			●				●									●	●	●
JUNIPERUS X MEDIA 'OLD GOLD' (juniper)			●			●	●	●					●									●	●	●
JUNIPERUS SABINA 'TAMARISCIFOLIA' (juniper)		●				●			●				●									●	●	●
LEONTOPODIUM ALPINUM (edelweiss)		●				●	●				●			●	●					●		●	●	
LEWISIA COTYLEDON		●				●	●				●		●		●		●	●	●	●		●		
LEWISIA REDIVIVA (bitter-root)	●					●	●				●				●		●		●	●		●		
LEWISIA TWEEDYI	●					●	●				●	●					●		●	●		●		
LITHODORA DIFFUSA	●					●			●	●	●		●					●		●		●		
LYCHNIS VISCARIA 'SPLENDENS PLENA' (double-flowered campion)		●				●	●	●			●						●			●		●		
MUSCARI AUCHERI		●			●	●	●	●			●						●	●	●			●	●	
MUSCARI BOTRYOIDES (common grape hyacinth)		●			●	●	●	●			●				●		●	●	●			●	●	
MUSCARI LATIFOLIUM		●			●	●	●	●			●						●	●	●			●	●	
OENOTHERA MISSOURIENSIS (Ozark sundrops)		●					●	●	●	●	●					●				●	●	●	●	●
OMPHALODES VERNA (blue-eyed Mary)	●					●		●			●						●	●	●			●	●	
ONOSMA ALBOROSEA	●					●	●	●			●	●	●		●		●		●			●	●	
ONOSMA TAURICA	●					●	●	●			●	●	●			●			●			●	●	
PHLOX ADSURGENS	●			●		●				●	●						●		●	●		●	●	
PHLOX AMOENA	●			●		●		●			●						●		●	●		●	●	

Column groups: **PLANT HEIGHT** · **LIGHT NEEDS** · **GROWTH HABIT** · **SPECIAL TRAITS** · **FLOWER COLOUR** · **FLOWERING SEASON** · **SOIL NEEDS**

Name	Under 15 cm (6 in.)	15 to 30 cm (6 to 12 in.)	30 to 90 cm (1 to 3 ft)	Over 90 cm (3 ft)	Shade	Partial shade	Full sun	Upright	Spreading	Trailing	Flowers	Distinctive foliage	Evergreen	Decorative fruit	White to green	Yellow to orange	Pink to red	Blue to purple	Spring	Summer	Autumn	Acid	Neutral	Alkaline
PHLOX DOUGLASII	●					●			●		●						●	●	●			●	●	●
PHLOX STOLONIFERA (creeping phlox)		●				●			●		●						●	●	●			●	●	
PHLOX SUBULATA (moss phlox)	●					●			●		●		●		●		●	●	●			●	●	●
PICEA ABIES 'NIDIFORMIS' (dwarf Norway spruce)		●					●		●				●						●					
PICEA ABIES 'PUMILA' (dwarf Norway spruce)			●				●	●					●						●					
PICEA GLAUCA 'CONICA' (dwarf Alberta spruce)			●				●	●					●						●					
PICEA MARIANA 'NANA' (dwarf black spruce)		●					●	●					●						●					
POTENTILLA ALBA (white cinquefoil)		●					●		●		●	●			●					●		●		
POTENTILLA TRIDENTATA (cinquefoil)		●					●		●		●		●		●					●		●		
PRIMULA AURICULA (auricula)	●					●	●		●		●			●		●	●		●				●	
PRIMULA DENTICULATA (drumstick primrose)		●				●			●		●				●	●	●	●	●			●		
PRIMULA JULIAE	●					●			●		●						●	●	●					
PRIMULA SIEBOLDII		●			●	●			●		●				●		●	●	●	●		●		
PRIMULA VERIS (cowslip)		●				●			●		●					●			●			●		
PRIMULA VULGARIS (primrose)		●				●			●		●					●			●			●		
PULSATILLA VERNALIS (pasque flower)	●					●			●		●		●	●			●		●			●	●	
PULSATILLA VULGARIS (pasque flower)		●				●			●		●			●			●	●	●			●		
RAMONDA MYCONI	●				●				●		●						●	●	●			●		
RANUNCULUS MONTANUS (mountain buttercup)	●					●	●		●		●					●			●			●		
RHODOHYPOXIS BAURII	●					●	●		●		●						●		●	●	●	●		
SAPONARIA X 'BRESSINGHAM' (soapwort)	●						●		●		●						●			●			●	
SAPONARIA OCYMOIDES (soapwort)		●					●		●	●	●						●			●		●		
SAXIFRAGA COCHLEARIS (saxifrage)	●					●			●		●				●					●		●		
SAXIFRAGA COTYLEDON (saxifrage)			●			●			●		●				●					●		●		
SAXIFRAGA KABSCHIA HYBRIDS (saxifrage)	●					●			●	●	●			●	●	●	●		●			●		
SAXIFRAGA MARGINATA (saxifrage)	●					●			●		●	●			●		●		●			●		
SAXIFRAGA PANICULATA (saxifrage)		●				●			●		●	●			●				●	●		●		
SAXIFRAGA STOLONIFERA (saxifrage)	●	●				●			●	●	●	●			●					●		●		
SEDUM CAUTICOLUM (stonecrop)	●					●	●		●	●	●	●	●				●			●	●	●	●	●
SEDUM EWERSII (stonecrop)	●					●	●		●		●	●	●				●			●		●	●	●
SEDUM REFLEXUM (stonecrop)		●				●	●		●	●	●	●	●			●	●			●		●	●	●
SEDUM SIEBOLDII (stonecrop)		●				●	●		●		●	●	●			●				●	●	●	●	●
SEDUM SPATHULIFOLIUM (stonecrop)	●					●	●		●	●	●	●	●			●	●			●		●	●	●
SEDUM SPURIUM (stonecrop)		●				●	●		●		●	●	●		●		●			●		●	●	●
SEMPERVIVUM ARACHNOIDEUM (cobweb houseleek)	●				●	●		●	●		●	●	●				●			●		●		
SEMPERVIVUM TECTORUM (common houseleek)		●			●	●		●	●		●	●	●				●			●		●		
SEMPERVIVUM HYBRIDS		●			●	●		●	●		●	●	●				●			●		●		
SILENE ALPESTRIS (alpine catchfly)		●					●		●		●				●					●		●		
SILENE MARITIMA (sea campion)	●					●	●		●		●				●					●		●		
SILENE SCHAFTA	●					●	●		●		●						●	●		●	●	●	●	
THYMUS X CITRIODORUS (lemon-scented thyme)		●					●		●		●	●					●			●		●	●	
THYMUS PRAECOX (thyme)	●						●		●	●	●	●					●	●		●		●	●	
TRILLIUM ERECTUM (wood lily)		●			●			●			●			●			●	●	●			●		
TRILLIUM GRANDIFLORUM (wake robin)		●	●		●			●			●		●	●	●		●		●			●		
TRILLIUM OVATUM (wood lily)		●			●			●			●			●	●	●	●		●			●		
TSUGA CANADENSIS 'ARMISTICE DWARF' (dwarf eastern hemlock)		●				●		●	●				●						●					
TSUGA CANADENSIS 'COLE' (dwarf eastern hemlock)	●					●			●				●						●					
TSUGA CANADENSIS 'JERVIS' (dwarf eastern hemlock)			●			●		●					●						●					
TSUGA CANANDENSIS 'MINIMA' (dwarf eastern hemlock)			●			●			●				●						●					

Characteristics of 56 bog and water plants

Plant	Bog	Aquatic	Floating	Upright	Flowers	Distinctive foliage	Evergreen	Under 0°C (32°F)	0° to 21°C (32° to 70°F)	Over 21°C (70°F)	Moist bog conditions	2.5 to 15 cm (1 to 6 in.)	15 to 30 cm (6 to 12 in.)	Under 30 cm (1 ft)	30 to 90 cm (1 to 3 ft)	Over 90 cm (3 ft)	White to green	Yellow to orange	Pink to red	Blue to purple	Multicolour	Spring	Summer	Autumn
ACORUS CALAMUS 'VARIEGATUS' (variegated sweet flag)		●		●	●	●		●			●				●		●						●	
ACORUS GRAMINEUS		●		●	●	●			●		●	●			●		●						●	
APONOGETON DISTACHYUS (water hawthorn)		●	●		●	●			●	●			●		●		●					●	●	
BUTOMUS UMBELLATUS (flowering rush)		●		●	●				●				●		●				●				●	
CALLA PALUSTRIS (water arum)		●		●	●				●		●			●			●						●	
CALTHA PALUSTRIS (marsh marigold)	●			●	●			●			●		●					●				●	●	
CRASSULA RECURVA	●	●	●		●	●		●			●			●			●						●	
CYPERUS ALTERNIFOLIUS (umbrella grass)	●	●		●		●				●	●				●		●						●	
CYPERUS HASPAN	●	●		●		●				●	●				●		●						●	
CYPERUS LONGUS	●	●		●		●			●		●				●		●						●	
CYPERUS PAPYRUS (papyrus)	●	●		●		●				●					●	●	●						●	
EICHHORNIA CRASSIPES (water hyacinth)		●	●		●	●				●	●	●	●							●			●	
ELODEA CANADENSIS (Canadian pondweed)		●	●		●		●					●												
ELODEA CRISPA		●	●		●							●												
ERIOPHORUM ANGUSTIFOLIUM (cotton grass)	●			●	●			●			●			●			●						●	
ERIOPHORUM LATIFOLIUM (cotton grass)	●			●	●			●			●			●			●						●	
ERIOPHORUM SCHEUCHZERI (cotton grass)	●			●	●			●			●			●			●						●	
HOTTONIA PALUSTRIS (water violet)		●	●	●	●	●		●				●							●		●			
HYDROCHARIS MORSUS-RANAE (frogbit)		●	●		●	●		●				●									●			
IRIS KAEMPFERI (Japanese iris)	●			●	●			●	●		●					●			●	●	●		●	●
IRIS LAEVIGATA	●	●		●	●			●			●					●			●	●			●	
JUNCUS EFFUSUS 'SPIRALIS' (corkscrew rush)	●			●		●	●	●			●					●	●							
LOBELIA CARDINALIS (cardinal flower)	●			●	●				●		●				●				●				●	●
LOBELIA SIPHILITICA (blue cardinal)	●			●	●				●		●				●		●			●			●	
LYSICHITUM AMERICANUM (yellow arum)	●			●	●	●		●			●			●	●	●					●			
LYSICHITUM CAMTSCHATCENSE	●			●	●	●		●			●				●		●				●			
MENYANTHES TRIFOLIATA (bogbean)		●		●	●	●		●			●		●		●		●						●	
MIMULUS CUPREUS	●			●	●				●		●				●				●		●		●	

Acknowledgements

The editors would like to extend special thanks to Mrs. Lizzie Boyd, Kingston-upon-Thames, Surrey. They also wish to thank the following: Dr. Robert J. Armstrong, Kennett Square, Pa.; Ernesta D. and Frederic L. Ballard, Chestnut Hill, Pa.; Morris Berd, Media, Pa.; Bozidar Berginc, West Allis, Wis.; Greg Boop, San Anselmo, Calif.; Dr. Alexej B. Borkovec, Silver Spring, Md.; Eleanor Brinckerhoff, Oliver Nurseries, Fairfield, Conn.; Jesse Brown, National Agricultural Library, Beltsville, Md.; Mr. and Mrs. Francis H. Cabot, Stonecrop Nurseries, Carmel, N.Y.; Mr. and Mrs. T. Emmott Chase, Orting, Wash.; Dr. Horace Clay, Honolulu, Hawaii; Roy Davidson, Seattle, Wash.; Mr. and Mrs. Richard Dresel, Greenbrae, Calif.; Don and Felicity Drukey, Format Design, Malibu, Calif.; Edwin Eberman, New Canaan, Conn.; Harold Epstein, Larchmont, N.Y.; Mrs. Robert C. Erb, New Canaan, Conn.; Mrs. Sara Faust, Stonecrop Nurseries, Carmel, N.Y.; Nora Fields, New York Botanical Gardens, Bronx, N.Y.; Marion M. Flook, Wilmington, Del.; Roxie E. Gevjan, Newton Square, Pa.; Liz Goodman, London; Harold Greer, Greer Gardens, Eugene, Ore.; Harland Hand, El Cerrito, Calif.; Pamela Harper, Seaford, Va.; Wallace Jackson, London; Mrs. John S. Kistler, West Chester, Pa.; Don Korsmo, Seattle, Wash.; Mr. and Mrs. Robert Edmund Lee, Washington, D.C.; Lornie Leete-Hodge, Devizes, Wiltshire; Eloise Lesan, Cos Cob, Conn.; Jane Liu, Cos Cob, Conn.; Professor MacDougall, Dumbarton Oaks Garden Library, Washington, D.C.; James A. Minogue, American Rock Garden Society, Bentonville, Va.; Elizabeth A. Mosimann, Assistant Librarian, Hunt Botanical Library, Carnegie-Mellon University, Pittsburgh, Pa.; Winona O'Connor, London; Oehme, Van Sweden & Associates, Inc., Washington, D.C.; John P. Osborne, Westport, Conn.; James Pendleton, Good Earth Nursery, Burke, Va.; Roger Perry, London; William Platt, Platt, Wyckoff & Coles, Architects, New York, N.Y.; Dr. Gordon Pollock, New Canaan, Conn.; Robert Scace, Librarian, Royal Horticultural Society, Wisley, Surrey; George Schenk, Bothell, Wash.; Bruce Schmidlin, William Tricker, Inc., Saddle River, N.J.; Carol Ruth Shepherd, New Canaan, Conn.; Mrs. Walter Simpson, Director, Longue Vue Gardens, New Orleans, La.; Joel W. Spingann, Baldwin, N.Y.; Edith Stern, Longue Vue Gardens, New Orleans, La.; Martin Stoelzel, San Rafael, Calif.; Powers Taylor, Rosedale Nurseries, Hawthorne, N.Y.; Charles B. Thomas, Lilypons Water Gardens, Lilypons, Md.; Pat Tookey, London; Milly Trowbridge, London; Bill and Carol Uber, Van Ness Water Gardens, Upland, Calif.; Mr. and Mrs. Leo Vollmer, Baltimore, Md.; Eulalie M. Wagner, Tacoma, Wash.; Dr. Richard Wagner, Torrence, Calif.; John Warwick, Superintendent of the Rock Garden, Royal Horticultural Society, Wisley, Surrey; Olga Wolhaupter, Los Angeles, Calif.; John A. Wood, El Rancho Tropi-Cal, Thermal, Calif.; Madeline Zilfi, Professor of Middle Eastern Studies, University of Maryland.

Species	Bog	Aquatic	Floating	Upright	Flowers	Distinctive foliage	Evergreen	Under 0°C (32°F)	0° to 21°C (32° to 70°F)	Over 21°C (70°F)	Moist bog conditions	2.5 to 15 cm (1 to 6 in.)	15 to 30 cm (6 to 12 in.)	Under 30 cm (1 ft)	30 to 90 cm (1 to 3 ft)	Over 90 cm (3 ft)	White to green	Yellow to orange	Pink to red	Blue to purple	Multicolour	Spring	Summer	Autumn
MIMULUS LUTEUS (monkey musk)	●			●	●				●		●			●				●			●		●	
MIMULUS RINGENS (lavender water musk)		●		●	●				●		●			●						●			●	
MIMULUS VARIEGATUS	●			●	●		●		●		●			●							●		●	
NELUMBO NUCIFERA (sacred lotus)		●	●	●	●	●			●				●	●	●	●	●						●	
NYMPHAEA ALBA (water lily)		●	●		●	●	●						●				●						●	
NYMPHAEA COLORATA (water lily)		●	●		●	●				●			●							●			●	
NYMPHAEA HARDY HYBRIDS (water lily)		●	●		●	●	●						●				●	●	●		●		●	
NYMPHAEA TROPICAL HYBRIDS (water lily)		●	●		●	●				●			●				●	●	●	●	●		●	●
NYMPHOIDES PELTATA (water fringe)		●	●		●	●			●				●					●					●	
ORONTIUM AQUATICUM (golden club)		●	●	●	●	●			●		●	●	●				●	●					●	
PISTIA STRATIOTES (water lettuce)		●	●			●				●	●	●	●										●	
PONTEDERIA CORDATA (pickerel weed)		●	●		●				●		●			●						●			●	●
PRIMULA BEESIANA	●			●	●				●		●			●					●	●			●	
PRIMULA BULLEYANA	●			●	●				●		●				●			●	●	●			●	
PRIMULA FLORINDAE	●			●	●				●		●				●			●					●	
PRIMULA FRONDOSA	●			●	●				●		●		●	●					●			●		
PRIMULA JAPONICA (Japanese primrose)	●			●	●				●		●				●				●		●	●	●	
PRIMULA PULVERULENTA	●			●	●				●		●				●				●		●		●	
RODGERSIA AESCULIFOLIA	●			●	●	●			●		●				●		●		●				●	
RODGERSIA PINNATA	●			●	●	●			●		●				●				●				●	
RODGERSIA TABULARIS	●			●	●	●			●		●				●		●						●	
SAGITTARIA SAGITTIFOLIA (arrowhead)		●		●	●	●			●		●			●			●						●	
STRATIOTES ALOIDES (water soldier)		●	●	●	●	●			●		●	●		●			●						●	
TROLLIUS EUROPAEUS (globe flower)	●			●	●				●		●			●				●				●		
TROLLIUS LAXUS (globe flower)	●			●	●				●		●			●				●				●		
TYPHA ANGUSTIFOLIA (reedmace)		●		●	●	●			●							●			●				●	
TYPHA LATIFOLIA (reedmace)		●		●	●	●			●							●			●				●	
TYPHA MINIMA (reedmace)		●		●	●	●			●						●				●				●	

Picture Credits

Bibliography

Allan, Mea, *Plants That Changed Our Gardens*. David & Charles, 1974.

Anderson, Alice S., *Our Garden Heritage*. Dodd, Mead & Co., 1961.

Ashberry, Anne, *Miniature Gardens*. David & Charles, 1977.

Bartrum, Douglas, *Water in the Garden*. John Gifford Ltd., 1968.

Berrall, Julia S., *The Garden: An Illustrated History*. Penguin Books, 1978.

Birdseye, Clarence and Eleanor, *Growing Woodland Plants*. Dover Publications, 1973.

Bohm, Cestmir, *Rock Garden Plants*. The Hamlyn Publishing Group, Inc., 1970.

Brooklyn Botanic Garden, *Dwarf Conifers*. BBG, 1973.

Brooklyn Botanic Garden, *Handbook on Miniature Gardens*. BBG, 1976.

Brooklyn Botanic Garden, *Handbook on Rock Gardens*. BBG, 1973.

Brooklyn Botanic Garden, *Rhododendrons and Their Relatives*. BBG, 1971.

Calkins, Carroll, *Gardening with Water, Plantings and Stone*. Walker & Co., 1974.

Chittenden, Fred J., editor, *The Royal Horticultural Society Dictionary of Gardening*. Oxford University Press, 1956.

Clifford, Derek, *A History of Garden Design*. Praeger Publishers, 1963.

Coats, Peter, *Great Gardens of the Western World*. Spring Books, 1968.

Cox, E. H. M., *Farrer's Last Journey*. Dunlau & Co. Ltd., 1926.

Cuthbert, *Guide to Growing Rock Plants*. Cassell & Co. Ltd., 1953.

Dulta, Reginald, *Water Gardening Indoors and Out*. Crown Publishers, Inc., 1977.

Edwards, Alexander, *Rock Gardens*. Abelard-Schuman Ltd., 1958.

Eliovson, Sima, *Gardening the Japanese Way*. Harrap, 1971.

Elliot, Roy, *Alpine Gardening*. Vista, 1963.

Farrer, Reginald, *The English Rock Garden*. Theophrastus, Sakonnet, R.I., 1928.

Farrer, Reginald, *My Rock Garden*. EP Publishing, 1977.

Farrer, Reginald, *The Rainbow Bridge*. Edward Arnold & Co., 1921.

Foster, H. Lincoln, *Rock Gardening*. Houghton Mifflin Co., 1968.

Griffith, Anna N., *A Guide to Rock Garden Plants*. E. P. Dutton & Co., Inc., 1965.

Gwynn, Stephen, *Claude Monet and his Garden*. The Macmillan Company, 1934.

Healey, B. J., *The Plant Hunters*. Charles Scribner's Sons, 1975.

Heath, Royton E., *Miniature Rock Gardening in Troughs and Pans*. W. H. & L. Collingridge Ltd., London, 1957.

Heath, Royton E., *Rock Plants for Small Gardens*. Collingridge Books, 1969.

Heritage, Bill, *Lotus Book of Water Gardening*. Hamlyn, 1973.

Hills, Lawrence D., *Alpines Without a Garden*. Faber & Faber Ltd., 1953.

Hills, Lawrence D., *Miniature Alpine Gardening*. Faber & Faber Ltd., 1945.

Hornibrook, Murray, *Dwarf and Slow-Growing Conifers*. Country Life Ltd., 1923.

Huxley, Anthony, *An Illustrated History of Gardening*. Paddington Press Ltd., 1978.

Huxley, Anthony and Toogood, Alan R., *Garden Perennials and Water Plants*. Blandford Press, 1971.

Ingwerson, Will, *Ingwerson's Manual of Alpine Plants*. Will Ingwerson & Dunsprint Ltd., 1978.

Jekyll, Gertrude, *Wall and Water Gardens*. Charles Scribner's Sons, 1901.

Jellicoe, Susan and Geoffrey, *Water: The Use of Water in Landscape Architecture*. Black, 1971.

Kolaga, Walter A., *All About Rock Gardens and Plants*. Doubleday & Co., Inc., 1966.

Kramer, Jack, *Water Gardening: Pools, Fountains and Plants*. Charles Scribner's Sons, 1971.

Krutch, Joseph Wood, *The Gardener's World*. G. P. Putnam's Sons, 1959.

Macself, A. J., *Simple Rock Gardening*. W. H. & L. Collingridge Ltd., 1949.

Masters, Charles O., *Encyclopedia of the Water-lily*. T.F.H. Publications, Inc., Ltd., 1974.

Miles, Bebe, *Bluebells and Bittersweet: Gardening with Native American Plants*. Van Nostrand Reinhold Co., 1969.

Perry, Frances, *The Garden Pool*. Great Albion Books, 1972.

Perry, Frances, *Water Gardening*. Country Life, 1938.

Proudley, Brian and Valerie, *Heathers in Colour*. Blandford Press, 1974.

Puttock, A. G., *Rock Gardening*. Magna Print Books, Litton, Yorkshire, 1975.

Reader's Digest Association, Ltd., *Reader's Digest Encyclopaedia of Garden Plants and Flowers*. RDA Ltd., 1975.

Rickett, H. W., *Wild Flowers of the United States*. McGraw-Hill Book Co., 1975.

Robinson, William, *The English Flower Garden*. John Murray, London, 1956.

Rockwell, F. F., *Rock Gardens*. The Macmillan Company, 1928.

Sanders, T. W., *Rock Gardens and Alpine Plants*. W. H. & L. Collingridge, London, 1922.

Schenk, George, *Rock Gardens*. Lane Book Co., 1970.

Schimper, A. F. W., *Plant-Geography*. Weldon, 1960.

Shewell-Cooper, W. E., editor, *Alpine and Rock Gardening*. Seeley Service & Co. Ltd., London, 1961.

Shewell-Cooper, W. E., *Rock Gardens and Pools*. Drake Publishers, 1973.

Skinner, Henry T., *The Rock Garden*. N.Y. State College of Agriculture at Cornell, 1977.

Staff of the L. H. Bailey Hortorium, Cornell University, *Hortus Third: A Dictionary of Plants Cultivated in the United States and Canada*. Collier-Macmillan, 1977.

Stark, Francis B. and Link, Conrad B., *Rock Gardens and Water Plants in Color*. Doubleday & Co., Inc., 1973.

Stetson, Paul, *Garden Pools*. T.F.H. Publications, Inc., 1963.

Stodola, Dr. Jiri, *Encyclopedia of Water Plants*. T.F.H. Publications, Inc., 1967.

Sunset Editors, *Garden Pools, Fountains and Waterfalls*. Lane Publishing Co., 1976.

Swindells, Philip, *Water Gardening*. Michael Joseph, 1975.

Symons-Jeune, B. H. B., *Natural Rock Gardening*. Charles Scribner's Sons, 1933.

Taylor, N., editor, *Encyclopedia of Gardening*, 4th edition. Houghton Mifflin Co., 1961.

Thomas, Dr. G. L., Jr., *Goldfish Pools, Water-lilies and Tropical Fishes*. T.F.H. Publications, Inc., 1965.

Thomas, H. H., *Rock Gardening for Amateurs*. Cassell & Co. Ltd., 1926.

Thornton, Archie, *Rock Garden Primer*. A. T. DeLaMare Co., Inc., 1931.

Underhill, Terry, *Heaths and Heathers*. David & Charles, 1971.

Vivian, John, *Building Stone Walls*. Garden Way Publishing, 1978.

Whittle, Tyler, *The Plant Hunters*. Heinemann, 1970.

Wilder, Louise B., *The Rock Garden*. Doubleday & Co., Inc., *Garden*. Garden City Publishing Co., Inc., 1928.

Wilder, Louise B., *The Rock Garden*. Doubleday & Co., Inc., 1935.

Wright, Richardson, *The Story of Gardening*. Garden City Publishing Co., Inc., 1938.

Wyman, Donald, *Wyman's Gardening Encyclopedia*. Macmillan Publishing Co., Inc., 1977.

Zander, *Handwörterbuch der Pflanzennamen*. Verlag Eugen Ulmer, 1972.

Index

Numerals in italics indicate an illustration of the subject mentioned.

A

Accent points, 42
Achillea, 88
Achillea aurea, 88
Achillea chrysocoma, 88
Achillea tomentosa, 88
Acidity, soil, 26, 34, 87
Aconite, winter, 37
Acorus, 131
Acorus calamus, 75
Acorus calamus 'Variegatus', 131
Acorus gramineus, 131
Adaptation, plant, 14, 20, 21
Adder's tongue. *See Erythronium*
Aeration, water, 83
Air circulation, 21
Air pockets, 34, 38
Ajuga, 37, 46, 88
Ajuga pyramidalis, 88
Ajuga reptans, 88
Alberta spruce, dwarf. *See Picea*
Algae, 51, 74, 82, 83
Algicides, 83
Alhambra, 8
Alkalinity, soil, 35, 87
Allium, 89
Allium beesianum, 89
Allium moly, 89
Allium senescens, 89
Allium sikkimense, 89
Allium tuberosum, 89
Alpine aster. *See Aster*
Alpine catchfly. *See Silene*
Alpine clematis. *See Clematis*
Alpine dandelion, *14*
Alpine flora, 14
Alpine Flowers for Gardens, 14
Alpine Garden Society, 17
Alpine gardens, *18*, 19-47
Alpine geranium, 37
Alpine greenhouses, 21
Alpine meadows, 7, 19, 26, 40, 87
Alpine pink. *See Dianthus*
Alpine plants, 7, 10, *11-13*, 14, 16, 19, *24-25*, 28, *32-33*, *86*, 88-130
Alpine plants, buying, 17
Alpine plants, flowering seasons, 37
Alpine plants, foliage, 37
Alpine plants, growing conditions, 21
Alpine plants, planting, 34, 36
Alpine plants, planting pot-grown, 38
Alpine plants, positioning, *39*
Alpine plants, spring-flowering, 36, 37
Alpine poppy, 39
Alpine poppy, soil for, 35
Altitudes, 19
Alyssum, *41*, 89
Alyssum montanum, 89

Alyssum saxatile, *25*, 89
Alyssum spinosum, 89
Alyssum, spiny, *13*
Anacharis. See Elodea
Anacyclus, 90
Anacyclus depressus, 90
Androsace, 22, 90
Androsace carnea, 90
Androsace sarmentosa, 90
Androsace, soil for, 35
Anemone, 91
Anemone apennina, 91
Anemone blanda, 91
Anemone nemorosa, 91
Anemone pulsatilla. See Pulsatilla
Anemone, rue. *See Anemonella*
Anemone thalictroides. See Anemonella
Anemone, wood. *See Anemone*
Anemonella, 91
Anemonella thalictroides, 91
Animals in pools, 51
Aphids, 84
Aponogeton, 131
Aponogeton distachyos, 131
Aquatic baskets, *75*, 76, 81, 82
Aquatic plants, 7, 8, 9, 16, 49, 51, 60, 70, 71-85, *86*, 131-145
Aquatic plants, fertilizing, 84
Aquatic plants, marginal, 54, 55
Aquatic plants, oxygenating, 74
Aquatic plants, planting, 75
Aquatic plants, planting distances, 82
Aquatic plants, pools for, 57
Aquatic plants, pruning, 84
Aquatic plants, winter protection, 84
Aquilegia, 92
Aquilegia bertolonii, 92
Aquilegia canadensis, 92
Aquilegia flabellata, 92
Aquilegia scopulorum, 92
Arabis, 92-93
Arabis albida, 92
Arabis alpina, 93
Arabis caucasica, *92*, 93
Arabis ferdinandi-coburgii, 93
Arctostaphylos, 93
Arctostaphylos uva-ursi, 93
Arenaria, 93-94
Arenaria grandiflora, 94
Arenaria montana, *93*, 94
Arisaema, 94
Arisaema atrorubens, 94
Arisaema candidissimum, 94
Arisaema dracontium, 94
Arisaema sikokianum, 94
Arisaema triphyllum, 94
Armeria, 95
Armeria caespitosa, 95
Armeria juniperifolia, 95
Armeria maritima, 95
Arrowhead, 8, 75, *86*. *See also Sagittaria*
Artemisia, 95

Artemisia schmidtiana 'Nana', 95
Arum, 56
Arum, bog, 75
Arum, water. *See Caltha*
Arum, yellow. *See Lysichitum*
Asarum, 96
Asarum canadense, 96
Asarum caudatum, 96
Asarum europaeum, 96
Asperula, 96
Asperula gussonii, 96
Asperula odorata, 96
Asperula suberosa, 96
Aster, 97
Aster alpinus, 97
Aster natalensis, 97
Aster tibeticus, 97
Astilboides. See Rodgersia
Atlas daisy, 87. *See also Anacyclus*
Atragene. See Clematis
Aubrieta, *18*, *25*, *41*, 46, 97
Aubrieta deltoides, *25*, 97
Aubrieta, planting, *39*
Auricula. See Primrose
Autumn alpines, 37
Autumn clearing, 39
Autumn colours, 37
Autumn planting, 37
Autumn shades water lilies, 71
Avens. See Geum
Avens, mountain, *86*. *See Dryas*
Azaleas, 20, 26

B

Baits, slug, 38
Balance, 42
Banks, moist, *6*
Bark, shredded, 27, 40
Barrel pools, 52
Barrenwort. *See Epimedium*
Basins, catch, 8, 51, *53*
Baskets, aquatic, *75*, 76, 81, 82
Bean, sacred. *See Nelumbo*
Bearberry. *See Arctostaphylos*
Beds, moraine, *37*
Beds, raised, 19, 22, 29, 30, *31*, 40
Beds, raised peat, 31
Beds, raised wooden, 30
Bell flower. *See Campanula*
Bellis, 98
Bellis perennis, 98
Bellis rotundifolia, 98
Berberis, *13*
Bird baths, 51
Bishop's hat. *See Epimedium*
Bitter-root. *See Lewisia*
Black spruce, dwarf. *See Picea*
Bleeding heart, fringed. *See Dicentra*
Blocks, concrete, 30, 31, 56
Blue cardinal. *See Lobelia*
Blue-eyed Mary. *See Omphalodes*
Bluebell of Scotland. *See Campanula*
Bog arum, 75
Bog gardens, 10, *11*, *48*, 52

Bog gardens, construction, 56
Bog gardens, water supplies for, 56
Bog plants, 8, 49, 52, *53*, 74, 75, *86*, 131-145
Bog plants, planting, 82
Bog primrose, *53*
Bogbean, 75. *See also Menyanthes*
Bombsite gardens, 16
Bone-meal, 34, 36, 39, 75, 76
Boulders, glacial, 26, 40
Bowls, pool, 57
Brick pool edges, 55
Bricks, 56
Bridges, pool, 60, *68*
Broom. *See Cytisus*
Bruckenthalia, 98
Bruckenthalia spiculifolia, 98
Buckbean. *See Menyanthes*
Bugle. *See Ajuga*
Bugleweed, *13*
Building drystone walls, *31*
Building rock gardens, 15, *23*
Building wall gardens, 29
Bulbs, 19, 37
Butomus, 132
Butomus umbellatus, 132
Buttercup, mountain.
     See Ranunculus
Butyl rubber, 54

C

Calla, 132
Calla palustris, 132
Callirhoë, 99
Callirhoë involucrata, 99
Calluna, 99
Calluna vulgaris, 99
Caltha, 56, 132-133
Caltha palustris, 133
Caltha polypetala, 132
Campanula, 37, 100, 108
Campanula carpatica, 100
Campanula cochleariifolia, 100
Campanula garganica, 100
Campanula, planting, *39*
Campanula pusilla, 100
Campanula rotundifolia, 100
*Campanula serpyllifolia. See
     Edraianthus*
Campanula zoysii, 100
Campion. *See Lychnis*
Campion, sea. *See Silene*
Canadian pondweed. *See Elodea*
Canals, 40, 60
Candytuft, 16, *24*, *41*, *47*. *See also
     Iberis*
Carbon dioxide, 74
Cardinal flower, *48*. *See also Lobelia*
Carp, 83
Carpathian bell flower. *See
     Campanula*
Cascade pools, 56
Catch basins, 8, 51, *53*
Catchfly, alpine. *See Silene*

Cedar, dwarf Japanese. *See
     Cryptomeria*
Cells, leaf, 20
Cement, 31
Cement paints, 57
Cerastium, 100, 101
Cerastium tomentosum, *100*, 101
Ceratostigma, 37, 101
Ceratostigma plumbaginoides, 101
Chamaecyparis, 101-102
Chamaecyparis lawsoniana 'Minima
     Aurea', 101
Chamaecyparis obtusa 'Nana', 101
Chamaecyparis obtusa 'Nana
     Gracilis', 101
Chamaecyparis obtusa 'Pygmaea', 101
Chamaecyparis pisifera 'Compacta',
     102
Chamaecyparis pisifera 'Plumosa
     Compacta', 102
Channels, water, 8, 60
Chatsworth, 9
Chelsea Physic Garden, 14
Cherry, weeping, *12-13*
China, sacred flower, 10
Chippings, limestone, 35
Chips, stone, 22, 23, 28, 34, 36, 40
Chrysogonum, 102
Chrysogonum virginianum, 102
Chutes, water, *62*
Cinquefoil. *See Potentilla*
Circulation, air, 21
Clay, 34, 76
Clay soil, 22
Clematis, 102
Clematis alpina, 102
Climate, 20
Club, golden. *See Orontium*
Cobweb houseleek. *See Sempervivum*
Colours, 42
Colours, autumn, 37
Colours, pool bottom, 51
Columbine, *47*. *See also Aquilegia*
Common daisy. *See Bellis*
Common grape hyacinth. *See
     Muscari*
Common houseleek. *See
     Sempervivum*
Compost, garden, 76
Compost, mushroom, 39
Concrete, 16, 51, 53
Concrete blocks, 30, 31, 56
Concrete, colouring, 31
Concrete, curing, 34, 58
Concrete, mixing, 31
Concrete, moisture for, 34
Concrete pools, 56
Concrete, pouring, 58
Concrete, ready-mixed, 58
Concrete sealers, 58
Concrete troughs, 31, *32-33*, 34
Conifers, *44*, *45*
Conifers, dwarf, *18*, *39*
Construction, rock garden, 15, 17,
     23, 37

Container rock gardens, 31, *32-33*
Containers, water, 52
Containers, water lily, 81
Copper, 53, 81
Corkscrew rush. *See Juncus*
Cornish heath. *See Erica*
Corydalis, 103
Corydalis bulbosa, 103
Corydalis cashmeriana, 103
Corydalis lutea, 103
Corydalis solida, 103
Cotton grass. *See Eriophorum*
Cotyledon, *18*
Courtyard gardens, 8
Cowslip. *See Primula*
Crane's-bill. *See Geranium*
Crassula, 133
Crassula recurva, 133
Creeping phlox. *See Phlox*
Crocks, 34
Crocus, 37, 103
Crocus chrysanthus, 103
Crocus speciosus, 103
Crocus tomasinianus, 103
Cross-leaved heath. *See Erica*
Cryptomeria, 104
Cryptomeria japonica 'Globosa
     Nana', 104
Cryptomeria japonica 'Lobbii
     Nana', 104
Cryptomeria japonica 'Vilmoriniana',
     104
Curing concrete, 34, 58
Cushion plant, 15
Cyclamen, 37
Cyperus, 133
Cyperus alternifolius, 133
Cyperus haspan, 133
Cyperus longus, 133
Cyperus papyrus, 133
Cypress, *65*
Cypress, false. *See Chamaecyparis*
Cypress, Lawson's, *13*
Cytisus, 104, 105
Cytisus decumbens, 105
Cytisus x *kewensis*, *104*, 105

D

Daisy, Atlas, 87. *See also
     Anacyclus*
Daisy, common. *See Bellis*
Dams, 52, *55*
Dandelion, alpine, *14*
Dandelion, lowland, *14*
Daphne, 105
Daphne arbuscula, 105
Daphne blagayana, 105
Daphne cneorum, 105
Daphne mezereum, 105
Daphne petraea, 105
Daphne retusa, 105
Daphne rupestris, 105
Debris, rock, 35
Depth, pools, 50, 51

Depth, water, 87
Depths, simulated, 51
Dianthus, 106
Dianthus alpinus, 106
Dicentra, 103, 106
Dicentra canadensis, 106
Dicentra cucullaria, 106
Dicentra eximia, 106
Dicentra formosa, 106
Dielytra. See Dicentra
Diseases, 84
Distances, planting, 36
Division, 85
Dog's-tooth violet. *See Erythronium*
Double-flowered campion. *See Lychnis*
Draba, 107
Draba dicranoides, 107
Draba mollissima, 107
Draba repens, 107
Draba rigida, 107
Draba sibirica, 107
Draba, soil for, 35
Dragon, green. *See Arisaema*
Dragonflies, 51
Drainage, 21, 22, *23*, 29, 30, 31, 34, 35, 36, 37, 39, 54
Drainage, improving, 22
Driftwood, *33*
Drought, 38
Drought resistance, 43
Drumstick primrose, *24. See also Primula*
Dryas, 107
Dryas octopetala, 107
Dryas x suendermannii, 107
Drystone walls, 19, 29
Drystone walls, building, *31*
Drystone walls, planting, 30
Dust, golden, *25. See also Alyssum*
Dutchman's-breeches. *See Dicentra*
Dwarf Alberta spruce. *See Picea*
Dwarf black spruce. *See Picea*
Dwarf conifers. *18. 39, 45*
Dwarf eastern hemlock. *See Tsuga*
Dwarf Japanese cedar. *See Cryptomeria*
Dwarf juniper. *See Juniperus*
Dwarf Norway spruce. *See Picea*
Dwarf plants, 20
Dwarf shrubs, 19, 38
Dwarf trees, 38

E

Eastern hemlock, dwarf. *See Tsuga*
Ecology, 82, 83
Edelweiss. *See Leontopodium*
Edraianthus, 108
Edraianthus pumilio, 108
Edraianthus serpyllifolius, 108
Edraianthus, soil for, 35
Edraianthus tenuifolius, 108
Egyptian paper rush. *See Cyperus*
Egyptian water gardens, 60, *61*

Eichhornia, 133-134
Eichhornia crassipes, 74, 134
Eichhornia speciosa, 133
Elodea, 74, 134
Elodea canadensis, 134
Elodea crispa, 134
English Rock Garden, The, 16
Epimedium, 108
Epimedium grandiflorum, 108
Epimedium macranthum, 108
Erica, 109
Erica carnea, 109
Erica herbacea, 109
Erica tetralix, 109
Erica vagans, 109
Erigeron, *33*, 110
Erigeron aureus, 110
Erigeron compositus, 110
Erigeron uniflorus, 110
Eriophorum, 134
Eriophorum angustifolium, 134
Eriophorum latifolium, 134
Eriophorum scheuchzeri, 134
Eritrichum nanum, 15, 19
Erosion, rock, 27
Erosion, soil, 40
Erythronium, 110
Erythronium americanum, 110
Erythronium dens-canis, 110, *111*
Erythronium hendersonii, 110
Erythronium revolutum, 110
European water lily, 10
Evaporation, 51, 84
Evening primrose, 16
Expeditions, plant, 15
Exposure, 20, 22
Extension, flowering season, 36, 37, 45

F

False cypress. *See Chamaecyparis*
Farrer, Reginald, 14, 15, 17, 19, 23
Fawn lily. *See Erythronium*
Feeder roots, 21
Feeding, 39, 84
Ferns, *6*, 15, 16, 19, *41*, *47*, 52
Fertilizer, 34, 76
Fertilizing. 8. 39, 84
Fibreglass, 53
Filters for pools, 83
Fish, ornamental, 17, 50, 74, 76, 83, 85
Fish, ornamental, feeding, 83
Fish, pool, 53, 57
Flag, sweet, 7, 75. *See also Acorus*
Flagstone paths, *13*
Flagstone pool edges, 55
Fleabane, 16. *See also Erigeron*
Floating heart. *See Nymphoides*
Flora, alpine, 14
Flower size, 20
Flowering rush. *See Butomus*
Flowering seasons, 20
Flowering seasons, extending, 36, 37, 45

Flowers, wild, 7, 20, 21
Foliage alpines, 37
Footbridges, *11*
Forget-me-not, *47*
Forget-me-not, water, 56
Formal pools, 50
Forms, rock, 31, 34
Fountains, *8*, 51, 52, 59, 60, *62*, *66-67*
Fountains, jet, *64*, 65, *66-67*
Fountains, wall, 49
Fragrance, 9
Fringed bleeding heart. *See Dicentra*
Frogbit. *See Hydrocharis*
Frogs, 51, 82
Fungicides, 38

G

Galium. See Asperula
Garden designs, Japanese, 16
Garden fountains, *8*, 51, 52, 59, 60, *62*, *66-67*
Garden hygiene, 38
Garden loam, 34
Gardener's Chronicle, 9
Gardens, bog, 10, *11*, *48*, 52
Gardens, bombsite, 16
Gardens, Moorish, 8
Gardens, moraine, 36
Gardens, Persian, 8
Gardens, scree, 36
Gardens, trough, 19
Gardens, wall, 29, 40
Gardens, water, *48*, 49-69
Garland flower. *See Daphne*
Gases, harmful, 50, 76
Generalife, 8, *64-65*
Gentian, *41*, *86*, 87. *See also Gentiana*
Gentiana, 111
Gentiana acaulis, 111
Gentiana clusii, 111
Gentiana farreri, 16, 111
Gentiana kochiana, 111
Gentiana septemfida, 111
Gentiana sino-ornata, 111
Gentiana, soil for, 34
Gentiana verna, 111
Geranium, 49, 112
Geranium, alpine, 37
Geranium dalmaticum, 112
Geranium farreri, 15
Geranium lancastriense, 112
Geranium renardii, 112
Geranium sanguineum, 112
Geranium sanguineum var. *prostratum*, 112
Germination, 24
Geum, 112-113
Geum borisii, 112
Geum coccineum, 113
Geum reptans, *112*, 113
Ginger, wild. *See Asarum*
Ginkakuji gardens, *68-69*
Glaciers, 35, 37

Globe flower. *See Trollius*
Gneiss, 26
Gold dust, *25*. *See also Alyssum*
Golden club. *See Orontium*
Golden orfe, 83
Goldfish, 83
Granite, 26
Granite rocks, *44*, *46-47*
Grape hyacinth. *See Muscari*
Grass, cotton. *See Eriophorum*
Grass, umbrella. *See Cyperus*
Gravel, 22, 23, 28, 30, 34, 35, 36, 38, 39, 57, 58
Green dragon. *See Arisaema*
Greenhouses, alpine, 21
Grottoes, 8, 14
Ground covers, 20
Groundsel, 16
Group plantings, 36
Growing conditions, alpine plants, 21
Gypsophila, 113
Gypsophila cerastioides, 113
Gypsophila repens, 113
Gypsophila tenuifolia, 113

H

Hairs, leaf, 20
Hampton Court, 8
Harebell. *See Campanula*
Hawthorn, water, 7. *See also Aponogeton*
Hazards for children, 51
Heart, bleeding. *See Dicentra*
Heart, floating. *See Nymphoides*
Heat, 20, 21, 22
Heaters, pool, 17, 85
Heath. *See Erica*
Heath, spike. *See Bruckenthalia*
Heather, *13*, 26, 37, *47*. *See also Calluna and Erica*
Heathers, soil for, 34
Heaths, soil for, 34
Helianthemum, 113-114
Helianthemum chamaecistus, 113
Helianthemum nummularium, *113*, 114
Heliosperma. *See Silene*
Hemlock, dwarf eastern. *See Tsuga*
Hemlock, weeping, *44*, *47*
Hepatica, 114
Hepatica nobilis, 114
Hepatica transsylvanica, 114
Hepatica triloba, 114
Herbs, 19
Himalayan primrose, 87
Hindu lotus. *See Nelumbo*
Hinoki false cypress. *See Chamaecyparis*
Holes, planting, 38
Hot-house pools, 9
Hottonia, 135
Hottonia palustris, 135
Houseleek. *See Sempervivum*
Humidity, 21, 38

Humus, 34
Hutchinsia, 114-115
Hutchinsia alpina, 114
Hyacinth, grape. *See Muscari*
Hyacinth, water, 74. *See also Eichhornia*
Hybridization, 9, 10
Hybrids, water lily, 9, 10
Hydrocharis, 135
Hydrocharis morsus-ranae, 135
Hydrocleys nymphoides, 74
Hygiene, garden, 38

I

Iberis, 115
Iberis saxatilis, 115
Iberis sempervirens, *24*, 115
Illumination, pool, 59
India, sacred flower, 10
Indoor pools, 49
Insects, 24, 83
Installations, water, *13*, *37*
Insulation, snow, 20
Iris, 37, 115-116, 135
Iris cristata, 115
Iris gracilipes, 116
Iris, Japanese, 8, 51, 56
Iris kaempferi, 135, *136*
Iris laevigata, 135
Iris pumila, 116
Iris verna, *115*, 116
Iris, water, 75
Irrigation, 8
Irrigation, underground, 36, *37*

J

Jack-in-the-pulpit. *See Arisaema*
Japanese dwarf cedar. *See Cryptomeria*
Japanese garden designs, 16
Japanese iris, 8, 51, 56. *See also Iris kaempferi*
Japanese larch, *12*
Japanese primrose. *See Primula japonica*
Japanese water gardens, 60, *68-69*
Jasmine, rock. *See Androsace*
Jets, 8, 60, 83
Jets, fountain, 59, *64*, *65*, *66-67*
Joke fountains, 8
Juncus, 136
Juncus effusus 'Spiralis', 136
Juniper, dwarf. *See Juniperus*
Juniper thrift. *See Armeria*
Juniperus, 116
Juniperus communis 'Compressa', 116
Juniperus communis 'Depressa Aurea', 116
Juniperus horizontalis 'Bar Harbor', 116
Juniperus horizontalis 'Blue Rug', 116

Juniperus horizontalis 'Wiltonii', 116
Juniperus x *media* 'Old Gold', 116
Juniperus sabina 'Tamariscifolia', 116

K

Kabschia saxifrages, 36
Kew broom. *See Cytisus*
Kingcup. *See Caltha*
Koi carp, 83
Koran, The, 62

L

Lagarosiphon. *See Elodea*
Lakes, Japanese, 60, 68, *69*
Larch, Japanese, *12*
Larkspur, 16
Latour-Marliac, Bory, 9
Lava, 14, 26, *35*
Lavender water musk. *See Mimulus*
Lawson's cypress, *13*
Laydekeri water lilies, 73
Leaching, 82
Leadwort. *See Ceratostigma*
Leaf cells, 20
Leaf hairs, 20
Leaf pores, 20
Leaf-mould, 23, 34, 35, 36, 39, 76, 87
Leaves, dangers from, 50
Leaves, shapes, 20
Leaves, texture, 20
Ledges, 19, 21, 35, 40, *43*, *53*
Ledges, building, 27, *29*
Ledges, planting, *39*
Lemon-scented thyme. *See Thymus*
Leontopodium, 117
Leontopodium alpinum, 117
Lettuce, water, 74. *See also Pistia*
Lewisia, 117
Lewisia cotyledon, 117
Lewisia rediviva, 117
Lewisia tweedyi, 117
Light, 49
Lighting pools, 59
Lights, water, 17
Lily, fawn. *See Erythronium*
Lily pads, 9
Lily pond, 10
Lily pools, *11*
Lily pools, siting, 49, 50
Lily, water. *See Water lily and Nymphaea*
Lily, wood. *See Trillium*
Lime, 26, 58
Lime, leaching, 34, 58
Limestone, 26, 29, 34, 35, 53, 87
Limestone chippings, 35
Limnanthemum. *See Nymphoides*
Liners, plastic, 56
Liners, pool, 16, 17, 53, 54, 56
Ling. *See Calluna*
Lithodora, 118
Lithodora diffusa, 118

Lithospermum. See Lithodora
Loam, 34, 35, 36, 75
Lobelia, 136
Lobelia cardinalis, 75, 136
Lobelia siphilitica, 136
Loss, moisture, 14
Lotus, 8, 10, *70*, 74. *See also Nelumbo*
Lotus, planting, 82
Lowland dandelion, *14*
Lowland plants, 19
Lychnis, 118
Lychnis viscaria 'Splendens Plena', 118
Lysichitum, 136-137
Lysichitum americanum, 136, *137*
Lysichitum camtschatcense, 137
Lysichitum japonicum, 136

M
Mallow, 16
Manure, 76
Manure, dried, 34, 39
Marginal plants, 8, 54, 55
Marigold, marsh, *11*, 75. *See also Caltha*
Marliac water lilies, 9, 10, 71
Marsh marigold, *11*, 75. *See also Caltha*
Marshes, 52
Mary, blue-eyed. *See Omphalodes*
Meadows, alpine, 7, 19, 26, 40, 87
Menyanthes, 137
Menyanthes trifoliata, 137
Mildew, 21, 38
Mills, water, 8
Mimulus, 137
Mimulus cupreus, 137
Mimulus luteus, 137
Mimulus ringens, 137
Mimulus variegatus, 137, *138*
Mineral matters, 34
Miniature pools, 50, 51
Miniature rock gardens, *32-33*
Miniature sunken pools, 52, 53
Miniature water lilies, 8, 52, 71, 73
Miniature water lilies, planting, 81
Moisture, 14, 21
Moisture for concrete, 34
Moisture loss, 14
Moisture retention, 26
Moisture-loving plants, *6*, 7
Monet, Claude, 10
Monkey musk. *See Mimulus*
Moorish water gardens, 8, 60, *64-65*, *66-67*
Moraine beds, 35, 36, *37*
Mortar, 19
Mosquitos, 83
Moss peat, 31, 34, 35, 56, 76, 84, 87
Moss phlox, *25*. *See also Phlox*
Mossy saxifrage, *24*
Moulds, rock, 31, 34
Mountain avens, *86*. *See also Dryas*
Mountain buttercup. *See Ranunculus*

Mountain shrubs, 20
Mountain trees, 20
Movement of rocks, 28
Mulches, 28, *32*, 38
Muscari, 119
Muscari aucheri, 119
Muscari botryoides, *118*, 119
Muscari latifolium, 119
Muscari tubergenianum, 119
Mushroom compost, 39
Musk mallow, 16. *See also Mimulus*
My Rock Garden, 14, 15
Myriophyllum, 74
Myrtle, *65*

N
Names, botanical, 87
Names, common, 87
Names, Latin, 87
Nelumbium. See Nelumbo
Nelumbo, 10, 139
Nelumbo nucifera, *138*, 139
Nelumbo speciosum, 139
Nightshade, 16
Nomenclature, 87
Norway spruce, dwarf. *See Picea*
Nuphar, 10
Nurseries, specialist, 17
Nutrients, 22, 76, 82, 84
Nymphaea, 10, 71, 139-141
Nymphaea alba, 9, *138*, 139
Nymphaea 'Attraction', 73, *138*
Nymphaea 'Blue Beauty', *79*
Nymphaea 'Chromatella', 73
Nymphaea colorata, 140
Nymphaea 'Comanche', *140*
Nymphaea x *daubenyana*, 73
Nymphaea 'Director George T. Moore', 73, *139*
Nymphaea 'Emily Grant Hutchings', *140*
Nymphaea 'Evelyn Randig', *79*
Nymphaea hardy hybrids, 140
Nymphaea 'Isabelle Pring', 73
Nymphaea x *laydekeri*, 140
Nymphaea mexicana, 10
Nymphaea micrantha, 73
Nymphaea 'Missouri', *78*
Nymphaea odorata, 9, 140
Nymphaea odorata 'Gigantea', *72*
Nymphaea odorata 'Rosea', 10
Nymphaea 'Panama Pacific', *79*
Nymphaea polychroma, 139
Nymphaea pygmy hybrids, 140
Nymphaea tropical hybrids, 140
Nymphoides, 141
Nymphoides peltata, 74, 141

O
Oenothera, 119
Oenothera missouriensis, 119
Oleander, *65*
Omphalodes, 119-120

Omphalodes verna, 119
Onosma, 120
Onosma alborosea, 120
Onosma taurica, 120
Orchid pots, 81
Orfe, golden, 83
Ornamental fish, 17, 50, 74, 76, 83, 85
Orontium, 142
Orontium aquaticum, 142
Outcrops, rock, *42-43*, *46-47*
Oxygen, 74, 85
Oxygenators, 74, 83
Ozark sundrops. *See Oenothera*

P
Pads, lily, 9
Paper rush, Egyptian. *See Cyperus*
Papyrus, 87. *See also Cyperus*
Pasque flower. *See Pulsatilla*
Paths, *13*
Paths, paved, 22
Paths, rock garden, 27, 28, 40
Patterns, planting, 36
Paving stone pool edges, 55
Paxton, Joseph, 9
Peat beds, raised, 31
Pebbles, *32*
Perlite, 31
Persian water gardens, 8, 60, *62-63*
Pest control, 8
Pesticides, 38
Pests, 38, 83
Phlox, *18*, 120
Phlox adsurgens, 120
Phlox amoena, 120
Phlox douglasii, 120
Phlox, moss, *25*
Phlox stolonifera, 120
Phlox subulata, *25*, *42*, 46, 120
Phosphorus, 34
Picea, 121
Picea abies 'Nidiformis', 121
Picea abies 'Pumila', 121
Picea glauca 'Conica', 121
Picea mariana 'Nana', 121
Pickerel rush, 75
Pickerel weed, 52, 87. *See also Pontederia*
Pine needles, 40
Pink. *See Dianthus*
Pinks, soil for, 35
Pipes, water, 17
Pistia, 142
Pistia stratiotes, 74, 142
Plant adaptation, 14, 20, 21
Plant expeditions, 15
Planting, 30, 34, 36
Planting distances, 36, 82
Planting holes, 38
Planting mixtures, 34, 35, 36, 76
Planting patterns, 36
Planting pockets, 21, 30, 31, 34, *35*, *39*, 46, 52
Planting seasons, 37

Planting techniques, 38, *39*
Plastic, 16
Plastic pool liners, 51, 56
Plastic sheeting, 54
Plumbago. *See Ceratostigma*
Pockets, air, 34, 38
Pockets, planting, 21, 30, 31, 34, 35, *39*, 46, 52
Pollination, 21, 24
Polythene pool liners, 54
Polyvinyl chloride, 54
Pond lily, 10
Ponds, 11, 16
Ponds, depth, 51
Ponds, Japanese, 60, *68*
Ponds, natural, 55
Ponds, woodland, 49
Pondweed, Canadian. *See Elodea*
Pontederia, 142
Pontederia cordata, 142
Pool containers, 52
Pool cracks, sealing, 85
Pool edges, camouflaging, 53, 55, 56
Pool finishes, 51
Pool heaters, 85
Pool liners, 16, 17, 53, 54
Pool shells, prefabricated, 53
Pool shells, shapes, 53
Pools, *6*, 7, 10, *11, 12-13*, 17, *48*, 60
Pools, ancient, 8
Pools, animals in, 51
Pools, barrel, 52
Pools, bathtub, 52
Pools, bowl-shaped, 57
Pools, bridges, 60, *68*
Pools, cascade, 56
Pools, classic, 60, *61-69*
Pools, cleaning, 54, 58, 85
Pools, cloudy, 83
Pools, concrete, 56
Pools, depth, 50, 51
Pools, draining, *57*, 85
Pools, drainpipes for, 59
Pools, drains for, 54, 58, 59
Pools, enclosures, 56
Pools, excavations for, 54, 57
Pools, filling, 54, 55, 59, 84
Pools, filters, 83
Pools, formal, 49, 50, 52, 54, 55, 56
Pools, hot-house, 9
Pools, ice prevention, 85
Pools, indoor, 49, 72
Pools, informal, 52, 54
Pools, installation, 53, 54, 55, 56, 57
Pools, lighting for, 59
Pools, lily, *13*
Pools, masonry, 56
Pools, miniature, 50, 51
Pools, miniature sunken, 52, 53
Pools, natural, 52
Pools, ornamental fish for, 17, 50, 74, 76, 83, 85
Pools, overflow, 59
Pools, painting, 57
Pools, planting, 76, 82

Pools, plantings, *68-69*
Pools, positioning, 50
Pools, pumps for, 83
Pools, raised, 55, 56
Pools, reflections, *50*
Pools, scum, 82, 83
Pools, shapes, 17, 56
Pools, shelter for, 50
Pools, sink, 52
Pools, siting, 49
Pools, stains, 51
Pools, sunken, 53
Pools, tropical, *80*
Pools, water changes, 82
Pools, waterproofing, 58
Pools, winter protection, 85
Poppies, 16
Poppy, alpine, 39
Poppy, alpine, soil for, 35
Poppy, water, 74
Poppy, Welsh, 15
Pores, leaf, 20
Porosity, 26
Portland cement, 31, 58
Positioning alpines, *39*
Positioning pools, 50
Potentilla, 121-122
Potentilla alba, 122
Potentilla tridentata, *121*, 122
Pot-grown alpines, planting, 38
Primrose, *47. See also Primula*
Primrose, bog, *53*
Primrose, drumstick, *24*
Primrose, evening, 16
Primrose, Himalayan, 87
Primula, 122-123, 142, 143
Primula acaulis, 122
Primula auricula, 122
Primula beesiana, 143
Primula bulleyana, 143
Primula denticulata, *24*, 122
Primula florindae, 143
Primula frondosa, 143
Primula hirsuta, 122
Primula japonica, 143
Primula juliae, 122
Primula officinalis, 122
Primula x *pubescens*, 122
Primula pulverulenta, 143
Primula sieboldii, 122
Primula veris, 123
Primula vulgaris, 123
Pring, George, 76
Propagation, 85
Propagation by plantlets, *73*
Prostrate broom. *See Cytisus*
Protection, winter, 8, 20
Pruning, 8
Pruning of aquatic plants, 84
Ptilotrichum. See Alyssum
Pulsatilla, 123
Pulsatilla vernalis, 123
Pulsatilla vulgaris, 123
Pumps, 17, 83
Pumps, submersible, 16, 52, 59

Pumps, water, 13
Purdom, William, 15
PVC pool liners, 54, 55
Pygmy water lilies, 73, 76, *79*

R

Railway sleepers, 28, 30, 56
Rainwater, 22, 27, 29
Raised beds, 19, 22, 29, 30, *31*, 40
Raised beds, peat, 31
Raised beds, wooden, 30
Ramonda, 12, 124
Ramonda myconii, 124
Ramonda pyrenaica, 124
Ranunculus, 124
Ranunculus geraniifolius, 124
Ranunculus montanus, 124
Reeds, 75
Reedmace, 8. *See also Typha*
Reflections, pool, 49, *50*
Reproduction, 20
Rhizomes, 71, 72, 81, 85
Rhododendrons, *13*, 20
Rhodohypoxis, 124
Rhodohypoxis baurii, 124, *125*
Risers, 28
Robinson, William, 14
Rock debris, 35
Rock erosion, 27
Rock gardening, 14, 16
Rock gardens, 10, *11-13, 18*, 19-47, 55
Rock gardens, construction, 15, 17, *23*, 37
Rock gardens, containers, 31, *32-33*
Rock gardens, definition, 19
Rock gardens, designs, 36
Rock gardens, miniature, *32-33*
Rock gardens, Oriental, 8
Rock gardens, paths, 27, 28, 40
Rock gardens, planning, 17
Rock gardens, planting, *39*
Rock gardens, plants for, 88-130
Rock gardens, routine care, 38, 39
Rock gardens, scale, 14
Rock gardens, siting, 21
Rock gardens, spring care, 39
Rock gardens, steps, 27, 28
Rock gardens, terraced, *43*
Rock gardens, types, 19
Rock gardens, upkeep, 8
Rock gardens, wild, 16
Rock gardens, woodland, 40
Rock jasmine. *See Androsace*
Rock outcrops, *42-43, 46-47*
Rock rose. *See Helianthemum*
Rock steps, 28
Rock, types, 23, 26
Rockeries, 14
Rocks, *6*, 7, 8, 14, *18*, 19, *23, 33*, 34, 40, 42, 49
Rocks, artificial, 31, 34
Rocks, bedding, 27
Rocks, cleaning, 21
Rocks, granite, *44, 46-47*

Rocks, lava, *35*
Rocks, moving, 26, *28*
Rocks, placing, 27
Rocks, sizes, 23
Rock strata, 17
Rocks, structure, 27, 29
Rocks, texture, 26
Rocks, tilting, 29
Rocks, use of, *6, 7*
Rocks, volcanic, 26
Rodgersia, 143
Rodgersia aesculifolia, 143
Rodgersia pinnata, 143
Rodgersia tabularis, 143
Roots, 21, 38
Rosa farreri, 15
Rose, rock. *See Helianthemum*
Rosemary, *43*
Roses, *65*
Routine care, 38, 39
Royal Botanic Gardens, 9
Royal Geographical Society, 9
Royal Horticultural Society, 10
Rue anemone. *See Anemonella*
Rush, corkscrew. *See Juncus*
Rush, Egyptian paper. *See Cyperus*
Rush, flowering, 75. *See also*
Butomus

S

Sacred bean. *See Nelumbo*
Sacred lotus, 8. *See also Nelumbo*
Sagittaria, 74, 144
Sagittaria sagittifolia, 144
Sand, 22, 23, 34, 35, 39, 54, 56, 58
Sand-pits, temporary, 51
Sandstone, 26, 29
Sandstone rocks, 11
Sandwort. *See Arenaria*
Saponaria, 125
Saponaria x 'Bressingham', 125
Saponaria ocymoides, 125
Sawara false cypress. *See*
Chamaecyparis
Saxatile, 21
Saxicoline, 21
Saxifraga, 22, *41*, 125-126
Saxifraga aizoon, 125
Saxifraga burseriana, 126
Saxifraga cochlearis, 125
Saxifraga cotyledon, 125, *126*
Saxifraga hypnoides, *24*
Saxifraga Kabschia hybrids, 36, 125,
127
Saxifraga marginata, 126
Saxifraga, mossy, *24*
Saxifraga paniculata, 126, *127*
Saxifraga sarmentosa, 125
Saxifraga, soil for, 35
Saxifraga stolonifera, 126
Saxum, 21
Schist, 26, *41*
Schomburgk, Robert, 9
Scottish Rock Garden Club, 17

Scree gardens, 35, 36
Screens, shade, 38
Sculpture, 49
Sea campion. *See Silene*
Sea pink. *See Armeria*
Sea shells, crushed, 35
Sealers, concrete, 58
Seasons, flowering, 20
Sedum, 15, *33*, 126-128
Sedum cauticolum, 126
Sedum ewersii, 126
Sedum reflexum, 126, *127*
Sedum rupestre, 126
Sedum sieboldii, 126, *127*
Sedum spathulifolium, 126
Sedum spurium, 126
Seeds, 24
Self-seeding, 39
Sempervivum, *33*, 37, *39*, 128
Sempervivum arachnoideum, 128
Sempervivum hybrids, 128
Sempervivum tectorum, 128
Shade, 21, 22, 82
Shading, 38
Shale, 26
Shapes, leaf, 20
Sheeting, plastic, 54
Shells, crushed sea, 35
Shells, pool, 53
Sho-ami, 68
Shrubs, alpine, 7, 19, 38
Shrubs, mountain, 20
Silene, 128
Silene alpestris, 128
Silene maritima, 128
Silene schafta, 128
Silt, 51, 58
Sink pools, 52
Sink rock gardens, 31
Sinks, stone, 19
Size, flower, 20
Slopes, 22, *23*, 35, *42*
Slug baits, 38
Slugs, 28, 38
Snow insulation, 20
Snowdrops, 37
Snow-in-summer. *See Cerastium*
Soapwort. *See Saponaria*
Soil acidity, 26, 34, 87
Soil alkalinity, 35, 87
Soil, clay, 22
Soil erosion, 40
Soil mixtures, 23, 30, 34, 35, 36, 76
Soils, 21
Soldier, water. *See Stratiotes*
Spatterdock, 10
Specialist nurseries, 17
Spike heath. *See Bruckenthalia*
Spiny alyssum, *13*
Spring care, 39
Spring gentian. *See Gentiana*
Spring planting, 37
Spring-flowering alpines, 37
Spruce. *See Picea*
Squirrel corn. *See Dicentra*

St. John's wort, 13
Stains, pool, 51
Stamens, *84*
Stepping stones, 40
Steps, 22
Steps, rock garden, 27, 28
Stone chips, 22, 23, 28, 34, 36, 40
Stone, crushed, 28, 30, 34, 38, 57
Stone sinks, 31
Stone walls, 7, 22, 29
Stonecrop. *See Sedum*
Stones, 22, 26, 51
Stones, stepping, 40
Strata, rock, 17, 27, 29
Stratiotes, 144
Stratiotes aloides, 144
Streams, 8, 16, 17, 19, 40, 51, *55, 56*
Streams, natural, 52
Structure, rock, 29
Succulents, 19, *32, 43, 45*
Succulents, planting, *39*
Sulphur, 38
Summer-flowering alpines, 37
Sun, 22
Sun, effects of, 20
Sun King, 8
Sundrops, Ozark. *See Oenothera*
Sunset shade water lilies, 71
Sweet flag, 7, 75. *See also Acorus*
Sweet woodruff. *See Asperula*

T

Tadpoles, 82
Talus, 35
Temperatures, 20
Temperatures, water, 9, 87
Tench, 83
Terraces, *13, 43*
Terraces, paved, 19
Textures, 42
Textures, leaf, 20
Thalictrum. See Anemonella
Thrift. *See Armeria*
Thyme. *See Thymus*
Thymus, 129
Thymus x *citriodorus*, 129
Thymus drucei, 129
Thymus praecox, 129
Tillaea. See Crassula
Timber pool enclosures, 56
Toads, 82
Topdressing, 38
Topsoil, 23
Towers, tufa, 35
Trailers, *33*, 40, 46
Trailers, planting, *39*
Transpiration, 14
Treads, 28
Tree line, 19
Trees, dwarf, 8, 38
Trees, mountain, 20
Trees, siting by pools, 50
Trillium, 129-130
Trillium erectum, *129*, 130

Trillium grandiflorum, 130
Trillium ovatum, 130
Trollius, 144-145
Trollius americanus, 144
Trollius europaeus, 145
Trollius laxus, 145
Trough gardens, 19, 31, *32-33*
Troughs, concrete, 31, *32-33*, 34
Tsuga, 130
Tsuga canadensis 'Armistice Dwarf', 130
Tsuga canadensis 'Cole', 130
Tsuga canadensis 'Jervis', 130
Tsuga canadensis 'Minima', 130
Tub pools, 52
Tubs, aquatic plants for, 8
Tufa, 26, *35*
Turf, 23
Typha, 75, 145
Typha angustifolia, 145
Typha gracilis, 145
Typha latifolia, 145
Typha minima, 145

U

Umbrella grass, *86. See also Cyperus*
Underground water systems, 36, *37*

V

Vallisneria, 74
Variegated sweet flag. *See Acorus*
Vermiculite, 31
Versailles, 8
Victoria amazonica, 9, 10
Victoria cruciana, 10
Victoria regia, 9, 10
Victorian water lily, *9*
Violet, dog's-tooth. *See Erythronium*
Violet, water. *See Hottonia*
Viscaria. See Lychnis
Viviparous, 73

W

Wahlenbergia, 108
Wake robin. *See Trillium*
Wall fountains, 49, *62*
Wall gardens, 29, 40
Wall gardens, planting, 30
Wall rock cress. *See Arabis*
Walls, drystone, 19, 29, 31
Walls, plants for, 7
Walls, retaining, *42*
Walls, stone, 22
Water, *6*, 7
Water aeration, 83
Water arum. *See Calla*

Water changes, 82
Water channels, 8
Water chutes, *62*
Water containers, 52
Water depths, 87
Water depths, simulated, 51
Water forget-me-not, 56
Water fringe, 52, 74. *See also Nymphoides*
Water gardening, 9, 16
Water gardens, *48*, 49-69
Water gardens, ancient, 8
Water gardens, classic, 60, *61-69*
Water gardens, equipment for, 17
Water gardens, geometric, 60, *64-65*
Water gardens, maintenance, 8, 83, 84
Water gardens, planning, 17
Water hawthorn, 7. *See also Aponogeton*
Water hyacinth, 74. *See also Eichhornia*
Water installations, *13, 37*
Water iris, 75
Water jets, 8
Water lettuce, 74. *See also Pistia*
Water lilies, *6*, 7, 9, *48*, 49, 60, *61*, 71, 72, 74, *86. See also Nymphaea*
Water lilies, basket, *75*, 76, 81, 82
Water lilies, changeable, 71
Water lilies, colour changes, 9
Water lilies, containers, 81
Water lilies, cut flowers, *84*
Water lilies, day blooming, 72, *77*, *79*, *80*
Water lilies, delivery, 75
Water lilies, depth, 87
Water lilies, European, 10
Water lilies, flowering season, 72, 73
Water lilies, flowers, 71, 72, *77-79*, 84
Water lilies, hardy, 71, 73
Water lilies, hybrids, 76, *77-79*
Water lilies, Laydekeri, 73
Water lilies, leaves, 71, 72, *78*
Water lilies, Marliac, 9, 10
Water lilies, miniature, 8, 52, 71, 73
Water lilies, miniature, planting, 81, 82
Water lilies, night blooming, 72, *77*, *79*
Water lilies, overwintering, 81
Water lilies, planting, 81, 82
Water lilies, planting depth, *75*, 81, 82
Water lilies, planting distances, 82
Water lilies, planting times, 72, 81
Water lilies, propagation, *73*, 85
Water lilies, pygmy, 73, 76, *79*
Water lilies, restricting, 81

Water lilies, rootstock, 71, 72, *75*
Water lilies, soil requirements, 75, 76
Water lilies, tropical, 71, 72, 73, 76, *77*, *78-79*, *80*, 87
Water lilies, tropical, feeding, 84
Water lilies, tropical, overwintering, 85
Water lilies, tropical, planting, 81
Water lilies, viviparous, *73*
Water lilies, winter protection, 84
Water lily pools, *13*
Water lily, Victorian, 9
Water mills, 8
Water musk, lavender. *See Mimulus*
Water plants, 131-145. *See also Aquatic plants*
Water poppy, 74
Water reflections, 49
Water, running, 51
Water soldier. *See Stratiotes*
Water systems, underground, 36, *37*, 56
Water temperatures, 9, 87
Water trough gardens, 31, *32-33*
Water violet. *See Hottonia*
Waterfalls, 8, 10, 14, 16, 17, 49, 51, 52, 59, *68*
Watering, 8, 27, 30, 38
Waterworks, ornamental, 8
Weeding, 8, 38
Weeds, 16, 34, 38
Weeping cherry, *12-13*
Weeping hemlock, *44, 46*
Welsh poppy, 15
White cinquefoil. *See Potentilla*
Wild flowers, 7, 20, 21
Wild ginger. *See Asarum*
Wild rock gardens, 16
Wilting, 38
Wind, 20
Wine-cup. *See Callirhoë*
Winter aconite, 37
Winter alpines, 37
Winter protection, 8, 20, 84
Winter temperatures, 20
Wisley Gardens, 10, *11-13*
Wisteria, *11*
Wood anemone. *See Anemone*
Wood lily. *See Trillium*
Woodland alpines, 87
Woodland rock gardens, 40
Woodruff. *See Asperula*
Woolly yarrow. *See Achillea*

Y

Yarrow. *See Achillea*
Yellow arum. *See Lysichitum*

Filmsetting by C. E. Dawkins (Typesetters) Ltd., London, SE1 1UN.
Printed and bound in Great Britain by Jarrold & Sons Ltd., Norwich.